AN EMERGENT THEOLOGY FOR EMERGING CHURCHES

Ray S. Anderson

IVP Books

An imprint of InterVarsity Press
Downers Grove, Illinois

InterVarsity Press
P.O. Box 1400, Downers Grove, IL 60515-1426
World Wide Web: www.ivpress.com
E-mail: mail@ivpress.com

InterVarsity Press® is the book-publishing division of InterVarsity Christian Fellowship/USA®, a student movement active on campus at hundreds of universities, colleges and schools of nursing in the United States of America, and a member movement of the International Fellowship of Evangelical Students. For information about local and regional activities, write Public Relations Dept., InterVarsity Christian Fellowship/USA, 6400 Schroeder Rd., P.O. Box 7895, Madison, WI 53707-7895, or visit the IVCF website at <www.ivcf.org>.

Design: Cindy Kiple
Images: Photodisc/Getty Images

ISBN-10: 0-8308-3391-9
ISBN-13: 978-0-8308-3391-9

Printed in the United States of America ∞

Library of Congress Cataloging-in-Publication Data

Anderson, Ray Sherman.
 An emergent theology for emerging churches / Ray S. Anderson.
   p. cm.
 Includes bibliographical references and indexes.
 ISBN-13: 978-0-8308-3391-7 (pbk.: alk. paper)
 ISBN-10: 0-8308-3391-9 (pbk.: alk. paper)
 1. Church—History of doctrines. 2. Theology. 3.
 Postmodernism—Religious aspects—Christianity. 4. Non-institutional
 churches. I. Title.
 BV598.A53 2006
 230'.046—dc22
                                                          2006013018

| P | 18 | 17 | 16 | 15 | 14 | 13 | 12 | 11 | 10 | 9 | 8 | 7 | 6 | 5 | 4 | 3 | 2 | 1 |
| Y | 21 | 20 | 19 | 18 | 17 | 16 | 15 | 14 | 13 | 12 | 11 | 10 | 09 | 08 | 07 | 06 |

CONTENTS

A bright young Fuller Seminary student once sent me this e-mail, telling me about someone she hoped I would meet:

> During 2002-2003 I spent every Tuesday evening with Ray [Anderson] in his Systematic Theology classes, as a part of completing my Fuller degree. Thankfully with Ray's inventive approaches to this topic I got through the required classes, but Systematic Theology is not a joyful topic of study for me. Much more fun were all the theological conversations I had with various classmates about the material we were studying.
>
> Ray has quite a few more years than his energy and quick mind would lead one to guess. . . . He has a huge heart and is much beloved by the Fuller community, including me.

When I finally did meet Ray, within five minutes I understood exactly what this student was saying. Youthful energy, quick mind, huge heart—she beautifully described the spirit of this retired-but-still-active professor of theology.

Some professors want to recruit new generations to defend and preserve the world of their own aging and fading generation. This is a noble task, as there is so much of value to be defended and preserved. Meanwhile, other professors take on another noble task: to invest the wisdom they've gained from previous generations to help new generations make their own new and better world. As you'll see in these pages, Ray is the latter kind of professor. This book is his generous offering to an emerging generation of thoughtful Christian leaders, and I hope it will be appropriately received and treasured.

Many of us are familiar with Tertullian's famous question: "What has Athens to do with Jerusalem?" The question warns us against the real and perennial danger of syncretism—in this case, domesticating the authentic and wild Christian faith with roots in Jerusalem by means of a refined but confining alien culture and philosophy rooted in Athens.

But in this book, Ray adds a new question: "What has Jerusalem to do with Antioch?"

This question warns us against another danger no less real than syncretism: stagnation, domination, containment. Jesus launched a movement that was supposed to begin in Jerusalem, but was intended to spread outward from there to Judea and Samaria, ultimately reaching the farthest corners of the earth. As the rings of its influence spread from its original center, it was to retain its essence: it would always be about relationship with the Father, Son and Holy Spirit (affirmed in baptism), and it would always be about training people to live in the ways of Jesus.

In other words, it was to begin in Jerusalem, but it couldn't be contained by Jerusalem—by its language, culture, customs, taboos, scruples or history. It couldn't be domesticated or dominated by Jerusalem any more than it could be tamed by Athens. It could not stagnate. After all, any movement that stops moving is an oxymoron, an impossibility. So when Jerusalem-centered Christians tried to limit the movement's daring expansion into and constructive engagement with other cultures, when they tried to contain it and control it and prune back its continuing emergence, Ray argues, Antioch became a new center from which the movement could move.

Looking back through history we might conclude that the headquarters of the faith's last expansion may always be tempted to limit and contain and control the next expansion. In this way, each Christian community must constantly choose between being a Jerusalem or an Antioch.

By the end of the book of Acts, Antioch is sending out teams of missionaries like Paul and Barnabas—bold innovators, creative explorers, daring boundary-crossers or, as my friend Erwin McManus has said, barbarians. Meanwhile, Jerusalem is too often sending out teams of critics, fault-finders, scolders and police. The city names change, but the story seems to be repeated again and again.

That's certainly not to say there is no room for dialogue and even debate between Jerusalem and Antioch. We see that kind of constructive communication in Acts 11 and again in Acts 15. We hear an echo of it in Galatians 2. If Jerusalem had gotten its way, there would only have been monologue, but because the Holy Spirit's work in Antioch was vigorous and unquenchable, there was a healthy dialogue and the movement launched by Jesus kept moving forward and outward. It kept emerging beyond old boundaries.

So perhaps we can put Tertullian's and Anderson's questions together in this way: are we going to follow an Athens-based faith, where our message is domesticated and diluted by new cultures it encounters? Are we going to follow a Jerusalem-based faith, where our message is tamed and contained by a dominant culture from the past? Or are we going to follow an Antioch-based faith, where our message never loses its wild, untamed essence (flames of fire, rushing wind), but like a spring of living water or vibrant new wine, it always flows and is never contained by old forms?

Ray's life has been invested in an Antioch-based faith, and this important and helpful book seeks to help emerging leaders never to lose the essence of the good news of Jesus Christ, but never to be contained by old cultural forms either.

Sometime in the late 1990s, I first heard my friend Andrew Jones (tallskinnykiwi.com) using the term "the emerging culture." He realized, wisely as usual, that the term *postmodern* had already become a dirty word in the mouths of some critics (from Jerusalem, so to speak), and "emerging culture" was a less negatively charged term. Soon people started using the term "emerging church" to describe churches that were seeking to engage constructively—in the Antioch way, so to speak—with this emerging culture.

Now, the terms *emerging* and *emergent* have taken on a negative charge for some Jerusalem-based critics, sometimes, no doubt, in reaction to people "from Antioch" who use the terms proudly or rudely or divisively. But I think for most people, these words still convey a gentle, humble and hopeful sense, a sense that the way of Jesus is a quiet but unstoppable movement, a never-ending journey, a faith that has a center but whose boundaries are always expanding into new frontiers.

In the end, Ray isn't asking us to pit Antioch against Jerusalem, or Jerusalem against Athens. All three cities are part of God's beloved world and God's emerging story. Ray invites us to participate in a vigorous, Christ-centered faith that emerges from, in and around Jerusalem, expands to and through Antioch, and becomes a transforming influence in Athens—and throughout the whole world beyond.

I thank God for the scholars and leaders of our older generations—people like Ray Anderson—who have decided not to rein in those who push the new frontiers, but instead have tried to encourage and resource them so the essence of their message remains true even as old boundaries are broken. We are all honored to learn from them, for they make theology a joyful thing.

Brian McLaren

Preface

WHAT HAS ANTIOCH TO DO WITH JERUSALEM?

My first reaction to the Internet bloggers touting the emerging church phenomenon, and the books on the subject that pastor friends suggested as "must reads," was one of curiosity mixed with skepticism. Having mentored doctor of ministry dissertations on the baby boomers, the post-baby boomers and the Gen-Xers, I had come to the conclusion that the church's attempts to surf the waves of contemporary culture in hopes of being relevant were fickle if not futile. Most surfers end up on the same shoreline they left unless they get caught in a riptide and disappear entirely. Others seemed to agree. The second wave of dissertations sought to catch the winds of postmodernity and sail out further from shore.

All of this, of course, was really an excuse. Having begun as more of a dogmatic theologian, followed by a theological midlife crisis and conversion to practical theology, I ended up in my own comfort zone of being a self-styled maverick theologian. My theological reflections began to take the form of musings rather than rigorous critical and analytical thinking. My musing is an exercise in thinking up questions that have no easy or final answers, but which, I concluded, had more the texture of the bread of everyday life than the hard substance of the philosopher's stone. Paraphrasing the late General Douglas MacArthur's final address to congress on his forced retirement—old soldiers never die they just fade away—I prepared my own self-indulgent and poignant farewell: maverick theologians never die they just find themselves amusing!

However, when I actually began to read some of the authors promoting the emerging church—most of whom, by the way, are also practicing pastors—my theological juices started to flow, somewhat like anticipating a bite into a dill pickle or, for those whose palate is a bit more educated, a seafood soufflé. In any event, when I came across a paragraph written by Brian McLaren my mouth began to water! "You see, if we have a new world, we will need a new church. We won't need a new religion per se, but a new framework for our theology. Not a new Spirit, but a new spirituality. Not a new Christ, but a new Christian. Not a new denomination, but a new kind of church in every denomination."[1] While I appreciated his evangelistic zeal for postmodernity, his passion for a new framework for theology put a growl in my stomach. It was Dan Kimball, though, who offered an enticing menu, one that whetted my appetite for some theological engagement with emerging churches. "The emerging church," wrote Kimball, "must redefine how we measure success: by the characteristics of a kingdom-minded disciple of Jesus produced by the Spirit, rather than by our methodologies, numbers, strategies, the cool and innovative things we are doing."[2] While I am a newcomer to the more recent discussion of the emerging church, in 1993 I did publish a book with a chapter titled "An Emerging Church." Little did I know at the time that the concept would later come to have a life of its own![3]

IS THIS BOOK ABOUT POSTMODERNITY?

Is this book about postmodernity? The short answer is no. To paraphrase

[1]Brian McLaren, *Reinventing Your Church* (Grand Rapids: Zondervan, 1998), p. 13.
[2]Dan Kimball, *The Emerging Church* (Grand Rapids: Zondervan, 2003), p. 15.
[3]Ray S. Anderson, "An Emerging Church," in *Ministry on the Fireline* (Downers Grove, Ill.: InterVarsity Press, 1993), pp. 135-48.

the prophet Amos, I am neither a philosopher nor the son of a philosopher. I am not the son of a theologian either, but, like Amos, this became
my calling. Though I was educated in dogmatic theology, perhaps because of the eleven years of pastoral ministry prior to that, and due to
the fact that I have served as pastor and preached to the same congregation for twenty-nine years while also serving as a full-time seminary professor, I am comfortable with being labeled a practical theologian.

I have no quarrel with those who espouse a postmodern theology and
envision a postmodern church. Postmodernity may well be—at the very
least—a healthy correction to the excessively abstract and universalizing
tendency of the post-Enlightenment period in Europe. I view postmodernity as a context in which we must do theology rather than as a hermeneutical tool. I have not found it to be an adequate theological and epistemological paradigm to capture the deeper dimensions of an incarnational
theology of the kingdom of God that draws the church out of its historical
past into its eschatological future. Myron Penner warns against turning toward a postmodern construct of reality that empties truth of any objective
content. "I am concerned that Christians who accept the postmodern turn
be careful not to become complicitous with certain forms of the postmodern turn that make a reactionary move toward subjectivity, which empties
it of the possibility of asserting anything as true."[4]

---

[4]Myron B. Penner, ed., *Christianity and the Postmodern Turn* (Grand Rapids: Brazos, 2005), p.
30. Someone once described *postmodernism* as a word that is forever chasing a meaning. Another suggested that postmodernism is like "intellectual velcro dragged across culture—an ad-
hesive label licking up anything at random that floats across the surface of our culture" (Graham Buxton, *Dancing in the Dark* [London: Paternoster, 2001], p. 178). Buxton goes on to say,
"The French social theorist, Jean-François Lyotard, argues that the essence of postmodernism
is the 'incredulity towards metanarratives': that there are no overarching explanations of the
human condition, such as those claimed by either Christianity or any other political or social
'order.' So free reign is given to relativism and subjectivity, and all are not only free, but encouraged, to believe whatever they wish, for there are no absolutes to life. Objective truth, according to postmodernists, is a myth, a viewpoint that conveys obvious ethical implications"
(ibid.). It might also be helpful to remember that *postmodernity* may well be a word that attempts to describes a state of development within intellectual history, while *postmodernism* is
more of a hermeneutical theory that claims explanatory power. See also John Franke and Stanley Grenz, *Beyond Foundationalism* (Louisville: Westminster John Knox, 2001).

My faculty colleagues Eddie Gibbs and Ryan Bolger have interviewed almost fifty emerging church leaders and identified a number of missiological principles that these ministries have in common with regard to the application of the gospel in a postmodern context.[5] Some have made the observation that the emerging church is a moving target, impossible to pin down. Brian McLaren likes to say that it is more of a conversation than a movement. While I will take note of some contemporary and (I hope) representative voices in the emerging church conversation, I view my role somewhat as an interlocutor in that dialogue. I am writing for all who are in some way connected to the emergent movement as well as for those who belong to or are curious about emerging churches.[6]

When I use the term "emergent church" in this book, I refer primarily to the first-century emerging church at Antioch, including the various churches that came into existence through Paul's ministry based in Antioch. When I refer to the emerging movement in our contemporary culture, I prefer to speak of "emerging churches," as I do not believe that there is any one emerging church but rather a rich variety emerging in both Protestant and Roman Catholic communities. I realize that there has been a great deal of confusion and even criticism, both within and outside the emergent movement.[7] I will not attempt to respond to these concerns or raise some of my own other than to point out, in a positive way, I hope, how an emergent theology drawn out of the early Antioch emerging community can fill what I perceive to be a need for a creative and constructive theological paradigm for the emerging church movement.

---

[5]Eddie Gibbs and Ryan K. Bolger, *Emerging Churches* (Grand Rapids: Baker, 2005).

[6]For information on the emergent movement and connecting links see the Emergent Village website at <www.emergentvillage.com/Site/index.htm>.

[7]For example, D. A. Carson, *Becoming Conversant with the Emerging Church* (Grand Rapids: Zondervan, 2005). See also Albert Mohler, "What Should We Think of the Emerging Church? Part One" <http://www.albertmohler.com/commentary_read.php?cdate=2005-06-29>, who applauds Carson's criticism of the emerging movement as biblically weak and theologically suspect, having caved in to postmodern relativism regarding truth claims; and R. Scott Smith, *Truth and the New Kind of Christian* (Grand Rapids: Zondervan, 2005).

Readers should not expect a critical discussion of epistemology (how we know what we know) or a philosophical critique of postmodernity. It is not that I question the importance of epistemology, for all versions of reality have to do with what it means to say that we have knowledge of that reality. As my former Ph.D. mentor, T. F. Torrance, liked to remind his students, those whose method is primarily philosophical tend to write the first chapter of their dissertation on epistemology, while those of a more scientific methodology, place their epistemology in the last chapter! My epistemology will emerge as an intrinsic aspect of a revelational theology rather than as a set of presuppositional assertions. My concern is not to trace out the contours of a church emerging in a postmodern context but to tease out an emergent theology that is truthful only because it is discovered along the journey (revelational), contextual only because it is currently being lived out (incarnational) and contemporary only because it viably takes us into the future (eschatological).

The emergent theology that I present in this book is certainly not a form of modern theology, nor is it merely postmodern; it is a vintage theology that is intended to remind emerging churches of their origins and lead them forward to fulfill their destiny to expand God's kingdom under the direction of the Lord Jesus, who is coming and who is present through the power and work of the Holy Spirit. As with all theologies, however, an emergent theology must be as devout as it is daring, and willing to be unprofitable as well as provocative. Perhaps it would look as if written by a maverick but taste like a vintage wine.

THE EMERGING CHURCH?

Is this book about the emerging church? The short answer is—partially. My interest in emerging churches was provoked by practitioners who prodded me for some theological reflection on the movement in which they were involved as well as by pastors who queried me about the ecclesial validity of that which was emerging on their very doorsteps. In my view emerging churches represent a contemporary expression of the first-century church's existence and mission in a postmodern world. While this book is about *emerging churches,* it is not intended to be another book on the emerging church. My focus in this book is not so much on the emerging-church movement but rather on an *emergent theology.*

Dan Kimball has helped me to see a distinction between *emergent* and *emerging.* He considers the term *emergent* to refer primarily to theological change and discussion while *emerging* has more to do with those who are "rethinking church and ecclesiology as any missionary would as we enter new cultures. Many emerging churches focus primarily on more ecclesiological rethinking and pragmatic change, whereas emergent is more about rethinking theology as a whole." Emerging churches who seek an authentic biblical and theological foundation are the ones who really are mission focused but also grappling with theological issues. "The distinction between 'emerging church' and 'emergent' is that 'emerging church' is a term used for churches who are emerging in this current culture and who are definitely passionate about rethinking what it means to be the church on a mission."[8]

I find this distinction helpful with regard to both an exploration of the church at Antioch in the first century as well as of many forms of churches that are emerging in our culture today. From this perspective, you should read this book as a contribution to the emergent theological discussion with a deep desire to be part of an ongoing dialogue within the emerging church community.

After reading Dan's book I began to think out loud about what the emerging church was about. Not being a leader or practitioner of an emerging church (though a participant!), I began my investigation and pursued my interest in emerging churches from a theological perspec-

---

[8]Dan Kimball, personal correspondence from November 2, 2005. Kimball, while continuing to participate in the broad stream of the emerging movement, views his own role as representing a conservative evangelical voice, with deep commitment to the Nicene Creed as a theological anchor along with a high view of Scripture as a source of "truth that you can hold on to."

tive. I began to muse a lot about what emerging churches might look like if they dared to view culture only as a context, the kingdom of God as the criterion and a kingdom-minded disciple as new kind of Christian Dan likes to use the concept "vintage Christianity," a thought that I found very intriguing. The word *vintage* took me back, not to something that was good merely because it was old but to what was true and authentic because it was there in the beginning and points the way into the future. "Jesus Christ is the same yesterday and today and forever" (Hebrews 13:8). That sounds vintage to me! The gospel of Christ is a vintage gospel, not just because it is old but because it is always true, and more than that, it leads us into the future! I suspect that Kimball's use of *vintage* follows a different line of thought, but this is how I intend to use the concept as a component of an emergent theology.

WHY ANTIOCH?

When I looked for some antecedent in the first-century church for what we today call the emerging church, my mind went immediately to the church at Antioch as one that emerged out of the church at Jerusalem and also that led to an emergent theology under the apostle Paul's ministry and teaching. Based on modern epistemological assumptions, the conservative evangelical tradition returned to the question originally put by Tertullian (A.D. 160-225) "What has Jerusalem to do with Athens?"[9] While Tertullian raised the question for the purpose of discrediting the academy, modern theology's concern for apologetics sought to integrate or at least to correlate revelation with reason, and the church with the academy. My own seminary library has more than twenty books with some variation of that title! I suspect that postmodern versions of the

---

[9]"What indeed has Athens to do with Jerusalem? What concord is there between the Academy and the Church? . . . Our instructions come from 'the porch of Solomon.' . . . Away with all attempts to produce a mottled Christianity of Stoic, Platonic, and dialectic composition! We want no curious disputation after possessing Christ Jesus!" (Tertullian *Prescription Against Heretics* 7).

Christian faith will add more titles of that genre.

The seminal issue for the church—and for Paul, I suspect—was not one that contrasted Jerusalem with Athens but Jerusalem with Antioch. The persecution of the followers of Jesus in Judea caused their dispersion as far north as Antioch, where the Holy Spirit led the church from its Jewish-oriented ministry and focus to include a number of Gentiles (Acts 11:19-26). The church at Jerusalem hearing of this, sent Barnabas to investigate and, we might surmise, based on later accounts of their concerns, to put the fire out with regard to the promiscuous inclusion of uncircumcised Gentiles. As it turned out, rather than bringing a fire extinguisher to Antioch, Barnabas brought an accelerant, for he was a "good man, full of the Holy Spirit," and a great many more were added to the church (Acts 11:24). Ignoring the elders in Jerusalem, Barnabas went to nearby Tarsus, found Saul, recently converted on the way to Damascus (not Jerusalem!), and for a year they ministered in the emerging church at Antioch, where the disciples were first called "Christians" (Acts 11:26). It was under the direction of the Holy Spirit that the church at Antioch set apart Saul and Barnabas for a mission that led to the establishing of churches throughout Asia Minor, Macedonia, Greece and even Rome (Acts 13:1-3).

An emergent theology was born, and along with it emerging churches. I am aware that the fluidity of thought and images in the emerging community may already have moved beyond the term "emerging church." In this regard, Will Samson comments, "Speaking of 'the church that is emerging,' Brian McLaren mentioned that this might be a better title than 'the emerging church.' I like that because it connects deeply into the Church at her root rather than speaking of the work we are participating in as some new expression."[10] This is exactly what I intend to do—go back to the root of the church that emerged out of Anti-

---

[10]Will Samson, "Hopes and Dreams of Emergent," emergent-us <http://emergent-us.type-pad.com/emergentus/2005/10/hopes_and_dream.html>.

och in the first century in order to anchor the church that is emerging in
our contemporary culture with a theology that emerged in the original
church

In following this track I was led to trace out the contours of the emergent theology that Paul developed through his ministry, often in direct
conflict with but also with intentional relationship to the church at Jerusalem. The emerging church at Antioch reached back toward Jerusalem
as far as the church there allowed, but the theology that emerged came
more out of the future than the past. If it became an emergent theology
it was precisely because it was a theology of the kingdom, not merely a
theology of the church. In the end, as Paul himself wrote, it is the kingdom of God that Jesus brings to completion and offers up to the Father,
not the church (1 Corinthians 15:24). The church in Jerusalem, as it
turned out, contributed virtually nothing to the emerging church, no
churches were planted out of Jerusalem and no theological writings of
substance were offered. At the same time, I do not intend to disparage
the Christian community at Jerusalem. It was the source of an incredible
spiritual force that resisted attempts to suppress and even destroy it.
When those who were dispersed, due to persecution, fled to other cities,
including Antioch, they carried with them the gift and power of the
Spirit along with the message of a crucified and risen Messiah. When I
contrast Antioch and Jerusalem throughout this book, it is for the purpose of sharpening the focus on the content and direction of the emergent theology uniquely envisioned and proclaimed by the apostle Paul.
This is an exercise in creative narrative theology rather than reconstruc-
tive historical theology. Therefore, this book is about an emergent theology more than it is about the emerging church.

WHAT IS AN EMERGENT THEOLOGY?

In what way can we distinguish an emergent theology from the emerging
church in such a way as to maintain the distinction but also preserve the
symbiotic relation between the two? Let me count the ways.

An emergent theology is messianic. An emergent theology is anointed and Spirit-led to point the way forward. An emergent theology is like the finger of John the Baptist, pointing into the world and saying, "Here is the lamb of God" (John 1:29).

Emerging churches are missional. Emergent churches only exist as the continuing mission of Christ (the Messiah) in the world. Emerging churches are like Jesus arising out of the water of baptism, anointed by the Spirit, and moving into the streets and market place to heal, promote justice and seek peace.

An emergent theology is revelational. An emergent theology is a theology of the Word; it is the bread come down from heaven; it speaks truth and opens minds and hearts.

Emerging churches are reformational. Emerging churches seek to put new wine into new wineskins; they want to renew the church that already exists and translate the older formulas of the faith into new paradigms of contemporary communication.

An emergent theology is kingdom coming. An emergent theology proclaims a new order of God's reign already present as a transforming spiritual, social and economic power of liberation and rehabilitation of humankind.

Emerging churches stress kingdom living. Emerging churches seek to be the gathering of all who seek the blessing of being grace-filled believers and the empowering community that sends them forth as Spirit-filled disciples.

An emergent theology is eschatological. An emergent theology has the mind of the risen and coming Christ as well as the heart and soul of the historical Jesus. It is a theology that keeps hope alive by preparing the way of the future into the present while, at the same time, keeping faith alive by looking "forward to the city that has foundations, whose architect and builder is God" (Hebrews 11:10).

Emerging churches are incarnational. Emerging churches' language is that of the people; their message is communicated through culture; their presence in the world is ordinary so as to get within arms length to embrace others with extraordinary love.

EMERGENT THEOLOGY AND EMERGING CHURCHES AS PARTNERS

An emergent theology without being embedded in emerging churches becomes isolated, speaking only to itself (solipsistic!), and living the monastic life of those whose windows to the world are not only stained glass but unable to be opened from the inside. In the end, it is pathetic.

Emerging churches without an embedded emergent theology wear their religion like a costume (always a change for the next act); they hoist their sails to catch a prevailing wind (but lack a rudder by which to steer); they live off the energy of others (having a battery but no generator). In the end, they become powerless.

The relation of emergent to emerging is somewhat like that of a seed to the soil. An emergent theology needs the soil of emerging churches in which to take root. One plants, the other waters, God gives the increase (1 Corinthians 3:6-9). An emergent theology is an embedded theology in the emerging church's mission. This book is meant to be somewhat of a manual for those who are emerging.

Who are my intended readers? They are my partners, not just readers.

Emerging churches are a Bible-teaching and a Bible-reading community. Even as the Protestant Reformation was sparked largely by the work of John Wycliffe (1330-1384)—among others—whose work of translation put the Bible into the hands of ordinary folk, so emerging churches are empowered by their members who read and study the Bible. Those who read the Bible (and this is not always an easy task!) are my readers and partners—church pastors and leaders too! But emergent theology is for ordinary folk who are also musing, always ready to ask pertinent questions!

When Barnabas was sent to Antioch by the elders of the church at Jerusalem, I believe it was because they were asking, What is the movement up there all about? The same question is being asked of emerging churches in our generation. I am concerned for what it is "all about," and the chapters that follow are my attempt to answer this question.

1   IT'S ABOUT THEOLOGY, NOT GEOGRAPHY

A friend who read an earlier version of this book said, "Well Ray, it looks like you may be reinventing the wheel! The Antioch Church already exists. You can save yourself a lot of trouble by converting to the Antiochian Diocese of the Orthodox Church and joining Peter Gillquist along with others from the Protestant evangelical movement." I replied, "This is exactly what I don't want to do—start another denomination!"[1] No, I don't look back to Antioch in order to find a new ecclesial community but an emergent theology that can shape the contours and stimulate the growth of a vital root structure for an emerging-church movement that appears to have more fluidity than focus. Something is going on, we need to know what it's about.

---

[1]Gillquist serves as head of the department of missions and evangelism for the Antiochian Diocese of the Orthodox Church. Gillquist, along with a group of former Campus Crusade for Christ leaders, set out in the late 1960s on a search for a church with deeper roots only to one day wind up on the doorstep of the Orthodox Church, seeking admittance. Gillquist told his own story in his book *Becoming Orthodox,* where he tracked the conversion of nearly a thousand evangelical Protestants to Orthodox Christianity in 1987. This mass conversion was one of the biggest events in modern American Orthodoxy, and Guillquist's book paints a vivid picture of the theological wrestling and jurisdictional complications that ended in the reception of the converts in the Antiochian Orthodox Church (Peter E. Gillquist, *Becoming Orthodox: A Journey to the Ancient Christian Faith* [Ben Lomond, Calif.: Conciliar Press, 1992]; see also, *Coming Home: Why Protestant Clergy Are Becoming Orthodox,* ed. Peter E. Gillquist [Ben Lomond, Calif.: Conciliar Press, 1995]).

The thesis of this book is simple and succinct. The Christian community that emerged out of Antioch constitutes the original form and theology of the emerging church as contrasted with the believing community at Jerusalem. I will argue that the emerging churches in our present generation can find their ecclesial form and their core theology by tracing out the contours of the missionary church under Paul's leadership based in Antioch. The difference between Antioch and Jerusalem is essentially a theological difference, not merely a geographical one.

MOMENTS AND MOVEMENTS

While the distance between Antioch and Jerusalem can be measured in miles, the difference can be understood in a moment. There are moments when, for something to emerge, a line must be drawn, a cord cut, a breaking away in order for the new to break in. The Greeks had a word for it—*kairos*—not a chronological sequence in time (*chronos*), but a "moment in time," as it were, the emergence of something new within the continuum of time and place. "See, now is the acceptable time *[kairos]*," wrote Paul, "see, now is the day of salvation" (2 Corinthians 6:2). The history of the Christian church includes both movements and moments. A movement is the development of a new strain out of an older batch! It is true that a moment can lead to a movement. But what is unique about a moment, as I use the term, is that it does not come by evolution but by revolution. Or, to use the language of change, a moment is second-order change while a movement tends to be first-order change.

First-order change is a change from one behavior to another within a given way of behaving as a response to a new environment or a new stimulus. First-order change has a high degree of continuity through the transition of change. The church community in Jerusalem, despite the "moment" of Pentecost, quickly incorporated this event into a movement with a high degree of continuity with the tradition of the Twelve. It carried a great deal of the DNA, to use a contemporary expression, of the historical past into the present.

Second-order change, on the other hand, produces a new system and a new way of behaving rather than a new behavior within the same system. It has a high degree of discontinuity through the transition of change. While first-order change appears to be based on common sense, second-order change may appear to be weird, unexpected and paradoxical. In second-order change there is less extrapolation out of the past and more of an attempt to restructure the present in terms of a perceived goal. Thus a moment, such as Paul's conversion and anointing with the Spirit as a result of the Damascus-road encounter with Jesus, was second-order change as contrasted with the evolving movement within the Jerusalem community of believers.[2]

The new evangelical movement came about during the middle of the twentieth century as some leading theologians and ministers felt the need to form a more positive and culturally relevant theology out of the older fundamentalism. The so-called new charismatic movement in the latter part of the twentieth century brought about a vigorous and sometimes contentious spirituality leading to the renewal of existing churches and the creation of new ones. Martin Luther, on the other hand, had a moment of spiritual and theological insight when he discovered the liberating and biblical teaching on justification by faith that led to the Reformation. John Wesley had a moment of deep personal and spiritual inner awareness of his salvation at Aldersgate that led to a theology of sanctification and holiness of life. While these moments also led to movements, these movements were more revolutionary in nature than evolutionary. The emerging church at Antioch was a moment, not a movement, leading to a new kind of church and a new gospel of grace; it did not evolve out of the Jerusalem community but was radically revo-

---

[2]Sources for the discussion of first- and second-order change can be found in Paul Watzlawick, John H. Weakland and Richard Fisch, *Change: Principles of Problem Formation and Problem Resolution* (New York: W. W. Norton, 1974). See also Ray S. Anderson, *Minding God's Business* (Grand Rapids: Eerdmans, 1986), chap. 3.

lutionary in nature, much to the alarm and concern of the elders at Jerusalem! The time (*kairos*) for the new messianic community had come, in Antioch rather than Jerusalem. Emerging churches can be understood as a *kairos* moment in our time.

The several hundred miles that separate Antioch from Jerusalem is not what is significant. It is the theological moment that emerged at Antioch that tells us what the new kind of church is about. Could the same event have occurred at the doorstep of Jerusalem? Would it have taken place in the same way in a suburban synagogue of Jerusalem, perhaps within walking distance of the temple? In one sense, yes, for the Spirit moves where it wills. In another sense, probably not, for, as Jesus said, new wine does not fit well in an old wineskin, nor can one put a new patch on an old coat without it tearing away (Mark 2:21-22). Thus it seems providential that through the persecution of the Jews in Jerusalem, a number of believing Jews ended up in Antioch where the Holy Spirit emerged in the form a new kind of community, including both Jews and Gentiles. But its difference was not only the inclusive nature of the new community, it was the theology that emerged through this community that became a "vintage theology," a theology that keeps its original flavor and increases in vigor as it leads the church closer to the coming day of the Lord.

THE CONTINUITY AND DISCONTINUITY OF THE EARLY CHRISTIAN COMMUNITY

There is a sense in which spatial distance from the womb of tradition appears to be necessary for the emergence of life beyond the womb. It was at Jerusalem that Pentecost occurred, an event that has often been noted as the rebirth of Israel as the Messianic community. In this new event there is both continuity and discontinuity. The formation of the believing Jews into a new community was based on two things. First, this community was constituted by the tradition of the Twelve. The original disciples were reconstituted as apostles through the breath of the Spirit following the resurrection of Jesus: "he breathed on them and said to them, 'Receive the Holy Spirit' " (John 20:22). Judas, of course, having taken his own life was not one of them. However, in their minds, the number twelve was a necessary structure of continuity, and after the ascension of Jesus, under Peter's leadership, they chose Matthias to take the place of Judas on the basis that he was among those who were followers of Jesus from the beginning and who was a witness to his resurrection (Acts 1:15-26). Thus the church at Jerusalem began to take shape even prior to Pentecost based on the felt need for continuity and the constitution of a central point of authority and control. It was into this already established community that the Holy Spirit came, leading to the multiplication of believers among the Jews. As it turned out, however, the moment (*kairos*) of Pentecost was subsumed in the time line (*chronos*) of historical continuity by the Jerusalem church. Both before and after Pentecost the tradition of the Twelve prevailed even as the witness and growth of the community expanded. What resulted was a messianic movement within the historical Jewish tradition where circumcision and observance of the Jewish law continued as the theological litmus test of conformity and community.

Meanwhile, it appears that the Spirit of the resurrected and ascended Jesus was already pushing the envelope of historical continuity and traditional thinking. Joseph, a native of Cyprus, was filled with the Spirit and became attached to the Twelve. Though he was an outsider, so to speak, he soon impressed the Twelve with his apostolic gift of encouragement and was renamed Barnabas, after his generous act of selling his property and giving the proceeds to the apostles for distribution to the poor. Later, Barnabas was recognized as an apostle in addition to the Twelve, indicating that the sharp lines of traditional authority were already beginning to be blurred as the defining structure of the early church.

The encounter between Saul of Tarsus and the risen and ascended Christ on the road to Damascus, however, threatened the authority and eventually the theology of the Jerusalem church (Acts 9). Returning to Jerusalem, Saul was met with suspicion by the Twelve because of his former activities against the believers, and only by the intercession of Barn-abas was he admitted into their fellowship. Threats against Saul led some of the believers to get him out of town and on his way back to his home in Tarsus (Acts 9:26-30). When Saul (who later assumed the Roman form of his name, Paul) reflected back on this experience, he added his name to the list of those within the line of historical continuity who were witnesses to the resurrected Jesus. His name, however, while appearing last, is not intended to be part of that tradition. "Last of all," he wrote, "as to one un-timely born, he appeared also to me" (1 Corinthians 15:8). While scholars speculate as to the significance of the rather unusual term "untimely" (*ektrōma*) that Paul used to describe his own encounter, it probably does not mean a "late birth" (i.e., one occurring at the end of a procession) but actually "premature" (i.e., one born ahead of time). Some translate the word as equivalent to an abortion—or a premature, extraordinary birth. All of the other witnesses to the resurrection encountered Jesus prior to his ascension, but Paul encountered Jesus after he had ascended to heaven. It's as if Paul wants us to understand that the Jesus who is to come at the end of the age had already appeared to him. No other human has yet experi-enced that encounter, only Paul. What a moment!

REVELATION AND RELIGION

My thesis is that the emerging church at Antioch is distinguished by its new theological orientation, not by its geographical distance from Jeru-salem, although distance sometimes allows what proximity denies. I will paint in broad brush strokes the theology of the emerging church at An-tioch in order to lay the foundation for what will follow in this book—an attempt to provide an emergent theology for a contemporary form of emerging churches that is biblically based and culturally relevant. In do-ing this I will contrast the emergent theology of the church at Antioch as a missionary church with the theology of the church at Jerusalem. In the remainder of this chapter I want to show why a theology based on reve-lation, such as that emerging out of Antioch, is a more "vintage" theology than a theology based on religion as represented by Jerusalem. It may appear that I am overgeneralizing at points and overstating certain assumptions in order to make my point. However, I believe that a fair reading of the New Testament documents will support my basic thesis.

What clearly set apart the emerging church at Antioch from the church at Jerusalem was a theology of revelation as contrasted with a theology of religion. The theology of the Jerusalem church was committed to historical precedent, crippled by religious scruple and controlled by a fortress mentality. Every venture out of Jerusalem, even by an apostle, was tethered to home base by a theological bungee cord. A prime example is Peter's encounter with Cornelius, a Gentile and a Roman soldier. Directed by a vision at the house of Simon in Joppa, Peter preached the gospel to Cornelius, his friends and relatives. During the sermon the Holy Spirit fell upon all who believed his word and as a result Peter baptized them. When the church in Jerusalem heard of this, they summoned Peter to account for his actions and criticized him for eating with Gentiles and baptizing the uncircumcised. Upon hearing Peter's lengthy explanation they consented saying, "Then God has given even to the Gentiles the repentance that leads to life" (Acts 11:18). This concession was a superficial one, as it turned out, for the leaders of the church in Jerusalem continued to criticize and oppose the ministry of Paul on a theology based on the law of Moses. Much later, Peter himself, while visiting the church in Antioch, was rebuked by Paul for separating from the uncircumcised Gentile believers under the influence of certain delegates of the church at Jerusalem who came to oppose the fellowship of Jewish believers with uncircumcised Gentiles (Galatians 2:11-14).

The emerging church at Antioch, in contrast, was oriented to a theology of revelation as led by Paul, whose own testimony was that he had received his gospel not from human sources but by revelation (Galatians 1:11-12). He made a special trip to Jerusalem in response to revelation (Galatians 2:2). He claims to have received his knowledge of the mystery of the gospel by revelation (Romans 16:25; Ephesians 3:3); he frequently refers to revelations in his correspondence with the Corinthian church (1 Corinthians 14:6, 26, 30; 2 Corinthians 12:1, 7). Paul refers to guidance by visions, dreams and direct intervention of the Holy Spirit in his missionary work (Acts 16:9; 22:17; 27:23). While the Old Testament Scriptures were the basis of his theological reflection, his interpretation and use of the Scriptures were guided by his revelational theology. He was often criticized for this and responded to his critics by saying that his theology and ministry were finally to be commended or judged by the Lord Jesus who was coming. "I do not even judge myself," he wrote. "I am not aware of anything against myself, but I am not thereby acquitted. It is the Lord who judges me. Therefore do not pronounce judgment before the time, before the Lord comes. . . . Then each one will receive a commendation from God" (1 Corinthians 4:1-5). This is more than a claim for apostolic authority, it was for him a method of doing theology. It was the content of his apostolic teaching, not merely his role as an apostle that he was defending. In fact, he was so bold as to say that if anyone, including he himself or an angel from heaven should preach a different gospel than what he had received by revelation they were to be accursed (Galatians 1:8-9).

Paul will not yield his authority as an apostle to those who heard the spoken words of Jesus prior to his death and resurrection. He fully accepts these teachings and acknowledges them in the context of his own teaching. But he claims that the same Jesus is now revealing his will through the mission of the Spirit, so that Paul can claim the same source for his teaching as an apostle as do those who have their source in the remembered words of Jesus.

This must have been an astounding claim at the time—that Paul first insisted on its veracity in the face of those who were eyewitnesses to what Jesus said and did before his resurrection and ascension! It would be one thing to say that the Spirit is the agent of redemption, whereby the hearts of men and women are opened to hearing the gospel of Christ. It is quite another thing to claim, as Paul did, that the Spirit is the very revelation of the work of Christ opening new dimensions of truth as a basis for theological reflection on what has already been revealed.

Paul's theology of the Holy Spirit goes far beyond a theology of renewal through an experience of the Spirit. There is an understanding of
the Pentecost experience among some that it results in a theology of a
Spirit-filled life or a theology of the baptism of the Spirit. For Paul, the
Spirit is the Spirit of Jesus Christ working to reveal truth, not merely to
express spiritual feelings and stimulate spiritual worship.

At the same time, however, Paul's theology of revelation through the
Spirit did not seem to be a kind of "word revelation" or "rhema revelation" that has popularity today among some Pentecostal Christians. The
Spirit may also have given revelation through the gift of discernment and
prophecy within the context of the Christian assembly. Paul does not
deny that this was also experienced by the Corinthians (1 Corinthians
12). But these words of revelation seem to be largely words that enhance
and enable other aspects of his ministry rather than becoming a basis for
theological reflection.

What is clear, however, is that Paul did not base his argument for his
apostolic authority on these private revelations alone but on the work of
the Spirit among those to whom he ministered Christ. What became un-
deniable, so that even those in Jerusalem had to acknowledge it, was that
the Spirit of Jesus was doing signs and wonders among the Gentiles, and
that many had come to believe that he was the Messiah through Paul's
ministry. This was a critical issue at the Jerusalem conference, where Paul
was sent by the church at Antioch, along with Barnabas and others, to
address the question of circumcision for the Gentile converts (Acts 15).
Paul didn't argue his case based on his personal revelation experience
but on the grounds of the manifestation of the Spirit of God through his
missionary activity among the Gentiles. What constitutes "revelation" for
Paul is not a private experience but an open, public and obvious work
of the Holy Spirit as the continuing ministry of Christ.

The fruit of the Spirit's work, for Paul, was the evidence for the work
of the Spirit. To the Christians at Thessalonica, Paul wrote, "our message

of the gospel came to you not in word only, but also in power and in the Holy Spirit and with full conviction" (1 Thessalonians 1:5). These early Christians "turned to God from idols, to serve a living and true God, and to wait for his Son from heaven, whom he raised from the dead—Jesus, who rescues us from the wrath that is coming" (1 Thessalonians 1:9-10).

This theology of revelation became the distinctive theology of the emerging church at Antioch and of the churches that emerged through Paul's missionary activity working out of Antioch. What Paul had to argue was that the emerging church was a continuation of the ministry of Jesus despite the clear break with the theology of religion as represented by the church in Jerusalem. This is an issue not only for the first century church but a theological issue for emerging churches in our present generation. Emerging churches must continually argue their theological continuity with Christ in the context of critical discontinuity with religious forms and historical traditions that, like the old wineskins that they are, can hardly contain the new wine.

THE CORNERSTONE OF CONTINUITY

The Jerusalem church sought to extend its own life as a movement out of the historical tradition of their own apostolic order. It is true that Paul well understood the significance of the foundation laid by the first apostles. Writing to the church at Ephesus he reminded them, "So then you are no longer strangers and aliens, but you are citizens with the saints and also members of the household of God, built upon the foundation of the apostles and prophets, with Christ Jesus himself as the cornerstone" (Ephesians 2:19-20). The continuity, however, as Paul envisioned it, was not in the historical link with the original apostles but due to the eschatological reality of the Jesus who was resurrected and ascended and present in the community through the Holy Spirit.

Jesus likened himself to the cornerstone that God had chosen. When his authority was questioned by those who were presumed to be guardians of the temple and the law, he replied: "Have you never read in the scriptures: 'The stone that the builders rejected has become the cornerstone; this was the Lord's doing, and it is amazing in our eyes'?" (Matthew 21:42; Psalm 118:22-23). As the first apostle, Jesus is the cornerstone for the apostolic foundation. Indeed, after his resurrection and ascension, Peter speaks of Christ as the "living cornerstone" and of members of the church as "living stones": "Come to him, a living stone, though rejected by mortals yet chosen and precious in God's sight, and like living stones, let yourselves be built into a spiritual house, to be a holy priesthood, to offer spiritual sacrifices acceptable to God through Jesus Christ" (1 Peter 2:4-5). Rather than viewing apostolic authority as vested only in the original Twelve, Paul viewed Jesus himself as the true apostle, as the author of Hebrews was later to articulate clearly: "Therefore, brothers and sisters, holy partners in a heavenly calling, consider that Jesus, the apostle and high priest of our confession, was faithful to the one who appointed him, just as Moses also 'was faithful in all God's house'" (Hebrews 3:1-2).

Following the resurrection of Christ, the early church was realigned to the living cornerstone, with the church comprising "living stones." We might picture Christ as both the historical cornerstone of the original apostles as well as the contemporary "living cornerstone" of the church as follows:

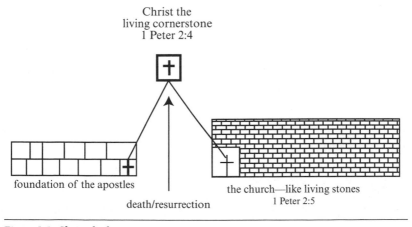

Figure 1.1. Christ the living cornerstone

The cornerstone connects the church to its apostolic foundation as the above diagram shows. At the same time, the risen Christ is the cornerstone of the church in every generation. As such, continuity with the apostolic foundation for the church at Antioch was well established through Christ as the cornerstone. This provided a theological criterion for Paul as he argued for the authority of the emerging church at Antioch over and against the demand by the Jerusalem church that he submit both his theology and his ecclesiology to their approval. This led Paul to suggest a quite radical discontinuity between the old order and the new order marked by the death and resurrection of Jesus Christ. The discontinuity relates to the side of historical, religious or ethnic priority. On the side of God's election and gracious covenant as fulfilled through Jesus Christ and the coming of the Holy Spirit, there is real continuity. Paul's own apostolic authority and commission rested on this fact; so did his theological hermeneutic.

No longer could circumcision be a criterion for belonging to the kingdom of God when the circumcised Messiah died and his circumcision did not save him. No longer can the regulations and rituals of the law bind persons with cultic power now that the Spirit of the resurrected Christ had become the new law (Romans 8). These things were only "shadows," but the "substance" belongs to the Christ who died and is now alive (Colossians 2:17). Through this Christological hermeneutic, Paul is able to find trajectories of theological tradition in the Old Testament that strongly support the theology of the emerging church.

There is a strong sense of continuity in Paul's theology, but this continuity rests solely in the relation between the Spirit given at Pentecost, the Spirit of Christ who confronted him on the Damascus road and the Spirit of the historical Jesus who died and was raised again. Thus Paul makes no clear distinction between Spirit of God, Holy Spirit, Spirit of Jesus and Spirit of Christ. Each of these ways of speaking refer to the unity of Word and Spirit as revealed through Jesus, descended from

David according to the flesh, and Jesus Christ, raised from the dead and declared to be "Son of God with power according to the spirit of holiness" (Romans 1:4).

For Paul, the nature of the church could only be established through continuity and discontinuity. His theology of the church was developed as a theology of the mission of the Spirit as the continuing mission of Jesus as Son of God. In his letter to the Roman church, in particular, Paul cites the faith of Abraham before he was circumcised as the basis for justification. So then it is through faith in the promise of God by which righteousness comes (continuity), not through the Mosaic law (discontinuity), as many of Paul's contemporaries claimed (Romans 4). Not only that, through faith both Jews and Gentiles become heirs of the promise given to Abraham by which "all the families of the earth" should be blessed. Through this Jesus Christ, who is descended from David according to the flesh but declared to be Son of God in power through the resurrection (Romans 1:4), a new relation of continuity is established between the Jew and Gentile as well as between the old covenant and the new covenant (Galatians 3:23-29).

The organic connection between the church (new covenant) and Israel (old covenant) is now established through Christ, even though the forms of the old cannot be required as a condition for participation in the new. Nor does one's standing in the former community of Israel grant automatically a place in the new community of the Spirit. "We [Jews]," says Paul, "have come to believe in Christ Jesus, so that we might be justified by faith in Christ, and not by doing the works of the law" (Galatians 2:16). Between Isaac and Ishmael is the barren womb of Sara, so that Isaac is the child of promise and grace. The continuity is solely due to the promise, fulfilled through grace, not due to natural process or religious standing.

In the same way, between the church and Israel is the empty tomb of the Messiah. The resurrected Christ is the "child of promise," so that both Jew and Gentile have access to the Father through him. Paul stresses the point that the offspring promised to Abraham was singular, not plural (Galatians 3:16). Christ is actually this offspring promised to Abraham. The continuity between the church and Israel is thus through Christ alone, so that all who belong to Christ through the Spirit, both Jews and Gentiles, are "Abraham's offspring, heirs according to promise" (Galatians 3:29). This continuity is not established through historical succession but through the resurrection of the Messiah (Christ) and the sending of the Holy Spirit. The emerging church of Antioch claims full apostolic authority and structure through direct continuity with Christ though the presence and power of the Holy Spirit. The basis for this, as Paul argued, is revelation not merely religious tradition or historical precedent.

EMERGING CHURCHES AS MISSION-MINDED COMMUNITIES

The book of Acts is the foundational document for the emerging church at Antioch and the expanding of God's kingdom as the continuing mission of Christ through the direction and power of the Holy Spirit. The establishing of communities of new believers westward throughout the Greek and Roman world of that day by teams sent out of Antioch marks the emerging church of every generation as a mission-minded community of Christ. Paul's letters to these churches during his own travels produced a narrative theology that to this day constitutes the theological core of the New Testament. Mission and theology are not adjunctive to the nature of emerging churches but constitute both their nature and purpose.

The church exists as the missionary people of God—that is its nature. The mission of the church is to embody in its corporate life and ministry, the continuing messianic and incarnational nature of the Son of God through the indwelling of the Holy Spirit. The nature of the church is determined in its existence as the continuing mission of Christ in and to the world. The church's nature, as well as its mission and ministry, have their source in the life of the triune God: Father, Son and Holy Spirit.[3]

This requires a theology that views the nature and mission of the church as a unity of theory and experience. This Paul was careful to do in his formulation "one body and one Spirit . . . one Lord, one faith, one baptism" (Ephesians 4:4-5). Paul makes it clear, the ministry of the Holy Spirit is essential to a knowledge of Jesus as the incarnate Lord. "No one speaking by the Spirit of God ever says 'Let Jesus be cursed!' and no one can say 'Jesus is Lord' except by the Holy Spirit" (1 Corinthians 12:3). But he also warns, "Anyone who does not have the Spirit of Christ does not belong to him" (Romans 8:9).

The nature of the church, argued Paul, could not rest solely upon a historical link with Jesus and the Twelve but upon the Spirit of the resurrected Christ who has "broken down the dividing wall . . . [of] hostility," and created in himself "one new humanity in place of the two" (Ephesians 2:14, 15). The critical phrase for Paul with regard to the nature of the church is "new creation" (2 Corinthians 5:17). This is "from God, who reconciled us to himself through Christ, and has given us the ministry of reconciliation" (2 Corinthians 5:18). The connection between the old covenant and the new covenant is a real one, but it's also one that is eschatological in nature. The relation is not predicated on historical necessity but on covenant faithfulness on the part of God.

When Paul was challenged as to the authority by which the Gentile churches were operating, he argued that with the death and resurrection of Jesus Christ a new age has broken into the old, so that these eras now overlap. Theologian David Ford says it well:

> The new is being realised now through the Holy Spirit, so the most urgent thing is to live according to the Spirit. It certainly involves present eschatological freedom, hope beyond death and the signif-

---

[3]See Charles Van Engen, *God's Missionary People* (Grand Rapids: Baker, 1991); and Darrell L Guder, *Be My Witnesses* (Grand Rapids: Eerdmans, 1985); Darrell L. Guder, *The Continuing Conversion of the Church* (Grand Rapids: Eerdmans, 2000); Darrell L. Guder, ed., *Missional Church* (Grand Rapids: Eerdmans, 1998).

icance of the Church in history. . . . If God is free to open history from the future then the future need not mirror the past. In the Church this combines with the message of the cross to allow for discontinuities and innovations.[4]

We are thus warned against seeking to establish direct links between historical events, even those that belong to the historical Jesus, and the being of the church in the contemporary age. The result of attempting to do this leads to the question of the authority by which the church is constituted. If the church is historically determined in its authority, it will either seek some kind of institutional connection with the past or in a strongly clerical ecclesiology based on a link with historical precedent, neglecting the role of the Holy Spirit as the present authority of Christ.

A THEOLOGY FOR EMERGING CHURCHES

When we grasp the heart of Paul's theology of the emerging church, we are impressed by several things. First, Paul became the theologian of Pentecost, transforming it from a festival into a foundation for the life and growth of the church. Second, Paul became the primary theologian of the early emerging church, defining the gospel of Christ as an imperative of mission before it becomes a subject of proclamation in the church. Third, Paul produced an authentic praxis theology, discovering anew the truth of the gospel in the context of Christ's ministry in the world.

Central to an emerging church theology is a view of God's mission through the Spirit by which the Spirit of God in creation is united with the Spirit of God through Christ seeking the restoration of the whole of God's creation. The theological formula—Christ Jesus—encompasses the whole of the messianic mission of God as the Father who sends the Spirit and begets the Son. Incorporated in this formula is the cosmic sig-

---

[4]David F. Ford, "Faith in the Cities: Corinth and the Modern City," in *On Being the Church,* ed. Colin E. Gunton and Daniel W. Hardy (Edinburgh: T & T Clark, 1989), p. 248.

nificance of Christ's death and resurrection as an atonement for the sins of the whole world and "life for all" (Romans 5:18). In saying Christ Jesus, Paul captures the liberating and reconciling power of the Spirit of God as a vital and compelling agent of transformation, overcoming the power of sin, canceling the power of evil, and creating a new humanity within every nation, tribe and culture (Ephesians 2:11-22).

Paul's theology originates in the mystery of God's own eternal and gracious election of all humanity through his own incarnate humanity, Christ Jesus. This theology culminates in the eschatological vision whereby God's gracious election of humanity through his Son is brought to fulfillment through the Spirit's work of effective calling so that "every knee should bend, in heaven and on earth and under the earth, and every tongue should confess that Jesus Christ is Lord, to the glory of God the Father" (Philippians 2:10-11). To know Christ Jesus is to experience the depth of the mystery of God's own love for the Son, the Son's own love for the Father and the Spirit's work of love in enabling us to also become children of God.

This is why Paul uses the language of adoption to indicate that even as Christ was raised from the dead to "become a Son of God" in power, so we too will become "joint heirs" with Christ through our resurrection and adoption. "The whole creation," says Paul, "has been groaning in labor pains until now; and not only the creation, but we ourselves, who have the first fruits of the Spirit, groan inwardly as we wait for adoption, the redemption of our bodies" (Romans 8:22-23). The Holy Spirit is the present and continuing work of God's redemption through adoption into the divine sonship of Christ. Christ continues his apostolic ministry as Lord, seated at the right hand of the Father (Colossians 3:1). Paul has no problem with this differentiation within the work of God, for God is known as the one God in all his working.

This apparently accounts for Paul's self-conscious distinction between words directly reported to him by the disciples and his own teaching that he claims as having the same authority. For example, to the Corinthians he writes, "To the married I give this command—not I but the Lord," then he goes on to state a teaching Jesus gave before his crucifixion. But then he adds, "To the rest I say—I and not the Lord"; here he does not have a direct citation from Jesus. This distinction is not made, however, for the purpose of giving greater authority to the words spoken by Jesus before his crucifixion than to the words that Paul speaks on behalf of Jesus. For he concluded by saying, "I think that I too have the Spirit of God" (1 Corinthians 7:10, 12, 40). "Now the Lord is the Spirit," wrote Paul, "and where the Spirit of the Lord is, there is freedom" (2 Corinthians 3:17). Paul wrote to the Corinthian Christians, who were in confusion regarding the freedom of the Spirit's gifts, reminding them that though there were a variety of gifts, there is but one and the same Spirit. There are varieties of service but the same Lord (Jesus), and there are a variety of workings but the same God who inspires them all in every one (1 Corinthians 12:4-6). This is an early trinitarian theology formulated as a means of grounding the manifestation of the Spirit in Christ, and the ministry of Christ in God the Father.

When we remember that Paul's ministry and the writing of this letter preceded the writing of the four Gospels, we see the emergence of a trinitarian theology from within mission theology. To be sure, what came to the early disciples following Easter as a commission directly from the risen Lord was part of the oral tradition that Paul would have learned immediately upon his conversion. Yet, more than any other witness to the resurrection, it was Paul who carried out this commission of Christ and so was led to develop a theology of the continuing mission of Christ through the Spirit.

The unity or oneness of God's being, for the Israelite, was not mathematical but organic and synthetic. God's work is one with his being, and so to praise his work is to praise him. To acknowledge the Spirit of Christ is to acknowledge Christ, and to acknowledge Christ is to acknowledge the Father, one God in all his works. Paul wrote to the Roman Christians, "I appeal to you, brothers and sisters, by our Lord Jesus Christ and by the love of the Spirit, to join with me in earnest prayer to God on my behalf" (Romans 15:30). This is a trinitarian understanding of the inner relations between God as Father, Son and Holy Spirit.

Here we see how the mission theology of the emerging church laid the foundations for what later became the trinitarian confession and theology of the church. Jesus claimed an identity between himself and the Father due to the works of the Father manifest in him. Later, John can remember Jesus saying, "Do you not believe that I am in the Father and the Father is in me? . . . Believe me that I am in the Father and the Father is in me; but if you do not, then believe me because of the works themselves" (John 14:10-11). The works and the words bind the identity of Jesus and the identity of the Father into a unity of divine revelation. In like manner, the Spirit claims identity with Jesus. Jesus promises that the Spirit, whom the "Father will send in my name," "will bring to your remembrance all that I have said to you" (John 14:26 NASB). When the Spirit does come, Jesus told them, "He will glorify me, for he will take what is mine and declare it to you. All that the Father has is mine. For this reason I said that he will take what is mine and declare it to you" (John 16:14-15).

We remember that these words of Jesus recorded by John were written long after Paul had developed the theology of the emerging church with its intrinsic trinitarian structure. What the disciples had first remembered concerning Jesus' promise of the Spirit, and no doubt shared as oral history, became for Paul an actual experience of hearing the words of Jesus as from the contemporary Lord.

The praxis of the Spirit of the risen Christ constituted the new school of theology for Paul. As he proclaimed the gospel of a crucified and resurrected Messiah, he witnessed the convicting and transforming power of the Holy Spirit. He reminded the church at Thessalonica of this compelling testimony to the power of the gospel when he wrote, "our message of the gospel came to you not in word only, but also in power and in the Holy Spirit and with full conviction. . . . [Y]ou turned to God from idols, to serve a living and true God, and to wait for his Son from heaven, whom he raised from the dead—Jesus, who rescues us from the wrath that is coming" (1 Thessalonians 1:5, 9-10).

On the one hand, the nature and mission of the church depend on the vital life that it shares with Christ. For this, the church receives and celebrates its life in the Spirit, for without the Spirit it cannot have its life rooted in Christ. On the other hand, the nature and mission of the church depend on its bearing the continuing ministry of Christ to the Father on behalf of the world. For this, the church receives and exercises the gifts of the Spirit through its members as the ministry of Christ. If the church were to abandon the mission and ministry of Christ that now take place in the humanity of the church's solidarity with the world, the church would forsake its share in the reconciliation of the world to God through Christ (2 Corinthians 5:18-21). If the church were to lose the presence and life of the Spirit as the source of its own existence and life, the church would sever its vital connection to Christ so that its worship would become worthless and its religion mere ritual.

The church is not only Spirit-filled, it is raised with Christ and through Christ has access to the Father in the one Spirit (Ephesians 2:17-18). As the inner life of Jesus in his relation to the Father is constitutive of Christology, so the inner life of the church in its experience of Jesus Christ by the presence of the Holy Spirit is constitutive of ecclesiology. The Spirit that creates the church through the renewal of life and faith is the Spirit of the resurrected Jesus Christ. As Jesus Christ was raised from the dead by God, the Father of glory, and so designated Son of God, we too have been made alive, argues the apostle Paul, as a dwelling place of God in the Spirit and so become children of God (Romans 1:3; Ephesians 1:5, 20; 2:2, 22).

This is emerging church theology!

CONCLUDING NONTHEOLOGICAL POSTSCRIPT

Emerging churches are often accused of lacking theological sophistication, critical intellectual competence and, occasionally, official clerical authorization. If that is the case today, it was also what the emerging church out of Antioch faced in its day. In the face of such criticism Paul responded with what we might call naive realism. I don't use naive realism in contrast to critical realism such as one finds in modern concepts of epistemology. In modern thought naive realism tends to be identical with idealistic or mental concepts of what is real, leading to a kind of arrogance. It leaves no room for mystery and does not depend on revelation. Postmodern critical realism approaches reality as something that involves more interaction between what is real and a person's perception of it. Paul Spaulding suggests that "modest realism" might be a better way to speak of the way that knowledge of reality involves something of the knower as well as openness to a more-than-meets-the-eye (or fills the mind) experience of reality. "Reality is the dynamic medium in which human knowing does its work. Both human knowing and the reality it knows are in a dynamic state.[5]

In 1979, as part of a team of theologians and Young Life leaders, I spent a week in Germany, where we presented papers and had discussion with German theologians and pastors concerning an incarnational approach to evangelizing German young people. At the end of the week I asked Professor Peter Stuhlmacher, "How is it that we can spend a week discussing the biblical basis for evangelism without having a New Testament scholar like your self from Tübingen challenge us as on the basis of recent textual criticism theories?" His response was rather stunning, I thought. "Some of us have concluded that redaction criticism of the text has come to a dead end and that we should simply accept the text as Word of God given to the believing community and read and use it as such!" I think that my own concept of naive realism began at that mo-

---

[5]Paul L. Spaulding, "Proclaiming Christian Truth in a Postmodern Culture" (D.Min. diss., Fuller Theological Seminary, 2005), p. 48. Spaulding goes on to say, "What is discovered in this process is *living truth*, that dynamic confidence that reality has been engaged, that a real connection has been made that is trustworthy and true" (ibid., p. 58).

ment! No one could accuse Stuhlmacher, an internationally respected scholar, of mere naiveté concerning the problems of the Scripture text. But when he approached the text as Word of God, the scaffolding of criticism dropped away and left the text to speak for itself.

By "naive realism" I refer to how Jesus, the Gospel authors and the apostle Paul used language in an unapologetic way—reality and knowledge were assumed to be true, not parts of the truth. I use the "naive realism" to express a view of knowledge as a "subjective experience of an objective reality." This kind of knowledge was represented by the Hebrew way of knowing as contrasted with the Greek. John Pedersen points out the difference between the Hebrew way of knowing as contrasted with our modern, post-Cartesian way of thinking.

> In the Hebrew dictionary we look in vain for a word which quite corresponds to our "to think." There are words which mean "to remember," "make present," and thus to act upon the soul. There are words expressing that the soul seeks and investigates; but by that is not meant an investigation which analyses and arranges according to abstract views. To investigate is a practical activity; it consists in directing the soul towards something which it can receive into itself, and by which it can be determined. One investigates wisdom, i.e. makes it one's own.[6]

---

[6]John Pedersen, *Israel: Its Life and Culture* (London: Oxford University Press, 1973), 1:108-9. Truth was grounded in being for the Hebrew in somewhat the same way that it was for the pre-Platonic period in Greek philosophy. Martin Heidegger argues that the original Greek concept of reality as "truth disclosing itself," was "humanized" by Plato when truth was subordinated to an idea. Prior to Plato there was a succession of logos to being. Truth (*alētheia*) was the "uncovering" or disclosing of logos through being. Following Plato, says Heidegger, logos became abstracted from being and became mere *nomos*, law or custom, and served as a standard of correctness (Martin Heidegger, *An Introduction to Metaphysics* [New Haven, Conn.: Yale University Press, 1959]; see also my essay "Theology as Rationality," in *Christian Scholar's Review*, 4, no. 2 [1974]: 132-33). Thus, Heidegger maintains, one can draw a line straight from Plato through Descartes to Nietzsche with an ultimate question mark raised over the role of metaphysics as a basis for knowledge (Heidegger, *Introduction to Metaphysics*, pp. 9, 18-19, 43; see also, L. Versényi, *Heidegger, Being and Truth* [New Haven, Conn.: Yale University Press, 1965], pp. 54-55).

Far from being guilty of mere naiveté, Paul moved beyond the complicated complexities raised by his critics to establish his theological assumptions as realities that carried their own apologetic to any one who demanded to know the source and truthfulness of his theology. "I am not out of my mind," Paul responded when charged with being insane when testifying to his personal encounter with Christ, "but I am speaking the sober truth" (Acts 26:25). When faced with the challenge of worldly wisdom he argued that "we have the mind of Christ" (1 Corinthians 2:16). Really! "Yes, really," he might respond. Paul could say as a matter of fact, in Christ "the whole fullness of deity dwells bodily" (Colossians 2:9). No philosophical proofs, no empirical data, no historical evidences were provided. What might appear as simply naive was for him profoundly simple and therefore real. Whereas modern epistemology looks for evidences of truth, Paul looked for evidences of reality. The reality of Christ was for him the basis for the truth of Christ.

The Gospel accounts of Jesus' ministry abound with naive realism. The man whom Jesus healed, who was blind from birth, was not swayed by his critics who challenged the authenticity of the healing and the authority of the one who healed him, but responded simply, "One thing I do know, that though I was blind, now I see." When challenged further as to the credentials of the one who healed him, he responded, "If this man were not from God, he could do nothing" (John 9:25, 33). "I am the resurrection and the life," claimed Jesus (John 11:25). "I am the way, and the truth, and the life," was his response to those who wanted him to point the way to God. "No one comes to the Father except through me" (John 14:6).

The revelation of God through Jesus Christ is so profound in its realism when grasped by faith and empowered by the Spirit that the critical mind becomes blind when attempting to challenge or even confirm it (John 9:39-41). Emerging churches have the truth on their side when they live and witnesses to the reality of Christ. Biblical truth stands as revealed truth on the reality of its effect not merely on the theory of its origin. The discipline of biblical scholarship and critical theological thinking is not disparaged by the emerging churches. But the theology of the Word of God goes deeper than textual criticism that only scratches the surface of Word of God and, as a result, yields superficial reasons rather than revelational reality.

My aim is to set forth a new vision for an emergent church theology that is biblically based and that is singed by the flames of a burning bush and touched by the tongues of fire lighted at Pentecost. This book is written for those who are hungry for a theology that is sweet and digestible as honey and who are sick to death of a fiber-filled bran where the kernel is gone and the husks pounded into indigestible wafers. I want to fan the fires of renewal already burning and light new ones among the underbrush of the church's institutional bureaucracy. I want the fire to burn back into the theological faculties and to reinvigorate weary and disheartened academicians, opening windows and throwing open doors through which men and women of the Spirit can learn from each other. I want our theological manuals and mission strategies to be opened for audit by those who have stories to tell of God's power and presence and, who themselves, have been transformed, healed, and empowered by the reality of Christ who comes where the two or three are gathered in his name.

This is what emerging churches are about. It is about theology, not geography. It is not about a new theology but a vintage theology—the same, yesterday, today and forever. It is about a theology that sings as well as stings, igniting the mind and stirring the heart.

2   IT'S ABOUT CHRIST,
NOT JUST CHRISTOLOGY

W̲ho do people say that the Son of Man is?" The disciples were a bit
nonplussed. Was there a right answer? Was he speaking of himself, or
was this some kind of theological trick question? Better to play it safe
and give multiple answers to a simple question: John the Baptist? Elijah?
Jeremiah? or one of the prophets? They gave Jesus several options to answer his own question! The second question could not be avoided: "But
who do you say that I am?" Peter had an inspiration: "You are the Messiah, the Son of the living God." Jesus responded, "Blessed are you, Simon son of Jonah! For flesh and blood has not revealed this to you, but
my Father in heaven" (Matthew 16:13-17). In other words, "Peter, you
are right, but you will never know why!" There it is: naive realism! The
truth is revealed in a confession before it is encoded in a creed.[1]

Emerging churches should continue to recite the creed, but their life
depends on a personal knowledge of Christ, not just having an orthodox
Christology. I realize that the creeds were a confession of faith—*credo* (I
believe). But the creeds confess *that* one believes and *what* one believes.
Is it not the case, all too often, I fear, that one can recite the creed without

---

[1]I cannot claim originality for this concept because Jaroslav Pelikan said something similar regarding the emergence of the doctrine of the Trinity in theological reflection after the church
rose from its knees to talk about the faith (see Jaroslav Pelikan, *The Christian Tradition* [Chi-
cago: University of Chicago Press, 1971]).

ever answering the question, "Who do you say that I am?"

Saul of Tarsus, stunned by the appearance of Christ on the road to Damascus, fell to the ground and cried out, "Who are you Lord?" The answer came, "I am Jesus, whom you are persecuting" (Acts 9:5). In this way the question is turned around and becomes a Christological question. That is, the original confession of Peter that Jesus was the Messiah was in response to the question put to him by Jesus. In the case of Saul, the question, Who? led to the revelation that Jesus was indeed the one who was crucified, risen from the dead and ascended to the right hand of the Father. This was the beginning of the "gospel" that Saul (Paul) received by revelation and that became the core theology of the emerging church.

THE CHRIST OF CHRISTOLOGY

I think that it would be fair to say that there is no formal Christology in the New Testament, though there are Christological statements.[2] For example, Paul's letter to the church at Philippi, according to many scholars, contains an earlier Christological hymn (Philippians 2:6-11). In 1 Timothy 3:16, there is also a brief Christological formula: "He was revealed in flesh, vindicated in spirit, seen by angels, proclaimed among the Gentiles, believed in throughout the world, and taken up in glory." However, we must say that the Christology of the New Testament is descriptive rather than analytical; it is embedded in narrative and proclamation rather than codified in creedal formulas.

Among the theologians of the early church, Christology became more of a formal, academic and even philosophical inquiry into and defense

---

[2]This is the view of C. Norman Krause: "Thus one does not find a standardized orthodox language system in the New Testament, but an appeal to apostolic witness. . . . And because the gospel does not give us a standardized christological formula, we test our descriptive statements, not by their conformity to some rational formula either in the New Testament or the creeds, but by their adequacy to describe Jesus as God's saving presence with us—Jesus as he is known in apostolic experience" (Jesus Christ Our Lord: Christology from a Disciple's Perspective [Scottdale, Penn.: Herald, 1987], p. 82).

of the person of Christ, particularly as to his divine and human natures as subsumed in one person. The first few centuries of the Christian church were wracked with Christological controversies, some of which resulted in the basic creeds of orthodoxy, such as Nicea (325), Constantinople (381) and Chalcedon (451). Throughout the medieval church, through the Reformation and to the present day the nature of the person of Jesus Christ has provoked controversy, division and a flood of books on Christological themes. Christian theology has generally begun with the revelation of God in Jesus Christ. Christology then developed by examining the person and work of Christ as foundational for a doctrine of atonement, justification, and sanctification through the indwelling of the Holy Spirit. This theological tradition has served the church well through the centuries, and has preserved the core of orthodox faith in the face of competing theories and theologies.

Yet where we look for consensus there remains conflict; where we seek clarity there remains confusion; where we expect light there is often darkness. Nor is it of much help when Karl Barth says, "All ecclesiology is grounded, critically limited, but also positively determined by Christology."[3] In the face of the confusion of tongues when it comes to Christological writings, I would add, all Christology is grounded and positively determined by Christ. No wonder emerging churches find more certainty in going back to the naive realism of the New Testament when they claim that it is more about Christ than just Christology. It is not my intention to supplant the formal dogma of Christology with a "Jesus only" experiential theology, but rather to suggest that the emerging church is about the contemporary presence of the historical Christ.

Dietrich Bonhoeffer reminded his students in his earlier lectures that the who question precedes the how and what questions when it comes to Christology. "The question 'Who are you?' is the only appropriate question. . . . If we look for the place of Christ, we are looking for the

---

[3]Karl Barth, *Church Dogmatics* 4/3 (Edinburgh: T & T Clark, 1962), p. 786.

structure of the 'Where?' within that of the 'Who?' We are thus remaining with the structure of the person. Everything depends on Christ being present to his church as a person in space and time."[4] In his earliest work Bonhoeffer set forth his basic axiom (more of an emergent church theology than a Christological formula!): "Christ exists as community."[5] Christ is our contemporary, he argued, not merely an historical person who disappears behind the futile search for the "historical Jesus" that has preoccupied much of modern Christology.

It is important to know that the Spirit that came upon the disciples at Pentecost is the Spirit of the resurrected and incarnate Son of God, Jesus Christ. In this way we avoid thinking that we can receive the Spirit in the same way that Jesus did. It is not the Spirit that provides continuity between the mission of God in Jesus and in the church, but it is Jesus Christ himself, through the coming of the Holy Spirit.

THE CHRIST OF PENTECOST

We cannot have a Pentecost without Christ. Pentecost is Christ's *parousia,* or manifestation in the world, empowering his disciples with his presence as they bear witness to him to the ends of the earth. This is in fulfillment of what he had promised before his crucifixion: "I will not leave you orphaned; I am coming to you" (John 14:18).

Nor can we have a Christ without Jesus of Nazareth. The anointing of Jesus by the Spirit to be the Messiah (Christ) was preceded by his conception and birth as the very incarnation of the Logos of God, existing with God before the world began (John 1:1-4). The divine Son of God came into the world through the historical and human birth of Jesus of Nazareth. The early Christians, of course, discovered his divine sonship only in retrospect. His mission revealed to them his origin as the "only begotten" Son of the Father, conceived by the Holy Spirit. Following his

---

[4]Dietrich Bonhoeffer, *Christology* (New York: Harper & Row, 1966), pp. 30, 61.
[5]Dietrich Bonhoeffer, *Sanctorum Communio* (Minneapolis: Fortress, 1998).

baptism, this trinitarian reality was secured in the tradition by the witness of John, "the Father loves the Son and has placed all things in his hands" (John 3:35), by the descent of the Spirit upon him, and the voice from heaven, "This is my Son, the Beloved" (Matthew 3:17).

Our vision of Christ is illuminated by the Spirit of Christ poured out at Pentecost (Acts 2). For those who were intimately acquainted with Jesus, such as the disciples, the Christ of Pentecost was familiar and friendly. If, on occasion, they sometimes longed for the days when they had him to themselves, they now lived for the days in which his power and presence could be experienced by so many others. Jesus Christ is alive and his life is given for all! And he continues his ministry in the world through the Holy Spirit that came upon the believers at Pentecost and that continues to abide with and empower Christians throughout the world.

I cannot overemphasize the importance of the continuity between the historical person Jesus of Nazareth and the Christ of Pentecost. If it isn't the same Jesus who wept at the tomb of Lazarus, who healed the eyes of the blind and who claimed to be the bread that came down from heaven, and who emerged out of the tomb, then the Spirit at Pentecost will be clothed with our own human understanding. And we all know of the disturbing distortions that plague the church when a different Christ emerges out of each new Pentecostal experience. The issue may not be which Christology is the right one, but which Jesus is the real one![6] The Lebanese poet and philosopher Kahlil Gibran once wrote, "Once every hundred years Jesus of Nazareth meets Jesus of the Christian in a garden among the hills of Lebanon. And they talk long: and each time Jesus of Nazareth goes away saying to Jesus of the Christian: 'My friend, I fear we shall never, never agree.'"[7]

It may well be that the primary reason for the forty days between the

---

[6]Brian McLaren discusses "the seven Jesuses I have known" in chapter one of *A Generous Orthodoxy* (Grand Rapids: Zondervan, 2004).
[7]Kahlil Gibran, *Sand and Foam* (New York: Alfred Knopf, 1954), p. 77.

resurrection of Jesus and his ascension was so this continuity could be stamped on the minds and hearts of the first disciples. While Luke does not expand on these days, he alludes to frequent meetings and convincing evidences that it was the same Jesus they knew before his death that now showed himself to him after his resurrection. "After his suffering he presented himself alive to them by many convincing proofs, appearing to them during forty days and speaking about the kingdom of God" (Acts 1:3).

Pentecost is the beginning point for a theology of Jesus Christ because the Holy Spirit reveals to us the inner life of God as the Father of Jesus and of Jesus as the Son of the Father. To receive the Spirit of God, wrote the apostle Paul, is to "have the mind of Christ" (1 Corinthians 2:10, 16). Jesus said, "All things have been handed over to me by my Father; and no one knows the Son except the Father, and no one knows the Father except the Son and anyone to whom the Son chooses to reveal him" (Matthew 11:27). The Holy Spirit is the revelation to us of the inner being of God as constituted by the eternal and ongoing relation between Father and Son.

Pentecost is also the beginning point for our own relationship with God through Christ, for apart from the Spirit we are alienated from the life of God. Paul wrote, "Any one who does not have the Spirit of Christ does not belong to him" (Romans 8:9). Pentecost is thus both a theological and experiential compass. Without true knowledge of God (theology) our experience can slip into delusion and even become demonic. Without authentic experience of Christ (faith), our theology can become vain and empty speculation. Without the light of Pentecost as the empowerment of Spirit, the resurrection recedes into mere historical memory. The eschatological reality of the risen Christ as the parousia (emergent One), empowering each contemporary event of faith and ministry, often tends to be replaced by historical theology on the one hand and pragmatic principles for institutional life and growth on the other. However, Pentecostal experience without a relation with Christ is like a sailboat with neither oars nor rudder—it can only move when there is a wind, though it cannot steer when it is moving. An orthodox Christology without Pentecostal experience is like a barge of coal anchored to shore. It has fuel but no fire, and even if it should burn, it has no engine to turn water into steam and steam into power. And so, not being able to transport people, it takes on more coal!

Emerging churches are not only Spirit-filled, they are raised with Christ and through Christ have access to the Father in the one Spirit (Ephesians 2:17-18). As the inner life of Jesus in his relation to the Father is constitutive of Christology, so the inner life of the church in its experience of Jesus Christ by the presence of the Holy Spirit is constitutive of a theology for emerging churches.

THE CHRIST OF EMERGING CHURCHES

I find it incredible that Paul, who had such a powerful and convincing experience of Jesus Christ, probably never met or even saw him on earth prior to his resurrection and ascension into heaven. If there were any occasions on which Saul of Tarsus personally heard Jesus of Nazareth speak or even came into the most casual contact with him, there is no evidence of this in Scripture, not even a clue in Paul's own writing. The disciples, on the other hand, who spent three years with Jesus prior to his death and resurrection and who met with him in his resurrection body over a period of forty days before his ascension say so very little about him after Pentecost! Scholars agree that the four Gospels were written after Paul had completed his missionary travels and probably had died, there is virtually little that the community of believers at Jerusalem contribute to our knowledge of Christ with respect to the church. Peter does say in his sermon at Pentecost, "Jesus of Nazareth, a man attested to you by God with deeds of power, wonders, and signs that God did through him among you, as you yourselves know. . . . This Jesus God raised up, and of that all of us are witnesses" (Acts 2:22, 32). Yes, Peter and John did perform miracles "in the name of Jesus Christ of Nazareth"

(Acts 3:6; 4:10). That's about it. The emphasis was on the Spirit of the Lord Jesus as a source of power rather than on Christ himself as their contemporary.

I say it is incredible to me that those who knew Jesus the best during his time on earth contribute so little to our theological understanding of Jesus as compared with Paul, who never ate with him, touched him or heard him preach to others. Have I missed something? Or did Luke leave out more than he brought in with his account of the beginnings of the church in Jerusalem? In any event, it is largely from Paul that we draw our knowledge of the Christ of the emergent church with its base in Antioch and its ministry flung out through their known world by Spirit-anointed ministry of Paul and others.

Paul reveals to us the very person of Christ through the presence of the Spirit, not merely the power of the Spirit of Christ. I marvel at the deep dimensions of Paul's knowledge of Christ. Of course he was well aware of the anecdotal material that was no doubt communicated to him directly by the disciples (oral tradition). Paul's references to "having a word of the Lord" in giving answers to questions put to him by members of the church in Corinth give evidence of this (1 Corinthians 7:10; 11:23). Did his fifteen-day stay with Peter in Jerusalem three years after his conversion contribute to this? I wonder what they talked about (Galatians 1:18)? The one thing that Paul makes clear is that he did not receive his gospel from those at Jerusalem but directly from the Lord by revelation (Galatians 1:11-12). Nor will he yield to their claim that only those who were witnesses to Jesus during his life have knowledge of him. Paul makes no distinction between knowledge of the historical Jesus and knowledge of the risen and ascended Christ. "Have I not seen Jesus our Lord?" he claims in defense of his own apostolic authority (1 Corinthians 9:1). The Lord Jesus is not only in heaven at the right hand of the Father, he is present where the Spirit is present. "Now the Lord is the Spirit, and where the Spirit of the Lord is, there is freedom" (2 Corinthians 3:17). The very knowledge of the glory of the Lord Jesus "comes from the Lord, the Spirit" (2 Corinthians 3:18).

In a remarkable bit of naive realism Paul wrote to the members of the church at Colossae encouraging them to know, "Christ in you, the hope of glory," while at the same time saying to them, "Your life is hidden with Christ in God" (Colossians 1:27; 3:3). Not only is the Spirit within the believers, Christ himself is in them by the Spirit. The fact that Christ himself is present in the community of believers is woven throughout Paul's letters. Believers are the "body of Christ" (1 Corinthians 12:27); they are a "holy temple in the Lord" (Ephesians 2:21); they are "one body in Christ" (Romans 12:5); their "bodies are members of Christ" (1 Corinthians 6:15). "Examine yourselves," Paul exhorts, "Do you not realize that Jesus Christ is in you?" (2 Corinthians 13:5).

The Christ of the emerging church at Antioch existed as a spiritual reality embedded in the concrete empirical reality of human persons. Or as Dietrich Bonhoeffer liked to put it, "Christ exists as community." Human persons exist as a social construct and spirituality is intrinsic to social life. Because the reality of spirit is first of all a social reality rooted in the nature of human personhood, Bonhoeffer argued that the social structure of human personhood is intrinsically spiritual. The Spirit of Christ does not constitute something alongside or merely inside of a person as an individual. Rather, the Spirit of Christ joins the human spirit at the core of its social reality.[8]

The emerging church at Antioch was not a post-Judaism development originating out of the legal absolutism of the Moses' tradition. Nor are emerging churches in our generation emerging out of the universalizing and absolutizing period of modernity. On the contrary, the Christ of the emerging church for Paul was pre-Moses, going back to Abraham, and even pre-Abraham, going back to Adam. This is an important distinction for it frees the emerging church from the criticism that it is just another version of modernity. It also provides a more theological than philosoph-

---

[8]Bonhoeffer, *Sanctorium Communio*, pp. 62, 66.

ical basis for the emerging church's engagement with cultural diversity and religious pluralism.

How did Paul counter the criticism brought by those sent out from the elders at Jerusalem who claimed that the Christ of the emerging church was more Gentile than Jewish and therefore not the real Messiah as promised? Not by arguing that the Christ of Pentecost was a post-Moses Jew but that he was a pre-Moses Gentile! Let me explain.

The basic charge against Paul was that he violated the law by not requiring circumcision on the part of believing Gentiles. He even labels them as the "circumcision faction" (Galatians 2:12). Rather than claiming a postcircumcision policy based on adaptation to a broader, non-Jewish culture, Paul argued for a precircumcision theology of grace based on Abraham. Those who argued for circumcision held that someone could not be righteous before God apart from circumcision as a sign of God's covenant. In a rhetorical slash of the sword Paul cut away the basis for that criticism by asking the question, "How was [righteousness] reckoned to Abraham? Was it before or after he had been circumcised?" Answering his own question, Paul wrote, "It was not after, but before he was circumcised." Paul went on to clinch his argument by reminding his critics, "He received the sign of circumcision as a seal of the righteousness he had by faith while he was still uncircumcised." Paul's argument was that if being an orthodox Jew as distinguished from a Gentile meant being circumcised, then Abraham was virtually a Gentile. And as such, Paul wrote, "The purpose was to make him the ancestor of all who believe without being circumcised and who thus have righteousness reckoned to them" (Romans 4:10-11).

Paul was not done. There still remained the question of how the Christ of the emerging church was related to Abraham and the promise given to Abraham that through him all the families of the earth would be blessed (Genesis 12). It is simple, wrote Paul. Those who believe, both Jew and Gentile, are descendants of Abraham. "God . . . declared the gospel beforehand to Abraham, saying, 'All the Gentiles shall be blessed in you.' For this reason, those who believe are blessed with Abraham who believed" (Galatians 3:7-9). Then comes the clincher. "Now the promises were made to Abraham and his offspring; it does not say, 'And to offsprings,' of many; but it says, 'And to your offspring,' that is, to one person, who is Christ" (Galatians 3:16). Christ is the "seed of Abraham," and thus the Christ of emerging churches is the one through whom all believers (those who are baptized into Christ) inherit the promise given to Abraham through faith. "And if you belong to Christ, then you are Abraham's offspring, heirs according to the promise" (Galatians 3:29).

In a theological debate that's what I call the *Wow* factor!

Christ does not negate the law, but fulfills it. Those who are in Christ are neither "lawbreakers" nor merely "post-lawkeepers" but they are "law-completed" to coin a term. The purpose of the law of Moses was that of a disciplinarian (pedagogue) until Christ came. "But now that faith has come," wrote Paul, "we are no longer subject to a disciplinarian" (Galatians 3:24-25). "As many of you as were baptized into Christ have clothed yourselves with Christ" (Galatians 3:27). In the Greek culture a pedagogue was not the teacher but a servant (usually a slave) whose responsibility was to take the child (*paidos*) from the home to the teacher. Once the child is with the teacher, the task of the pedagogue was over. In this way, Paul viewed the law as merely a servant: of God's promise in order to bring the "seed" (son) to the teacher—Christ. From Paul's perspective the Jews who viewed the law itself as an absolute and permanent principle of righteousness (truth) killed the teacher and made themselves "teachers of the law" (lawyers). "Woe also to you lawyers!" Jesus warned, "For you load people with burdens hard to bear, and you yourselves do not lift a finger to ease them" (Luke 11:46).

Is it a stretch of the imagination to read into Paul's discourse a Christological answer to the problem of modernity rather than to take a philosophical turn to postmodernity? I don't think so. Modernity claims a form of truth that is indubitable (too evident to be doubted) and universal moral principles that stand above human culture accessible solely by human reason. Postmodernity rejects those claims in favor of truth embedded in the narratives of the human community where there is no metanarrative that reconciles all narratives to a single, compelling moral truth. Such a claim, as some have pointed out, is really itself a metanarrative! And to say that there are no universal, absolute principles or truths is itself a claim to an absolute principle![9]

Paul avoids this by a theological exegesis of Genesis by which he identifies the Christ of the emerging church with a pre-Moses (premodern) revelation of God's purpose for humanity as found not only in Abraham but also in Adam, where it all began and where it all went wrong. The Christ of the emerging church is not only the seed of Abraham that precedes the Jew-Gentile religious and cultural divide within humanity, but Christ is the "second Adam." If the fundamental human dilemma can be traced back to the original humans through whom sin and death entered into humanity so as to distort the divine image in humans and destroy the fragile spiritual bond between humans and their Creator God, then Christ is the answer: not just a theological and intellectual answer to a problem but an existential and spiritual reverse of the curse and the reconciliation of humanity to God. "For if the many died through the one man's trespass,

---

[9]With respect to the issue of modernity and postmodernity, I defer to the clear and compelling discussion of what is meant by these terms offered by Brian McLaren, *A New Kind of Christian* (San Francisco: Jossey-Bass, 2001); see also his book *A Generous Orthodoxy* (Grand Rapids: Zondervan, 2004). In his unpublished open letter to Charles Colson, a response to Colson's essay "The Postmodern Crackup: From Soccer Moms to College Campuses, Signs of the End" (*Christianity Today*, December 2003, p. 72), charging that postmodernity was "dead," McLaren defended his own postmodern view as distinguished from postmodernism. "The postmodern culture is the world in which many of us live and work and minister, sharing the good news and following the good ways of Jesus Christ. The old modern apologetic simply doesn't work for us, or our children, or their friends." Available online at <http://www.youthspecialties.com/articles/topics/postmodernism/open_letter.php>. Jimmy Long has written an engaging and helpful book suggesting strategies of ministry to an emerging generation in the postmodern context, *Emerging Hope* (Downers Grove, Ill.: InterVarsity Press, 2005). I recommend also the book by my own faculty colleague Nancey Murphy, *Beyond Liberalism and Fundamentalism* (Valley Forge, Penn.: Trinity Press International, 1996); John Franke and Stanley Grenz, *Beyond Foundationalism* (Louisville: Westminster John Knox Press, 2000); and Dan Kimball, *The Emerging Church* (Grand Rapids: Zondervan, 2003), esp. chap. 1.

much more surely have the grace of God and the free gift in the grace of the one man, Jesus Christ, abounded for many." Paul goes on to nail this down in unmistakable language: "Therefore just as one man's trespass led to condemnation for all, so one man's act of righteousness leads to justification [righteousness] and life for all" (Romans 5:15, 18). The universal implications of Christ as the "second Adam" is made clear by Paul.

> All this is from God, who reconciled us to himself through Christ, and has given us the ministry of reconciliation; that is, in Christ God was reconciling the world to himself, not counting their trespasses against them, and entrusting the message of reconciliation to us. So we are ambassadors for Christ, since God is making his appeal through us; we entreat you on behalf of Christ, be reconciled to God. (2 Corinthians 5:18-20)

The universality of Christ as Reconciler is clearly stated by Paul; that meant for him that there are no cultural barriers, no ethnic boundaries, no gender restrictions on who are to be baptized into Christ by the Holy Spirit—the Redeemer (Galatians 3:27-28).

The Christ of emerging churches is not just culturally relevant but humanly relevant. Beneath and within every culture there are human beings who share the same human dilemma—spiritual estrangement. All humans, regardless of their cultural, ethnic or religious context, are part of what God intended at the beginning (to be image-bearers of the divine) and what went wrong at the beginning—"all . . . fall short of the glory of God" (Romans 3:23). The emerging church must be culturally relevant to be sure, but it also must be humanly real. Without cultural sensitivity the reality of Christ will be hidden behind cultural imperialism—if you aren't our kind of people, you don't know our Christ. There is, as I have written, a core social paradigm that lies behind every culture in which humans exist as they always have, with basic human needs, aspirations and longings.[10]

---

[10]Ray S. Anderson, "The Sociocultural Implications of a Christian Perspective of Humanity," in *The Shape of Practical Theology* (Downers Grove, Ill.: InterVarsity Press, 2001), pp. 161-77.

I want the reader to know that I have not forgotten the basic thesis for this book, which was stated at the beginning of the first chapter. The Christian community that emerged out of Antioch constitutes the original form and theology of the emerging church as contrasted with the believing community at Jerusalem. I have said that emerging churches in our present generation can find their ecclesial form and core theology by tracing out the contours of the missionary church under Paul's leadership based in Antioch. The difference between Antioch and Jerusalem is essentially a theological difference, not merely a geographical one. In this chapter I have focused more narrowly on the Christ of the emerging church, attempting to show that the Christ that Paul knew was not only his contemporary, despite the fact that he never met Jesus of Nazareth in person before the crucifixion, but that this is the Christ that connects us to humanity from the very beginning and in every generation.

WHAT IS A VINTAGE THEOLOGY?

My use of the term "vintage theology" was inspired by the subtitle of Dan Kimball's book *The Emerging Church: Vintage Christianity for New Generations*. He uses the word *vintage* primarily with respect to the worship service, while I use it more in a theological sense. Dan stresses the fact that vintage worship goes deeper than mere novelty and creativity. Authentic worship should recapture some of the original sense of the mystery of approaching and experiencing God. The concern is for a deeper ecclesiology and spirituality rather than a superficial and consumer-oriented religiosity stimulated by innovative and spectator-oriented methods. In this view, vintage Christian faith goes back to an essential spirituality that has always been constitutive of genuine relation with God, while at the same time, it is pluralistic and diverse with respect to the culture and context of a post-Christian age set in a postmodern mindset.

I am reminded of the insightful book by Robert Weber, *Ancient-Future Faith*. Weber writes from a Protestant evangelical perspective, though with deep appreciation for the rich heritage of tradition carried forward from the first century to the present. From a contemporary Roman Catholic perspective, Colleen Carroll suggests that young people today are seeking moral and spiritual truths that provide anchors for their faith amid the relativity and shifting values of a postmodern culture.

> These young adults are not perpetual seekers. They are committed to a religious worldview that grounds their lives and shapes their morality. They are not lukewarm believers or passionate dissenters. When they are attracted to tradition in worship or deepening their commitment to it, they want to do so whole-heartedly or not at all. When they are attracted to tradition in worship or in spirituality, they want to understand the underlying reality of that tradition and use it to transform their lives.[11]

What both Weber and Carroll point to is a felt need in our postmodern culture for a spiritual reality rather than mere religious tradition. At the same time, people are searching for a connection with God embedded in truth, not merely in experience. This is very close to what I mean by a vintage theology. It tries to avoid the faddishness of some attempts to create a postmodern church. At the same time, it grasps the searching spirit in our postmodern culture and baptizes it in the stream of revelational truth that flows out of God's own immersion in the world through his incarnation in the person of Jesus. As such, my attempt is to provide a deep theology, not only a deeper ecclesiology.

In this chapter I have traced out the contours of a vintage theology that emerged originally in the Antioch church and Paul's ministry, particularly though an "emergent Christ," to paraphrase a contemporary expression. What strikes me in this exercise is the fact that the Christ of the emerging church at Antioch is, in Paul's experience, a Christ who emerges in the present out of the future. The Pentecost event was a kairos moment that occurred within a specific historical time frame but that had

---

[11]Colleen Carroll, *The New Faithful* (Chicago: Loyola Press, 2002), p. 11.

an eschatological rather than a temporal origin. The early believers in Jerusalem did not seem to grasp this due to their historically conditioned mindset. Thus, they sought to extend the post-Pentecostal community in continuity with their own preresurrection status as disciples of Jesus and as necessarily an extension in some form of their Jewish religion. This was vintage Christianity with a vengeance, as it turned out!

Paul, on the other hand, being an outsider to this community and though formerly a zealous Pharisee, was disconnected from this tradition by his encounter with the Christ who had already ascended to heaven. This is where the eschatological priority over the historical occurred as a kairos event in his own life. What I have shown in this chapter is the remarkable way that Paul's knowledge of Christ as the coming One already present through the Holy Spirit not only inaugurated a new and creative edge for the kingdom of God in the world, it resolved the age-old and divisive split between the Jew and Gentile. More than that, the Christ of emerging churches touches the deeper core of the human dilemma originating in the Fall of the first humans so that what results is not just a deeper ecclesiology but a deeper humanity. This is what makes the Christ of the emerging church so relevant in our own generation, not because of contemporary music and culturally relevant media, but because the naive realism of a Christ and humanity (rather than Christ and culture) is edifying as well as stimulating.[12]

CONCLUDING NONTHEOLOGICAL POSTSCRIPT

I teach and worship in what is both an emerging and a traditional Lutheran church, where remnants of the older Lutheran form of worship are affirmed and spiritually fed within the context of their familiar robes and rituals at the early service. What interests me is what takes place in the

---

[12]I cannot but help here but echo the judgment of others, Brian McLaren included, that Richard Niebuhr's classic book *Christ and Culture* misses the mark as essentially a product of modernity itself. The critical issue is not how Christ relates to culture but how Christ relates to humanity in every culture. The emerging church seems to have found a way.

later, more contemporary worship service where, behind the façade of what might be only a superficial cultural event of stimulation, is a deeper, more vintage, if you please, spirituality that is compelling, convicting and edifying for those who participate. And I mean "participate," for the experience is highly and intentionally interactive, though driven by a worship and praise team and led by a pastor with a palm pilot! I sit there and ask, *What's going on here?* There are Bibles in most every hand, and they are opened in response to the cues from the preacher. Often, when a Bible text is referred to and participants in the service are asked to read it for themselves, they are reminded that the Bible is our norm here. We are a church that recognizes the Bible as Word of God and our final authority. There is no attempt to prove that the Bible is the inerrant Word of God, it is simply used as having authority. If one were to question the preacher as to issues of redaction criticism (who really wrote some of the letters of Paul) and inerrancy (is every word true?) the response would probably be, "We are too busy here doing kingdom of God work to spend time on such issues."

In this church the presence of the Holy Spirit is not only encouraged but expected! Christian faith is not only inculcated by sound teaching, but Christian living is empowered by receiving and manifesting the fruit of the Spirit. There is something going on here! In an age where everything seems to be in flux, with no certainty and security in life, I see those who experience this emerging church gripped by a reality that answers to their souls' anxious searching, not just for truth but for truthfulness, not just for a new Spirit but for a deeper spirituality that heals their humanity and holds them within arms length of God through Christ in their midst. Most of them will never read the standard authors on Christology (and those who have, no longer remember their names), but they are closer to Christ than they have ever been. Come Holy Spirit!

3

IT'S ABOUT THE SPIRIT, NOT JUST SPIRITUALITY

A young woman signed the guest register of the church where I recently was a pastor. Under the category of denomination, she wrote "spiritual." I rather liked that. But because she was a one-time visitor from out of the area, I did not have a chance to explore what she meant by *spiritual*. My hunch was that she was among the many in our society today who are turned off by the institutional church and avoid identifying themselves with a denominational label, but at the same time, they have deep longings for connection with God. She was there with her parents and appeared comfortable and quite at home in our "nondenominational" service. I hoped that she found us to be a spiritual people as well!

It may be, however, that she understood the word *spiritual* in quite a different way. Spirituality in our age can as often (more often?) be found outside the edges of institutional religion than within. Without doubt there is a craving for spirituality in our culture that finds little fulfillment in the more traditional churches. Darrell Guder points toward this when he says, "The postmodern openness to perceiving life in a variety of ways has contributed to the reemergence of spirituality as a viable and necessary part of the human struggle for meaning today. People are very secular, but they are often spiritual secularists."[1]

---

[1]Darrell L. Guder, ed., *Missional Church* (Grand Rapids: Eerdmans, 1998), p. 44.

The traditional forms of spirituality tend to be individualistic, highly structured and often based on pietistic forms of the classic *imitatio Christi* (imitation of Christ) model. This form of spirituality seeks to "empty the self" of human propensities for the sake of being filled with the divine impulses of a Christlike motivation.[2] Contemporary Protestant spirituality has tended to borrow heavily from the older forms of spirituality, in what I believe is often a theologically uncritical manner and can tend more toward the human spirit than the Holy Spirit. Evidence of this is the preoccupation with personal edification, use of the so-called spiritual disciplines and an internal rather than an external form of spiritual devotion.[3]

Brian McLaren has suggested that what is needed is "not a new Spirit, but a new kind of spirituality."[4] Dan Kimball also writes of the spirituality of emerging churches: "Since emerging generations really want to experience the spiritual, shouldn't our worship gatherings provide that for which they crave? Shouldn't it be a place to connect with God, to breathe, to slow down and experience some peace as they focus on God and lift up the name of Jesus."[5]

BUT NOT ALL SPIRITUALITY IS OF THE SPIRIT

There is a human dimension to the soul's spirituality that may not have any specific religious intent or content. Dietrich Bonhoeffer argued that human spirituality is the core of the self as it becomes a self

---

[2]Examples of writings on classic forms of spirituality are Thomas à Kempis, *The Imitation of Christ* (Nashville: Thomas Nelson, 1981); Ignatius of Loyola, *The Spiritual Exercises of St. Ignatius* (Chicago: Loyola Press, 1992); Thomas Merton, *The Wisdom of the Desert* (New York: New Directions, 1960); Teresa of Ávila, *The Interior Castle* (Garden City, N.Y.: Doubleday, 1961).

[3]As an example of some contemporary and well-known works on Protestant spirituality that, despite their value in providing guidance for spiritual development and growth, tend toward an inner rather than outer spiritual life, which is also more individual than social, see Richard Foster, *Celebration of Discipline* (San Francisco: Harper & Row, 1978); Dallas Willard, *The Divine Conspiracy* (San Francisco: HarperSanFrancisco, 1998).

[4]Brian McLaren, *Reinventing Your Church* (Grand Rapids: Zondervan, 1998), p. 13.

[5]Dan Kimball, *The Emerging Church* (Grand Rapids: Zondervan, 2003), p. 144.

through social relation with others.[6] Created in God's image through a divine inbreathing of Spirit (Genesis 2:7), humans have an intrinsic spiritual nature that has a drive toward health and wholeness. The French Jesuit philosopher, Pierre Teilhard de Chardin once said, "We are not human beings having a spiritual experience, but spiritual beings having a human experience."[7] There is a place for emotional, mental and even physical well-being and health that has a deeply spiritual core. However, if we agree that everything that is human is intrinsically spiritual, it must also be said that not everything that is spiritual is healthy for our humanity. The kind of spirituality that we embrace is dependent on the kind of spirit that we seek. Or it could be said another way. The kind of spirituality that overtakes us is dependent on the kind of spirit that possesses us. Indeed, I fear that spirituality without a clear understanding of the spirit that moves within us can be as dangerous in its final effect as it might be stimulating in its first impulse.

Forms of contemporary spirituality cross a wide spectrum, embracing outright secular and humanistic expressions of spirituality as well as intensely religious forms. Keith Miller extends spirituality to the entire spectrum of our earthly life:

> Spirituality begins with the renewing and satisfying of the soul, and extends to every aspect of the Christian's life before God and others. . . . In reality, spirituality encompasses all that we are and do—our Christian beliefs, heart connection to the Lord, relation-

---

[6]"Spirit," Bonhoeffer wrote, "is necessarily created in community, and the general spirituality of persons is woven into the net of sociality. We will find that all Christian-ethical content as well as all aspects of the human spirit are only real and possible at all through sociality. . . . It will be shown that the whole nature of human spirit [Geistigkeit], which necessarily is presupposed by the Christian concept of person and has its unifying point in self-consciousness (of which we will also be speaking in this context), is such that it is only conceivable in sociality" (Dietrich Bonhoeffer, Sanctorum Communio [Minneapolis: Fortress, 1998], pp. 62, 66).
[7]Pierre Teilhard de Chardin, cited in Gordon McDonald, The Life God Blesses (Nashville: Thomas Nelson, 1994), p. 76.

ships with others, how we use our money, our concern for the environment, and so on.[8]

On the same continuum of human-spirit spirituality, some are seeing new forms of spirituality emerging out of barren secularism and humanism. The so-called New Age spirituality arrived on a variety of fronts in the last decade of the twentieth century. While assimilating some forms of Eastern religion with a bent toward mystical self-transcendence, contemporary spirituality can also include more esoteric tendencies toward the channeling of spirits from another dimension as well as focus on meditation in search of inner peace.[9]

Matthew Fox, a contemporary Christian theologian and popular author identified with the New Age movement, advocates a form of "creation spirituality."[10] Psychologist Robert Grant has studied the effects of trauma on victims of work-place accidents, violence, rape and war. From his studies Grant concludes that there are many people who experience what he calls "trauma spirituality." When the fundamental beliefs and concepts on which people have built their lives crumble and fall apart, some people walk through the "metaphysical minefields" brought on by traumatic experience and emerge with an altered consciousness and new access to their spiritual core.[11]

---

[8]Keith Miller, *The Secret Life of the Soul* (Nashville: Broadman & Holman, 1997), p. 65.

[9]For example, see J. Gordon Melton, Jerome Clark and Aidan A. Kelly, *New Age Encyclopedia* (Detroit: Gale Research, 1990); Russell Chandler, *Understanding the Age* (Dallas: Word, 1988); Paul Heelas, *The New Age Movement* (Cambridge, Mass.: Blackwell, 1996); Wouter J. Hanegraaff, *New Age Religion and Western Culture* (New York: E. J. Brill, 1996); Kerry D. McRoberts, *New Age or Old Lie?* (Peabody, Mass.: Hendrickson, 1989); Ron Rhodes, *The New Age Movement* (Grand Rapids: Zondervan, 1995). See also my book *The New Age of Soul* (Eugene, Ore.: Wipf & Stock, 2001).

[10]Fox suggests that the persistent teaching of the "fall/redemption" motif in traditional theology fails to satisfy the contemporary spiritual seeker. "A devastating psychological corollary of the fall/redemption tradition is that religion with original sin as its starting point and religion built exclusively around sin and redemption does not teach trust. . . . What if, however, religion was not meant to be built on psychologies of fear but on their opposite—on psychologies of trust and ever-growing expansion of the human person?" (Matthew Fox, *Original Blessing* [Santa Fe, N.M.: Bear, 1983], p. 82).

[11]Robert Grant, "Trauma Spirituality," *Orange County Register,* October 14, 1999, p. 14. In his

This recalls the apostle Paul's experience in Athens when he came across the various altars erected to the different gods that they worshiped. Speaking to the Athenians he said: "I see how extremely religious [spiritual] you are in every way. For as I went through the city and looked carefully at the objects of your worship, I found among them an altar with the inscription, 'To an unknown god.' What therefore you worship as unknown, this I proclaim to you" (Acts 17:22-23). Paul then used the occasion to preach the gospel of Christ and his resurrection. Contemporary spirituality could be viewed as a form of worship at an altar labeled "To an unknown spirit." Spirituality without the Spirit of God may be as much a violation of our own humanity as a void in our religious experience. The bottom line of all such human-centered spiritualities is that the human self becomes its own center of spirituality and health.[12]

We must take care that emerging churches do not become just another form of spirituality but a movement of God's Spirit on the creative edge of the kingdom of God breaking into the various cultures of our present age, often in conflict with existing forms of spirituality.

A Ph.D. student whom I mentored recently is from Nepal. When he became a Christian, his own father chased him out of the house with a gun. He was put in prison by the authorities for his evangelistic work,

---

research he found that a traumatic experience can break a person, destroying trust in God and the world. Or it can provide a spiritual opening—a crack that opens the way to a deeper sense of life's meaning. Human beings, he says, have a tremendous resiliency under such conditions and discover spiritual depths that lead to greater faith and hope than they have every known. Not all have this experience, he admits, but it is more common than we realize.

[12]"Without a center that lies outside of the self," said theologian Emil Brunner, "there is a 'sorrow of heart' that experiences ultimately the disharmony of existence." To attempt to organize the self around its own center, warned Brunner, produces what might be called spiritual or psychological health, but "without a center that gives the self a place of hope in God beyond oneself, this 'health' is itself a form of madness, or insanity." "To place the central point of existence outside God, who is the true Centre, in the 'I' and the world, is madness; for it cannot be a real centre; the world cannot provide any resting-place for the Self; it only makes it oscillate hither and thither" (Emil Brunner, *Man in Revolt* [1939; reprint, Philadelphia: Westminster Press, 1979], p. 235]).

because the Christian religion was illegal in that country. Through his Spirit-filled life and testimony in prison, many of the prison guards were converted. He was finally released. His father came to know Christ and donated a parcel of land in the capital city in Nepal, where my future student began a Bible School. Following his Ph.D. work he returned to Nepal, and through his training program of lay pastors, he has planted scores of churches throughout Nepal, all based on a theology of spiritual power—signs and wonders, if you please. He told me that in the world-famous Valley of the Gods (Shangri La), there are more gods than people in the entire land. In a land where spirituality is woven into the very culture and embedded in its geography, the emerging church in Nepal, as in Antioch, is where the Holy Spirit of Christ is the power of the gospel.

Another of my students is from Nigeria and has established a Bible school and has trained scores of men and women who have planted more than two dozen churches, some meeting under large trees. His church and Bible school were burned down in the Muslim-Christian riots, and without any mission board or external support other than some "mission partners" in the United States, he has rebuilt both. Until recently he was without a car, having to walk or use public transportation in order to carry out his teaching and pastoral duties. This is an emerging church in Nigeria much like Antioch, where a Spirit-filled and Spirit-empowered ministry thrives. But in Europe the church is dying, and in North America the church is declining. Spirituality without the Spirit of God might be an illusion, the religiosity of a hallucinating secular culture magnifying the human spirit to fill the void left in the twilight of the gods.

A former student of mine from Norway who was mentored in ministry by people from the Vineyard Church while in the Los Angeles area went back to Trondheim, Norway, where he began an emerging-church ministry in the Antioch tradition. Through this church, where the presence and power of the Holy Spirit were evident, several hundred young people who had been drawn into the New Age movement came and experienced the reality of the Spirit of Christ. It was not a new kind of spirituality that drew them; these young people had already tried that in their attraction to the New Age philosophy and worldview. It was the Spirit of Christ who encountered them and drew them into an authentic Christian community of faith.

Eugene Peterson, well-known author and translator of the Bible (*The Message*), in an interview on "spirituality" said, "It's a kind of specialized form of being a Christian, that you have to have some kind of in. It's elitist. Many people are attracted to it for the wrong reasons. Others are put off by it: . . . I try to avoid the word." He continued, "Spirituality is not about ends or benefits or things; it's about means. It's about how you do this. How do you live in reality?" He concluded, "I'm rooted in pastoral life, which is an ordinary life. So while all this glitter and image of spirituality is going around, I feel quite indifferent to it, to tell you the truth. And I'm somewhat suspicious of it because it seems to be uprooted, not grounded in local conditions, which are the only conditions in which you can live a Christian Life."[13]

What he did not say, and what I think needs to be said, is that the religious life of a Christian and the Christian community is not just about spirituality, it's about the Spirit. Discernment of the Spirit is essential in the formation of a spiritual community. "Do not believe every spirit," wrote the apostle John, "but test the spirits to see whether they are from God. . . . [E]very spirit that does not confess Jesus is not from God" (1 John 4:1, 3). If we are to seek a new spirituality, as McLaren says, then we need to look for the kind of spirit that lies behind the spirituality of our contemporary emerging churches.

Spirituality can become a catchword without spiritual content. The Spirit, not just spirituality, emerges in and through a church that vibrates with the real presence of Christ. There is Godly spirituality, resulting

---

[13]Eugene Peterson, "Spirituality for All the Wrong Reasons," in *Christianity Today*, March 2005, pp. 46, 48.

from the coming of the Holy Spirit into the human spirit without displacing the human but empowering the human spirit to bear the fruit of the Spirit (Galatians 5:22-23). The Holy Spirit does not constitute something alongside or merely inside a person as an individual. Rather, the Spirit of God joins the human spirit at the core of its social reality in order to produce a Godly spirituality. Theologian Jürgen Moltmann says:

> The Holy Spirit does not supersede the Spirit of creation but transforms it. The Holy Spirit therefore lays hold of the whole human being, embracing his feelings and his body as well as his soul and reason. He forms the whole Gestalt of the person anew by making believers 'con-form' to Christ, the first born among many brethren (Romans 8:29).[14]

TOWARD AN EMERGENT THEOLOGY OF THE SPIRIT

Pentecost occurred at Jerusalem not Antioch. And Peter was filled with the Spirit and spoke in other tongues before Paul had that experience (Acts 2)! Peter was the theologian of Pentecost while Saul of Tarsus (Paul) was still raging against the new believers, "breathing threats and murder against the disciples" (Acts 9:1). The community of disciples following Pentecost expressed a two-dimensional spirituality—praising God and ministering to others. What does this then say about my thesis that Antioch, not Jerusalem is the source for an emergent theology of the Spirit?

The fact is, the community of believers at Jerusalem is the original source of the emerging church, not because of their own missiological convictions but rather due to the persecution that drove many of them to seek refuge in other places, including Antioch (Acts 8:1; 11:19). Paul had his own personal Pentecost, not on the road to Damascus, where he encountered the risen Christ, but in Damascus, after he remained without sight and without food for three days. Paul's Pentecost occurred

---

[14]Jürgen Moltmann, *God in Creation* (San Francisco: Harper & Row, 1985), p. 263.

when Ananias, a Spirit-filled disciple laid hands on him and prayed, with the result that Paul recovered his sight and was filled with the Holy Spirit (Acts 9:1-19). By his own testimony, Paul did not go back to Jerusalem for three years, and then only for about two weeks, during which time he stayed with Peter, and was only accepted into the band of disciples by the intervention of Barnabas (Galatians 1:18; Acts 9:26-27). Fourteen years passed (probably including the three years) before Paul went back again to Jerusalem. He makes this point in order to prove that he did not receive his gospel from the disciples at Jerusalem who preceded him in the faith, but directly by revelation through the Spirit. "Those leaders contributed nothing to me" (Galatians 2:6). Paul's emergent theology of the Spirit did not come from the emerging church at Jerusalem but directly from Christ through the Spirit. Paul's theology and missionary work was developed and affirmed in Antioch, not Jerusalem. For this reason I envision Antioch, rather than Jerusalem, as the source for an emergent theology for emerging churches.

A friend, in reading my manuscript asked, "Ray, why do you stress the book of Galatians so much in your development of an emergent theology? Why not talk more about Jesus, for those in emerging churches like to think of Jesus as one with whom they can identify more easily?" My response was that the apostle Paul completed his mission work and wrote his emergent theology through letters to the churches, and he died before any of the Gospels were written! Scholars agree that the earliest of the four Gospels (ordinarily assumed to be Mark) was written no earlier than A.D. 68, after Paul had completed his missionary journeys.[15] Of course, Paul would have known of the oral testimony of the disciples concerning Jesus' life and ministry, though he seldom made reference to

---

[15]Irenaeus (d. c. A.D. 200) wrote, "Mark wrote his Gospel 'after the departure [exodus] of Peter and Paul.' " *Departure* usually is used in this context to mean death, indicating that the early tradition of the church recognized that the written Gospels followed the life and ministry of Paul (G. E. Graham Swift, introduction to the book of Mark, in *The New Bible Commentary*, ed. D. Guthrie et al., 2nd ed. [London: Inter-Varsity Press, 1970], p. 851).

that (1 Corinthians 7:10, for example). Instead, Paul, having directly encountered the risen Lord Jesus and receiving the gift of the Spirit of Christ, claimed that he "had the mind of Christ" as the source for his teaching (1 Corinthians 2:16). This is not to say that the Gospels and the words of Jesus are not as important for emerging churches as the teaching of Paul, but it does mean that Paul is our primary source in the New Testament for an emergent theology for emerging churches. An emerging *theology* of the Spirit did not arise in Jerusalem, but in Antioch. And it was Paul's defense of that point in his letter to the Galatian church that stands as the basis for my own development of an emergent theology. The Spirit of Paul's Christ is that of the historical Jesus. In the name and power of that Spirit, Jesus speaks through the Gospels to us today. Emerging churches live by the life, teaching and presence of Jesus—but when they ask, "Who is the Spirit that fills and empowers us?"—Paul gives us the answer. The Holy Spirit is the Spirit of Jesus, the crucified, resurrected and risen Lord.

The emerging church at Antioch, not Jerusalem, leads us to discover an emergent theology of the Spirit. The church at Antioch was formed and existed only by the Spirit, unlike the church at Jerusalem that had a built-in structure to rest on. Jerusalem had the tradition of the Twelve, existing leaders, continuity with the past, a temple that they could use as a central gathering place, and synagogues in which they could experience and express their messianic Judaism. Yes, they were empowered by the Spirit at Pentecost, but their existence was held in place by the long line of continuity with their ethnic and religious tradition.

This was not the case at Antioch. Without the Spirit, they could not exist. Without the Spirit they had no Christ, no leadership, no history, no past and no future. For emerging churches the Holy Spirit is not an accessory but rather the engine that propels and the fuel that empowers. The emerging church at Antioch manifested a Spirit-directed life that issued in a messianic mission that was not found at Jerusalem. If the emerging church is about spirituality, it needs to know the name of the Spirit.

The apostle Paul's theology of the Holy Spirit as the Spirit of Jesus, and of Jesus as the divine Son of God the Father, is extraordinary. We are forced to ask, What did he know and how did he know it? The clearest testimony to the Spirit is found in the Gospel of John as that of Jesus Christ who breathed on the disciples. But we can assume that Paul had no knowledge of this Gospel, because he had completed his ministry and was dead by the time that John wrote it. Paul's brief contact with the apostles at Jerusalem was hardly the basis for a tutorial in John's theology of the Spirit. Besides, Paul explicitly rejects the notion that his gospel came from them or from any other human; it came from direct revelation. "For I want you to know . . . that the gospel that was proclaimed by me is not of human origin; for I did not receive it from a human source, nor was I taught it, but I received it through a revelation of Jesus Christ" (Galatians 1:11-12).

This reminds us that Paul encountered the risen and ascended Christ on the road to Damascus prior to his being filled with the Spirit through the ministry of Ananias (Acts 9:17). This surely accounts for the fact that Paul's theology and experience of the Holy Spirit is grounded in the person of Jesus Christ. Paul did not have a spiritual experience of a religious nature, but rather he had a Christ experience of a spiritual nature. The importance of this cannot be over emphasized for emerging churches. To have knowledge about Christ without the Spirit is still to be blind, if we follow the sequence of Paul's experience. The encounter with Christ through the dazzling light on the Damascus road left Paul blind. It was only in being filled with the Spirit that Paul's eyes were opened and he came to know Christ in a deep personal and spiritual way. "Brother Saul, the Lord Jesus, who appeared to you on your way here, has sent me so that you may regain your sight and be filled with the Holy Spirit" (Acts 9:17).

We can also say that a spiritual experience without relation to Jesus Christ is liable to be only a human form of spirituality, despite whatever religious manifestations might result. Our survey of the various kinds of spirituality earlier in this chapter revealed the possibility that what is behind many such forms of spirituality may only be a variation of the human spirit. Indeed, Paul's warning to the church at Corinth was that despite their often fanatical zeal for spirituality and the exercise of the spiritual gifts, if the result is not a deeper knowledge of Christ and the edification of the community through Christ, such spirituality might only be a sound without meaning and heat without light (1 Corinthians 14:10-11). Furthermore, without the love of Christ, what might be considered the highest form of spirituality may only be like a noisy gong or a clanging symbol, which in the end gains nothing (1 Corinthians 13:1, 3). "The Lord is the Spirit," was Paul's foundational theological axiom. Our knowledge of the Lord, Paul asserts, comes from the Lord, the Spirit (2 Corinthians 3:17-18). And when the Spirit shines in our hearts we receive "the light of the knowledge of the glory of God in the face of Jesus Christ" (2 Corinthians 4:6).

The church at Jerusalem did not seem to grasp this! Or if they did, it was only in reading Paul's letters to the churches that they would come to know it. The letters of Paul were emerging-church letters, and if there is one thing we know, the church at Jerusalem, while the original emerging church, had a theological lapse that appeared to have stunted their continued expansion.

WHY EMERGING CHURCHES NEED AN EMERGENT THEOLOGY

The church that is emerging today needs to remember that without a strong biblical basis and emergent theology, it will be like a sailing ship without a rudder, drifting aimlessly or even carelessly over the open waters of contemporary religiosity. Dan Kimball, for one, has recognized this and in his more recent writing points out the need not only for a deep ecclesiology but for a deeper theological undergirding for what emerging churches practices in their worship, evangelism and mission. He writes:

But the fact is that what we practice is based on our theology. Anything we do has a theological backdrop to it. . . . [A]bsolutely everything we do in church is a reflection of what we theologically believe, whether we are consciously aware of it or not. . . . We also need to be teaching the people in our churches to be understanding this, so they consider how theology impacts what they do and practice as well.[16]

Instead of inviting Paul to become a resident theologian in order to develop and deepen their emergent theology, the Jerusalem church resisted and sought to undermine the validity of the emerging churches through its attempt to invalidate the authority and apostolic authority of Paul. We know this to be the fact when we read of Paul's own admission that did not have the "letters of commendation" that others did who came out of Jerusalem. Because the emerging church at Corinth was somewhat uneasy over this fact, Paul wrote:

Surely we do not need, as some do, letters of recommendation to you or from you, do we? You yourselves are our letter, written on our hearts, to be known and read by all; and you show that you are a letter of Christ, prepared by us, written not with ink but with the Spirit of the living God, not on tablets of stone but on tables of human hearts. (2 Corinthians 3:1-3)

I have my ordination certificate, Paul told them, written and signed by Christ himself.

The emerging churches founded by Paul were not led by credentialed elders, nor did Paul train others to assume leadership roles, except with the possible cases of Timothy and Titus, for example. And even here, if Timothy was sent to give leadership to the church at Ephesus, as some think, his "credentialing" was not by an ordination certificate but by "the

---

[16]Dan Kimball, "Emerging into a Worshiping Community of Missional Theologians," prepublication manuscript, November 2005. Used by permission of the author.

gift of God that is within you through the laying on of my hands" (2 Timothy 1:6). Paul's confidence in the Holy Spirit as the Spirit of Christ to provide instruction, guidance and leadership for the emerging churches was bold and uncompromising, even though it sometimes led to some degree of confusion and even disorder. Despite all that, Paul did not write to the churches (at Corinth, for example), telling them to replace the leadership of the Spirit with a more top-down ecclesial system of authority. On the contrary, he simply reminded them that the unity of the Spirit and the mind of Christ given by the Spirit were to be sought by consensus. "There is one body and one Spirit, just as you were called to the one hope of your calling, one Lord, one faith, one baptism, one God and Father of all, who is above all and through all and in all" (Ephesians 4:4-6). Paul went on to say, "But each of us was given grace according to the measure of Christ's gift" (Ephesians 4:7). Really? Was each member of the body equal with regard to having authority to receive and dispense Christ's gift? Apparently so.

When the Corinthian church became exercised over the issue of baptism—some were evidently claiming baptismal privileges!—Paul reminded them that he himself did not baptize many, apparently leaving that to other members of the body (1 Corinthians 1:13-17). Who was allowed to baptize did not seem important to Paul; anyone filled with the Spirit of Christ was authorized to baptize in the name of Christ. Baptism was a function of the body of Christ itself, not restricted to those who held an office. Similarly, when Paul dealt with confusion and disorder at the Lord's Supper in the Corinthian church, he made did not make an issue of who was permitted to administer or serve the Lord's Supper but rather appealed to the respect and remembrance that each should have of the other as members of Christ's body (1 Corinthians 11). This does not mean that the church cannot and should not recognize and appoint within its own members those who represent the entire body of Christ in the ministry of Christ. Disorder and chaos is not a sign of spiritual freedom, as Paul reminded the church at Corinth. At the same time, ministry is first of all Christ's ministry through the whole body, and baptism into Christ is baptism into the ministry of Christ as well as fellowship with Christ.[17]

This is why the emerging-church movement today is not calling for another Reformation but a new kind of church. As Brian McLaren says, what is needed is "not a new denomination, but a new kind of church in every denomination."[18] But I maintain that what is also needed is a new kind of theology for emerging churches, an emergent theology that has its roots in the church at Antioch rather than in Jerusalem. Lazarus came out of the tomb but was still clothed with the grave clothes. "Unbind him, and let him go," said Jesus (John 11:44). This is what I am trying to do—attempting not to reform modernity by turning to postmodernity but to go back to the future, so to speak. I want to unbind the church of its wrappings so that the church of the future can emerge in our midst through the Holy Spirit, as Christ emerged from his tomb and is emerging from his future into our present.

CONCLUDING NONTHEOLOGICAL POSTSCRIPT

There was a time when I felt that I had my fill of "Spirit-filled" Christians. During the 1960s while serving as pastor of a new congregation, some came into our fellowship and pronounced that they were filled with the Spirit and began to question our credentials along that line, mine included! One such person approached me and said, "Pastor I realize that you are not anointed with the Spirit and so cannot understand our con-

---

[17]The concept of baptism as ordination for ministry is the thesis of the article "Christ's Ministry Through His Whole Church and its Ministers," produced by the Fourth World Conference on Faith and Order (July 1963). Originally published in *Encounter* 25, no. 1 (1964): 105-29, it has been republished in *Theological Foundations for Ministry*, ed. Ray S. Anderson (Grand Rapids: Eerdmans, 1979), pp. 430-57. "Through our baptism Christ incorporates us and ordains us for participation in his ministry. . . . For Jesus baptism meant that he was consecrated as Messiah. For us baptism means that we are consecrated as members of the messianic people. . . . According to this understanding of baptism, to be baptized means immediately to be called to the life of a servant" (ibid., p. 432).
[18]Brian McLaren, *Reinventing Your Church* (Grand Rapids: Zondervan, 1998), p. 13.

cerns for the church." Another couple secured a copy of our list of babysitters (teenage daughters of members of the church) and called them to come to their home to babysit. However, instead of leaving, they began to pressure the young girls to receive the Holy Spirit and to speak in tongues as evidence. Some parents became concerned about this and called it to my attention. When I visited the couple to talk about what they were doing, I heard the same refrain, "Pastor we know that you do not have the Holy Spirit, so you will not understand that the Holy Spirit has sent us to this church to help your young people be filled with the Spirit." I replied, I have no problem with that as long as the parents are informed, so I am going to send a letter to every parent informing them of your intention, and if they are willing to allow their daughters to come to your home under the pretext of babysitting, I have no problem with that." The couple became quite upset with this plan, but I implemented it, and they left the church never to return! I could never understand why the Holy Spirit, as they claimed, did not like that much openness!

I have had students tell me that they were concerned that I was not filled with the Spirit. I learned never to argue with them, for I discovered that the Spirit that had filled them was not interested in the Spirit that lived within me. When I tried to say that it was not a matter of my having all of the Spirit but that it was more a matter of the Spirit having all of me, and that I was working on that, I could sense immediately that this only confirmed their diagnosis. I think (hope!) that I have grown beyond reacting and responding in this way. I also sense that the Spirit of the emerging church where I encounter the Spirit of Christ is closer to what I was trying to say.

According to the apostle Paul every Christian has been baptized into the body of Christ by the Holy Spirit (1 Corinthians 12:13). Each Christian has the Spirit as the life of Christ within the self. The Spirit thus works from the inside out. In other words, the emphasis on the filling of the Spirit is not on how to get the Spirit inside of ourselves but allowing the Spirit who is already inside as a subjective reality to produce the fruit of the Spirit as an objective reality. There is a fullness of the Spirit-filled life that is part of our growth into the fullness of Christ (Philippians 3:12-16). While the fullness of the Spirit is within each of us, not all of us are at the same stage in experiencing that fullness, that is, growing into maturity in Christ (Ephesians 4:11-16).

For Paul the fruit of the Spirit was a singular, not a plural, word (Galatians 5:22). Paul liked the singular noun—he had earlier in that letter argued that the word *offspring* as used in Genesis to speak of the promise to be given through Sarah was singular, not plural, and thus referred to Christ (Galatians 3:16). In the same way, the "fruit of the Spirit" is singular, not plural and refers to Christ, who is the content of the fruit expressed through the human qualities of gentleness, kindness, peace, love and so on (Galatians 5:22-23). Don't ask me whether or not I have the spiritual fruit of kindness, ask those who live with me! I may think that I am kind, but I am not an authority on that. In the same way, I may think that I am filled with the Spirit, but I am not an authority on that either.

In the emerging church where I am at home, the Holy Spirit as the Spirit of Christ is allowed to live freely and openly as Christ himself is present in our midst. I thrive on the Spirit of Christ expressed through praise, proclamation and presence. This is pure gospel for me, never mind the polity.

4   IT'S ABOUT THE RIGHT GOSPEL, NOT JUST THE RIGHT POLITY

A number of years ago the moderator of the Presbyterian Church (PCUSA) visited our campus to meet with students and faculty. At a faculty luncheon I asked the moderator about a recent case where a presbytery affirmed the ordination of a man who denied the deity of Christ. This action had provoked considerable debate, not only in that presbytery but also across the nation. The moderator, with tongue firmly in check replied, "What you need to understand is that Presbyterians have more scruples about polity than about theology!" He went on to explain that it was ironic that some were willing to permit far more latitude concerning serious theological issues than about how the church should administer the sacraments and whether or not the elders were following the Presbyterian Book of Order. "We have had more dissention in some churches over the color of the choir robes," he added, "than about the content of the creed." More recently, of course, that same denomination (as well as others) has experienced internal strife and conflict over the issue of ordination for practicing homosexuals. While this issue has obvious theological concerns, ordination itself has as much to do with polity as it does with theology.

At the seminary where I teach, a communion service for our graduates is held on campus a few days before commencement. Some years ago a faculty member protested that practice and refused to participate on the grounds that only a church under the supervision of elders could properly conduct a communion service and administer the elements. In that our seminary represents a multitude of denominations, attempts to satisfy the polity of each would be impossible, even though we certainly share the same gospel. In so many cases right polity takes precedence over the gospel. Violation of polity may be our modern form of heresy.

I am not so innocent myself in that regard! While a resident doctoral student in Scotland, I worked with an elder of a Church of Scotland parish outside of Edinburgh, where we lived, assisting him in his work with young people of the parish who did not attend church. As the Christmas season approached, I suggested that we hold a Christmas Eve service, in the church, sponsored by the young people as a way of getting them involved. I told the group about the custom we had in our California church of passing out small candles to all who attended and then lighting them at the end of the service while singing the carol Silent Night. They thought that was a marvelous idea and the service was scheduled.

As I entered with my family, I noted that the candles were not being passed out but that some who had come early had theirs. The elder explained to me that one of the older elders was quite outraged and demanded we not use candles because, as he put it, "Our ancestors died to keep candles out of the church!" It then occurred to me that the Scots fought the English in the middle of the seventeenth century over the attempt by the Church of England to impose their liturgy on the Scottish churches! Thousands of the Scottish soldiers were killed in those battles that actually raged at the nearby Pentland Hills, which I could view from the second-story window of my study and on which stands the famous Martyr's Monument. As it turned out, I was probably the first person who attempted to introduce lighted candles in that very church for over three hundred years, as the church itself had been built on an old Druid worship site in the eighth century! I learned the power of polity to trump the gospel. I also discovered that I had chosen the wrong time and the wrong place to begin an emerging church ministry!

While apartheid was still the law of the land in South Africa, I was invited to speak in Pretoria at a theological conference. During that time I attended a synod meeting of the Dutch Reformed Church, where the issue of apartheid was debated—was it a sin for which repentance ought to be offered, or was it heresy, another gospel? One speaker reminded the synod that in the early years it was an interracial church in which whites and blacks worshiped together. Some white Afrikaners came to object to drinking out of the same cup as black Christians during the Lord's Supper. He said that the synod (annual general meeting) of 1857 proposed that as a concession to the prejudice and weakness of a few, it is recommended that the church serve one or more tables to the European members after the nonwhite members have been served. This recommendation came in spite of their recognition that the Bible taught that all Christians ought to worship together. In addition the synod recommended that if the weakness of some requires that the groups be separated, the congregation from the heathen should enjoy its privilege in a separate building and a separate institution. This concession soon grew into a policy of separating white and nonwhite churches.

The speaker went on to say that fifty years later the same synod held that the separation of the races was not only God's sovereign will for the land but that failure to carry out this principle in every aspect of society was to be considered disobedience to God. When the Afrikaner political party took control of the government in the middle of the twentieth century (1948), the first prime minister was an elder of the Dutch Reformed Church who made it his policy to imprint the separation of the races through civil law so deeply that it could never be removed. As it turned out, apartheid in South Africa had its origin in church polity leading to "another gospel."

I cannot think of an instance in the modern era where a polity decision by a church body led to more than a hundred years of suppression of millions of people by a religious minority, all done under the legal authority of a nation in bondage to a false gospel. We may smile a bit at the pathetic ironies of local congregational polities, but we should never underestimate the power of polity as a means of survival on the part of a church when it goes into a fortress mentality.[1]

I suspect that criticism and even resistance to the contemporary forms of emerging churches will not be so much from the standpoint of their theology but of their polity. This will come from those churches emerging within mainline denominations where institutional traditions, polities and bureaucratic structures will feel threatened. In the end it is not about the right polity but about the right gospel. Emerging churches will get it right if it gets the gospel right.

THE GOSPEL OF THE EMERGING CHURCH

The emerging church at Antioch, under Paul's leadership, lived and proclaimed a gospel of grace, including both Jews and Gentiles and free from the legalism of the law of Moses. Paul refers to this as "my gospel" (2 Timothy 2:8). It really was not Paul's gospel, of course, but the gospel that he had received directly from Jesus Christ by revelation. Some may proclaim another Jesus and another gospel, said Paul, but there is no other gospel; those who proclaim another Jesus and another gospel are to be treated as "anathema," or accursed (Galatians 1:6-11; see also 2 Corinthians 11:4). The "other gospel" Paul contended with came out of Jerusalem. The elders in the church at Jerusalem sent delegates to Antioch—Paul calls them "certain people from James"—in an attempt to force some aspects of the law of Moses on the Gentile believers (Galatians 2:12). In the church at Antioch both Jews and uncircumcised Gentile believers gathered in unity at

---

[1]Here is a comical example: "When the guru sat down to worship each evening the ashram cat would get in the way and distract the worshipers. So he ordered that the cat be tied during evening worship. After the guru died the cat continued to be tied during evening worship. And when the cat expired, another cat was brought to the ashram so that it could be duly tied during evening worship. Centuries later learned treatises were written by the guru's scholarly disciples on the liturgical significance of tying up a cat while worship is performed" (Anthony de Mello, *Song of the Bird* [New York: Doubleday, 1981], p. 63).

their common meals (and probably also the communion meal). This was considered an unacceptable practice and a serious violation of polity by the Jerusalem church. Not only did Peter yield to their influence by refus ing to eat with the Gentile believers but, as Paul wrote, "even Barnabas was led astray by their hypocrisy" (Galatians 2:13). The issue was polity behind which lurked "another gospel." Paul confronted Peter about this "to his face" and "before them all," charging him and the others with "not acting consistently with the truth of the gospel" (Galatians 2:14). What was at stake was the right gospel, not just the right polity.

Paul's argument in his letter to the Galatians that distinguished the emerging church at Antioch from the church at Jerusalem is one of the most profound pieces of theological reflection in the New Testament in my judgment. While the situation confronting him at Antioch was a local one, the implications were far reaching, as Paul seemed to realize when he confronted Peter so strongly.[2] At stake was not merely polity but the very na-

---

[2]The chronological issue with regard Paul's letter to the Galatians and the Acts 15 conference in Jerusalem has been debated by scholars for decades. If we assume an early date for the letter to the Galatians then it preceded the Jerusalem conference, so that Paul's rebuke to Peter in Galatians would have been based on some earlier occasion where Peter expressed agreement with Paul's position. However, if we assume that Paul wrote his letter to the Galatians after the Jerusalem conference, then the rebuke to Peter is especially sharp as Peter's actions (along with Barnabas's) would violate the terms of that agreement between the leaders at Jerusalem and Paul. I assume the later date for the letter as the best way to understand why Paul was so agitated by the continued attempts to undermine his ministry to the Gentiles following that conference. In personal correspondence on this point (11-02-2005), New Testament scholar Professor Seyoon Kim wrote, "In fact, your view is the majority view, and it is favored especially by the continental scholars and now also by the (mainly Anglo-American) New Perspectivists (those who advocate a new, 'anti-Lutheran' interpretation of Paul's theology in the light of E. P. Sanders' redefinition of Judaism as 'covenantal nomism'). A minority of scholars represented by F. F. Bruce (*Paul: Apostle of the Heart Set Free,* pp. 151-59) upholds the view of Southern Galatia/the Gal 2:1-10 = Acts 11:27-30 (famine relief visit) equation/the early date of Gal (48 A.D.)/the Jerusalem council of Acts 15 as precipitated by the agitation of Gal 2:11ff. and the Galatian controversy. I generally follow this minority view. However, I have argued that Gal 2:7-8 represents the personal agreement between Paul and Peter during Paul's first Jerusalem visit (Gal 1:18) and that Paul incorporates it in Gal 2:1-10 because it was endorsed by James and the other Jerusalem apostles during Paul and Barnabas's famine relief visit ("The Mystery of Romans 11:25-26 Once More," *New Testament Studies* 43 [1997], 426ff., reprinted in my *Paul and the New Perspective* [2002], 253-55)." Personal correspondence with Seyoon Kim, October 24, 2005.

ture of the gospel itself. Would the Christian church as we know it historically and in our present day exist if Paul had not established the
theological basis for the emerging church at Antioch? Only God knows. In
his providence it took place through Paul's missionary calling and work. If
it could have happened in a different way, we will never know. We do
know that the church at Jerusalem was virtually a movement within the
tradition of Judaism as a religion and with a compelling Jewish identity.
The church would likely never have emerged out of that community. Jesus
knew that, and the Holy Spirit knew that, and Paul knew that.

Paul viewed the difference between Antioch and Jerusalem as a theological matter over which the gospel was to prevail. While Paul proclaimed a gospel of Abraham, the Jewish leaders in the church at Jerusalem were promoting a gospel of Moses. The gospel of Abraham is an
emerging gospel of grace, and the emerging church at Antioch is born of
the free woman (Sarah) while the gospel of law promoted by the church
at Jerusalem is in bondage and seeks to bind others (Galatians 4:21-31).

In making his argument, Paul did not base his gospel on a new beginning and total discontinuity with the Jerusalem tradition and the law of
Moses. He might well have done that on the basis that his gospel was received directly from the risen and ascended Lord Jesus. Instead, Paul
showed that it actually was the Jerusalem tradition that had broken off
from the earlier gospel of grace with Abraham. In a bold thrust of theological insight clothed in a biblical allegory, Paul labeled the Jerusalem
church as the rejected Ishmael and claimed Isaac as the antecedent for
the emerging church at Antioch.

In effect, Paul told the Jerusalem elders that the mother of the Jerusalem
church was Hagar, not Sarah, and thus they were to be considered as slave
children. "Now Hagar is Mount Sinai [Moses] in Arabia and corresponds
to the present Jerusalem, for she is in slavery with her children. But the
other woman [Antioch] corresponds to the Jerusalem above; she is free,
and she is our mother" (Galatians 4:25-26). They are not going to like that!

The emerging church at Antioch, argued Paul, can trace its ancestry to

Abraham through Isaac, not Ishmael. God's gospel of grace emerged through Abraham as life out of death (a barren woman). The promised offspring came through grace, not law. The child of promise was Isaac, born of the barren Sarah, not Ishmael born of Hagar the slave woman. In this way, the law of Moses, including circumcision, is seen to be provisional and temporary. Even as Sarah produced the child of promise through grace, not through law, so Jesus was born of grace to put an end to law.

While circumcision was instituted with Abraham as a sign of God's covenant, it was intended to point to God's promise of blessing to "all the families of the earth" (Genesis 12:3). The promise was universal with regard to its extent and grounded in grace as to its source. It was in fact pure gospel. As I have pointed out in chapter two, Abraham may be considered to be virtually a Gentile, as he was circumcised after being declared righteous and before there were any Jews. Four hundred years later, Moses introduced the law with all of its legal requirements; circumcision became part of that law as far as the religious practice and distinctive theology of the Israelites were concerned. From this point on, the gospel of grace, as given to Abraham with its inclusive intent, was submerged in the legal and ceremonial rules and regulations of the law of Moses only to emerge again through Jesus who was "the end of the law" according to Paul (Romans 10:4). Jesus, as the obedient Son, respected the law of Moses; he did not come to abolish but to fulfill it (Matthew 5:17).

Based on this emerging gospel of grace through Christ, Paul rejected the argument that circumcision as part of the law was still required on the part of the Gentiles, for the law came to an end with the death and resurrection of Jesus. "If you let yourselves be circumcised, Christ will be of no benefit to you. . . . [N]either circumcision nor uncircumcision counts for anything," wrote Paul (Galatians 5:2, 6). However, for those who used the law as a basis for rejecting Jesus' claim to be the Messiah, Moses was their master. When they challenged Jesus over the healing of the blind man on the sabbath they claimed to be "disciples of Moses" rather than of the Messiah (John 9:28). In saying that he was the Lord of the sabbath, Jesus taught an emergent theology of the sabbath; the sabbath is intended for human welfare, humans are not made just to keep a legalistic sabbath (Mark 2:27-28). The critical issue for Jesus was God's work on the sabbath as a sign of a gospel of grace for the healing and hope of humanity. For Paul, the critical issue was the coming of the Spirit to uncircumcised Gentiles as a sign of the gospel of the Abrahamic covenant through which salvation and blessing would come to all humanity. In both cases, the gospel gives priority to persons over polity. It emerges from the future and liberates God's original purpose from the old wineskins in order that old wine may be served in new containers.

OLD WINE WITHOUT THE WINESKIN

When we trace out the emerging church during the period immediately following Pentecost, the struggle between the old wineskins of historical continuity and the fermenting, and sometimes explosive, power of the Spirit becomes evident. The emergent theology of Paul, originating out of Antioch, is clearly on the side of vintage quality wine in new containers, while the church at Jerusalem sought to keep the emerging church in old wineskins. The church does not emerge out of its past. When it attempts to do this, it resorts to strategies of resuscitation rather than experiencing the power of resurrection. Older wineskins may have many uses, but fermenting new wine is not one of them! Emerging churches are not carried into the future in the old containers. In its attempts to be contemporary, the church usually arrives a decade if not a generation too late. The renewed church emerges in the present out of its future. As in the case of everything related to the creative life and power of God, the future of the church exists first—and then its present.[3]

---

[3]"We must understand that God is the measure of all reality and propriety, understand that eternity exists first and then time, and therefore the future first and then the present, as surely as the Creator exists first and then the creature. He who understands that need take no offense here" (Karl Barth, *Church Dogmatics* 1/1, trans. G. W. Bromiley, 2nd ed. [Edinburgh: T & T Clark, 1975], p. 531).

The emergent theology of Jesus was like new wine; it could not be contained in the old wineskins. The gospel Jesus announced was finest vintage wine put in a new container to be served to all. The parable of the wine and the wineskins that Jesus told has an interesting twist at the end. At first it appears that his point was that the gospel is like new wine that must be put into new wineskins. But then he concludes by saying, "And no one after drinking old wine desires new wine, but says, 'The old is good' " (Luke 5:39).

So what is the point? It is that the gospel is itself "old wine" that has gone through the fermentation process and has acquired a taste and character that satisfies the most discerning and demanding palate! It is vintage gospel (see p. 13) And in what do you serve old wine? In any kind of vessel that you want! For the old wine does not demand that which is merely new but any kind of vessel—new or old—can be used. The gospel of the emerging church is vintage wine; it is the gospel of grace through Abraham. Older wineskins have carried it forward in history, but these are disposable when they have served their purpose.

The gospel was rediscovered by Luther and the other Reformers, served in vessels and carried forward with institutional structures, church polities and liturgical rules and regulations. But these are merely the wineskins, and when they have served their purpose, the original, vintage gospel can be served and tasted in new ecclesial forms—the emerging church, for instance. What Luther discovered and set in motion was not Lutheranism but the gospel. What Calvin proclaimed and taught at Geneva was the gospel, not Calvinism (not even Presbyterianism!). When the heart of Wesley was "strangely warmed" at Aldersgate, he did not spread Methodism but the inner and transforming power of vintage gospel. The wineskins now have names, denominational distinctives, polity manuals and books of order. What is needed is not new wine that does not taste as good and is likely to blow apart rather than build up existing structures. What is needed is the vintage gospel of Christ, the Spirit and the kingdom of God.

I sense that in making my point, it may appear that I am disparaging polity as against gospel. This is not the case. Polity is simply the way the church practices and presents the gospel. As I have said, if the gospel is vintage wine, it can be as well served in old wineskins—more traditional liturgical practices as well as in established rules of polity. Even emerging churches will soon have their own version of polity to hand over to the next (emerging) generation!

I have sensed in some of the more recent literature on the emerging church the taste of new wine rather than the vintage gospel. I hear much about new methods, innovative worship and multimedia approach to presenting the gospel as though preoccupation with new wineskins will by itself bring forth the kingdom of God. In some cases, I fear, this may be an attempt to tell good news without the gospel. When innovative methods become the means of worship without a clear and compelling story of the gospel, it may satisfy the need for stimulation, but like fiber without nutritious filling they lead to spiritual malnutrition. The gospel of the emerging church is a vintage gospel, not just new wine. For Paul, the content of the gospel is Christ. "Christ died for our sins, . . . he was buried, . . . he was raised on the third day. . . . He appeared also to me" (1 Corinthians 15:3-4, 8). This is the true gospel, it is the vintage gospel, and there is no other gospel.

THE GOSPEL OF CHRIST

I assume that Paul first came to know Christ (the Messiah) before he came to know Jesus of Nazareth. This was the exact opposite for the original disciples, who were called to be disciples of Jesus and only subsequently did they confess that he was also the Messiah (the Christ). They became followers (and later apostles) by the calling of Jesus and only later came to experience the grace of Jesus. Paul first experienced the grace of Christ and subsequent to that, his calling. Rather than beginning as a disciple, he began as an enemy of Christ, one who persecuted the church of God (Acts 26:9-11). It was through his encounter with Christ while engaged in this mission of persecution that he was overcome by grace. "By the grace of God I am what I am," Paul confessed (1 Corinthians 15:10).

In all of Paul's writings there is virtually no mention of the life and teaching of Jesus prior to his death and resurrection. This is somewhat surprising because John Mark, who wrote the Gospel of Mark was part of the team that accompanied Paul on his first missionary journey out of Antioch, and despite some problems with that relationship Mark was summoned at the end to spend time with Paul when he was imprisoned (2 Timothy 4:11). Luke, who wrote one of the four Gospels, was also part of that mission team and would no doubt have already begun to compile the material concerning the life and ministry of Jesus. From this we can gather that Paul did have access to the anecdotal material circulating among the apostles. There are indications in Paul's letter to the Corinthians that he had received some "words of the Lord," and it was through these contacts that he could pass on to them an answer to some of their questions (1 Corinthians 7:10). With regard to the issue of improper behavior at the Lord's Supper at Corinth, Paul gives them instruction based on what he had "received from the Lord" (1 Corinthians 11:23).

While Paul neither mentions the nativity of Jesus (found in Matthew and Luke) nor the incarnation of a preexisting divine Logos (found in John), he does say that "When the fullness of time had come, God sent his Son, born of woman, born under the law, in order to redeem those who were under the law" (Galatians 4:4-5). And as to Jesus being the Son of God, Paul affirms this as certified by Jesus' resurrection from the dead by the "spirit of holiness, . . . Jesus Christ our Lord, through whom we have received grace and apostleship" (Romans 1:4-5).

The Christ of the gospel is not first of all a doctrinal confession but a reality that we experience. This is why Christology, as an attempt by the early church to define Christ as both divine and human, strained philosophical credulity and produced theological controversy. Emerging churches exist by their confession of gospel truth, Christ made visible. Christ is both a personal reality whom we receive by grace as well as an eternal reality that places us within the life of God. It is "Christ in you," says Paul, which is "the hope of glory" (Colossians 1:27). Christ himself, Paul adds, dwells within us, not just through grace but as grace himself. Christ is the content of grace. The same Christ who is within us places something of us within the life of God. By grace our life is "hidden with Christ in God" (Colossians 3:3). "When Christ who is your life is revealed, then you also will be revealed with him in glory" (Colossians 3:4). Amazing grace!

THE GRACE OF CHRIST

When Barnabas came to Antioch to follow up reports that the church was including Gentile as well as Jewish believers, he rejoiced because he "saw the grace of God" (Acts 11:23). This is worth pondering—how does one see grace? Even as the first disciples came to see the grace of God through the life and ministry of Jesus, the emerging church at Antioch made the grace of Christ visible through the breaking down of the wall of division between Jew and Gentile. Grace that remains invisible is not the grace of Christ, nor is there a gospel of Christ where grace is not made visible.

For the emerging church at Antioch, Christ is the content of gospel, and grace is the gift of Christ. If there is no Christ, there is no gospel. If there is gospel, there is grace—the grace of Christ. Grace is not what God created as an antidote for our sin but an original creative impulse within God himself. "Grace is an inner mode of being in God Himself," says Karl Barth.[4] God's grace is a movement of his own heart toward us, expressed first as a creative act by which humanity came into existence. When humans fled behind the curtain of fear and guilt, God's grace then drew

---

[4]Karl Barth, *Church Dogmatics* 2/1, trans. G. W. Bromiley (Edinburgh: T & T Clark, 1964), p. 353.

them out of hiding and became visible in their reconciliation to one another and to God (Genesis 1—3). Just as Adam and Eve were clothed by God's grace rather than by their own handmade garments of shame and disgrace, we too are brought forth from the law that works death is us and are liberated by the grace of Christ.

Those who received the grace of Christ crossed over the boundaries of race, religion and ethnic identity to form "one new humanity" (Ephesians 2:15); they became the spiritual body of Christ, a holy temple, and the dwelling place of God (Ephesians 2:21-22). Emerging churches do not need well-defined boundaries because they have a real presence of Christ at the center. This again reveals the fact that it is about the right gospel, not the right polity. Where Christ is not clearly visible as the life of the community of faith, the boundary lines tend to be become more visible, often to the exclusion of those who are themselves ambiguous with regard to their spiritual identity. Emerging churches will often be a little messy around the edges—like the original followers of Jesus—but Christ can handle that!

For Paul, it wasn't just that the law of Moses was a religious inconvenience and burden, but it also made sin visible and brought him under condemnation and a sentence of death (Romans 7:8-11). The law killed me, said Paul, because it revealed the fact that I was not righteous before God. That was all that the law could do, bring persons to Christ in order that they could be brought from death to life in Christ. This is why Paul was led to find grace through Abraham before the law was introduced. The gospel of Abraham was a gospel of grace, the creation of God's promise out of nothing, as it were. Grace does "kill before it can make alive," as a former professor told us.[5] But what grace puts to death is what we create by our own religion based on a human and natural law,

---

[5]This was Professor Thomas Torrance in his Edinburgh lectures. He credited his former mentor for this insight; it was Karl Barth, Torrance told us, who reformulated Calvin's doctrine of grace as the very truth of God revealed to us through incarnation. The truth is, that God himself is given to us through the person of Jesus Christ, not just information about God. "It is this truth

which the law of God reveals as inhuman and enslaving. Through the grace of Jesus Christ we have access to grace (Romans 5:2).

Paul experienced grace as far more than exemption from the burden of the law; he experienced it as liberation from being slaves to the law. Grace does not lead to lawlessness and permissiveness, for grace binds us to Christ rather than merely freeing us from law. Grace is not permission to live without any law but to live with Christ under the law of the Spirit: "The law of the Spirit of life in Christ Jesus has set you free from the law of sin and of death" (Romans 8:2).

Paul says that we who once were estranged from God but are baptized into Christ by the Spirit are "clothed . . . with Christ" (Galatians 3:27). This, of course is a spiritual garment and not a literal one. But grace is a spiritual reality for which we must use metaphors and analogies to describe. The grace of forgiveness and healing from shame and guilt is itself an effect produced in us by Jesus Christ.

If Paul can be said to be the apostle of grace, it must also be said that he is the apostle of love. Love is not only the "more excellent way" with regard to the exercise of spiritual gifts (1 Corinthians 12:31), it is the norm by which every commandment of God can be fulfilled. "Owe no one anything, except to love one another; for he who loves has fulfilled the law. . . . Love does no wrong to a neighbor; therefore, love is the fulfilling of the law" (Romans 13:8, 10). To know the love of Christ is to have the fullness of God (Ephesians 3:19). How does this really work? It works because "God's love has been poured into our hearts through the Holy Spirit that has been given us" (Romans 5:5).

The gospel of Christ is a gospel of the Holy Spirit. It was while the church at Antioch was worshiping the Lord that the Holy Spirit revealed to them that Saul and Barnabas were to be set apart for the extension of the church beyond their own common life. "So, being sent

---

which kills and makes alive," wrote Barth (*Church Dogmatics* 4/2, p. 579). Barth also said of God's work of grace through Christ, "He kills the old man by introducing the new, and not conversely" (ibid., p. 577).

out by the Holy Spirit," they went on their way, the beginning of the first missionary journey (Acts 13:2-4). The Spirit of Christ is the Holy Spirit. This is vintage gospel. Christ becomes our contemporary; we become the vessels, some of us are rather common and ordinary, some odd shaped, others cracked and marred, but each Spirit-filled (see 2 Timothy 2:20)!

THE SPIRIT OF CHRIST

While Paul does not specifically refer to the coming of the Holy Spirit at Pentecost, it is clear that he has experienced a personal encounter with the Spirit of the risen Christ in his own personal Pentecost. It is Paul's clear testimony to the power of the Spirit of Christ in his life and thought that provides the basis for saying that Paul begins his theological reflection out of the Pentecost event as a continuing reality and presence of the Spirit of Christ.

Emerging churches not only find freedom from old wineskins that bind them to the past but also experience the liberation and freedom of the Spirit of Christ. Paul did not merely seek to demolish the old wineskins but rather to allow the wine of the Spirit of Christ to flow into new channels of human life, "as the Spirit chooses" (1 Corinthians 12:11). The church is neither free to follow every spirit nor "every wind of doctrine" (Ephesians 4:14). Being freed from the law of sin and death, we are under the "law of the Spirit of life in Christ Jesus," wrote Paul (Romans 8:2). The Holy Spirit does not only abide in each individual member of the church but in the body as a whole. It is not enough for individual members to be filled with the Spirit; the church must be filled with the Spirit as well.

The church is not only Spirit-filled, it is raised with Christ, and through Christ has access to the Father in the one Spirit (Ephesians 2:18). As the inner life of Jesus in his relation to the Father is constitutive of our knowledge of Christ, so the inner life of the church in its experience of Jesus Christ by the presence of the Holy Spirit is constitutive of emerging churches. The Spirit that creates the church through the renewal of life and faith is the Spirit of the resurrected Jesus Christ. As Jesus Christ was raised from the dead by God, the Father of glory (Ephesians 1:20), and so designated Son of God (Rom 1:4), we too have been made alive, argues the apostle Paul, as a dwelling place of God in the Spirit (Ephesians 2:22), and so become children of God (Ephesians 1:5).

Emerging churches begin by allowing the Spirit to give new shape and vitality to the church's life and ministry. The church must be prepared to lose its identity as an institution and find it again in the Spirit-filled community. It begins with its new birth from above. At the same time, the church is free to use whatever is serviceable, even in some cases, old wineskins, allowing them to carry and serve the vintage wine of the gospel at the banquet where those gathered from "the streets and the lanes . . . the poor, the crippled, the blind, and the lame" are brought in by the Spirit of Christ (Luke 14:21).

UNBINDING THE CHURCH

The raising of Lazarus (John 11) might be viewed as a parable of the emerging church. The lament of the sisters upon greeting Jesus expresses so well the mentality of the church whose programs and methods become rituals for the baptizing of the dead rather than celebrating life. "Lord, if you had been here, my brother would not have died" (John 11:32). This is as if to say, "Lord, we were faithful and did our best. We left it in your hands and now it is too late." Even when Jesus attempted to break through this cordon of negativity by saying, "Take away the stone," they attempted to stop his ministry! "Lord, already there is a stench because he has been dead four days" (John 11:39). In the end, however, Lazarus emerged when his name was called, though he was still bound with strips of cloth. "Unbind him," said Jesus, "and let him go" (John 11:44).

There is a sense in which the work of the Holy Spirit represents the unbinding of the church from its grave clothes. With a bit of frustration and not a little bit of sarcasm, Paul wrote to the church he had planted in Galatia. "Are you so foolish? Having started with the Spirit, are you now ending with the flesh? . . . For freedom Christ has set us free. Stand firm, therefore, and do not submit again to a yoke of slavery" (Galatians 3:3; 5:1).

The church at Jerusalem allowed Christ to come out of the tomb, but one wonders whether they continued to view him as bound with the wrappings with which he was buried. The elements of the law that they continued to wrap around the body of Christ that existed after Pentecost as the new community of faith, Paul viewed as a yoke of slavery. "For freedom Christ has set us free," he urged the Galatians (Galatians 5:1). I have the feeling that the emerging church appears a bit naked to those who see it unencumbered by the traditional institutional forms and polity of the church. The vestments of the pastoral office, though often vibrant with color, may still carry the musty odor of the tomb.

The gospel is not really naked, but clothed with Christ in the form of human need and human aspirations. Thomas Torrance says it eloquently when he writes:

> The Church cannot be in Christ without being in Him as He is proclaimed to men in their need and without being in Him as He encounters us in and behind the existence of every man in his need. Nor can the Church be recognized as His except in that meeting of Christ with Himself in the depth of human misery, where Christ clothed with His Gospel meets with Christ clothed with the desperate need and plight of men.[6]

The Spirit of God does not come to us unclothed, as it were, but comes clothed with the very humanity of Christ. Every feeling and every sensation that Jesus experienced as a complete human being became an

---

[6]Thomas Torrance, "Service in Jesus Christ," in *Theological Foundations for Ministry,* ed. Ray S. Anderson (Grand Rapids: Eerdmans, 1979), p. 724.

expression of the divine being, revealing the truth of God through the humanity of God. Every feeling, need and aspiration of the human spirit has its correspondence in the humanity of Jesus that bears all human experience directly into the divine heart.

The humanity of God as expressed through Jesus Christ makes God an ally of those who are bereft of love, who are betrayed and who are stricken and oppressed. Wherever Jesus was found, the humanity of God was found on the same side as humanity under distress. As James Torrance has eloquently said:

> Christ does not heal us by standing over against us, diagnosing our sickness, prescribing medicine for us to take, and then going away, to leave us to get better by obeying his instructions—as an ordinary doctor might. No, He becomes the patient! He assumes that very humanity that is in need of redemption, and by being anointed by the Spirit in our humanity, by a life of perfect obedience for us, by dying and rising again, our humanity is healed in him.[7]

CONCLUDING NONTHEOLOGICAL POSTSCRIPT

One of my former students began an emerging-church ministry out of a large denominational church in Texas. Called Mercy Street, they met on Saturday evenings with only a couple of dozen people attending. The church reached out intentionally to draw close to those who were victims of drug abuse and who felt estranged from the church due to their often dysfunctional lifestyle. Today there are several hundred attending who are involved in ministry to persons in prison; the members also provide assistance, food and shelter to those caught in economic distress. When I asked him what held this group together, he said that it was not

---

[7]James Torrance, "The Vicarious Humanity of Christ," in *The Incarnation-Ecumenical Studies in the Nicene-Constantinopolitan Creed A.D. 381,* ed. Thomas F. Torrance (Edinburgh: Handsel Press, 1981), p. 141.

the contemporary music or the innovative style of worship, but simply Jesus. Every sermon and the central focus of the community is on Jesus Christ. "This is our gospel," he told me, adding, "You better not try this unless you have a Spirit-filled community where the power and presence of Jesus creates a healing center and lives on the broken edges."

This is what the emerging church is about.

5   IT'S ABOUT KINGDOM LIVING, NOT KINGDOM BUILDING

As a student at Fuller Theological Seminary from 1956 to 1959, I had the rare opportunity of sitting in the lectures of Professor George Ladd who, at that time, was in his prime as a scholar and teacher. Those were heady days! Not only was his theology of the kingdom of God emerging right before our eyes, he was striking at the very heart of a dispensational theology that was not only held by some of his faculty colleagues but also was being taught and preached by Charles E. Fuller, one of the founders of the seminary! We did not have to wait for the 11 p.m. news for reports of theological skirmishes involving pretribulation and posttribulation rapture! As a testimony to Ladd's seminal work on the kingdom of God, when I later arrived at the University of Edinburgh to do my doctoral work (1970-1972), I checked in the university library for references to some of the evangelical scholars that were at the forefront of the new evangelical movement beginning in the middle of the twentieth century, some of whom had been my teachers. I found only the works of George Ladd listed. I discovered that Ladd was one of a very few number of North American evangelical scholars that caught the attention of European and British scholars. You cannot discuss the kingdom of God without beginning with George Ladd!

In his classic work on New Testament theology, Ladd wrote, "the

Kingdom of God is the redemptive, dynamic rule of God exercised in Christ's total Messianic mission to bring order to a disorganized universe, to accomplish God's total redemptive purpose."[1] The term "kingdom of God" was not used in the early part of the Old Testament and only then as a theme in Psalms and later prophets, pointing to God's dynamic rule and dominion over all the earth. The Hebrew concept of the kingdom of God (*malkut*) has the dynamic idea of reign, rule or dominion.

> They shall speak of the glory of your kingdom,
>> and tell of your power. . . .
> Your kingdom is an everlasting kingdom,
>> and your dominion endures throughout all generations.
>> (Psalm 145:11, 13)

> The LORD has established his throne in the heavens,
>> and his kingdom rules over all. (Psalm 103:19)

Because Paul was first trained in what we call the Old Testament Scriptures, we can assume that his view of the kingdom of God was informed by this perspective as well as by revelation received directly from Christ.

In the New Testament, the word "kingdom" (*basileia*) is sometimes rendered as "kingship" or "kingly power" (Luke 19:12; 23:42; John 18:36; Revelation 17:12). The coming of the kingdom for which we pray in the Lord's Prayer is that God's will be done on earth, that is, that his rule be perfectly realized (Matthew 6:10). The kingdom that Jesus appointed for his disciples is royal rule (Luke 22:29-30). As such, the kingdom of God is both future and present. When the disciples asked when the kingdom was to come, Jesus replied enigmatically that the kingdom was already in their midst, but in an unexpected form (Luke 17:20). The

---

[1]George Ladd, *A Theology of the New Testament,* ed. Donald Hagner, rev. ed. (Grand Rapids: Eerdmans, 1993), p. 450.

signs of the kingdom were not to be found in the political realm but in the spiritual rule of the Messiah over evil and supernatural powers, such as disease, demons and even death (Matthew 12:28).

As the anointed One, Jesus (the Messiah) manifested the power of the kingdom of God to forgive sin, banish demons, heal the sick and raise the dead. Jesus constantly pointed to the work that God performed through him that testified to the power of God. Even if his contemporaries did not believe in him, Jesus counseled them to "believe the works" so that they might know that "the Father is in me and I am in the Father" (John 10:37-38). The kingdom of God that was to come into the present out of the future was already present in a provisional form through the person and work of Jesus Christ as the power of the Spirit.

Jesus came announcing the reality of the kingdom of God as the eschatological reality and power of God that is the revelation (apocalypse) of God's power and healing presence. Through his death and resurrection, the powers and evils of this age were brought under divine judgment, and total victory and healing is accomplished. The gift of the Holy Spirit is the eschatological inauguration of the new age and the seal and promise of salvation, with healing ultimately assured through the resurrection of the dead.

For forty days the resurrected Jesus Christ moved in and out of the lives of those who had known him in his living and dying, and who now came to know him in his resurrection presence and power. While appearing to them, he confirmed to them the reality of his living presence as that of the same Jesus who had died, and spoke to them of the kingdom of God (Acts 1:3).

Extending the concepts of George Ladd, Darrell Guder developed the theme of God's kingdom reign.

> A significant recovery of "reign of God" or "kingdom of God" language has been evident within the field of scholarship. . . . Typical Christian conversation on this subject speaks of "building" or "ex-

tending" the reign of God. . . . But the grammar by which the New Testament depicts the reign of God cuts across the grain of these North American culture bound ways of seeing things. The verbs *to build* and *to extend* are not found in the New Testament grammar for the reign of God. The New Testament employs the words *receive* and *enter*."[2]

The church represents the divine reign or *sign* and *foretaste*. The church also represents the divine reign as its *agent* and *instrument*.[3]

THE MISSION OF THE KINGDOM

The church's mission is not to build up an empire or kingdom that it controls but to experience and express the kingdom of God through the lives of its members as well as the various groups and organizations that they form. The church finds its being in its kingdom mission, under the guidance and power of the Spirit. Its intention and direction is oriented to the rule of the kingdom in the world that God loves and to which it is sent. When the church prays, "thy kingdom come," it reveals that its nature is open to the coming of the kingdom and thus is a witness to the reality of the kingdom already manifest through the Holy Spirit.

Guder stresses the point that "Churches are called to be bodies of people sent on a mission rather than the storefront for venders of religious services and goods in North American culture."[4] The church exists in the context of its own culture in every age, but the kingdom demands that the church be willing to be divested of its own particular cultural forms and practices in order to be an authentic missional community in other cultures. In his analysis of the post-Constantine era of fourth-century Christianity, Tony Jones argues that the Christian faith became the pre-

---

[2]Darrell L. Guder, ed., *Missional Church* (Grand Rapids: Eerdmans, 1998), pp. 93-94. See also his earlier work *Be My Witnesses* (Grand Rapids: Eerdmans, 1985).
[3]Ibid., pp. 101-2.
[4]Ibid., p. 108.

dominate faith of the Western world. As a result, "Christianity was as much a culture as it was a faith."[5] This marriage of church and culture persisted through the Reformation and can be found in various versions, such as "Christian America."

John Franke says that the church not only has a mission but is missional by its very nature. "The move from church with a mission to missional church has significant implications for the character of theology. Like the church, the impulses and assumptions that have shaped the discipline of theology in the West are those of Christendom rather than the mission of God."[6]

Guder calls for a conversion of the church out of its culture in order to recover its true missional existence in the world. "The calling of the church to be missional—to be a sent community—leads the church to step beyond the given cultural forms that carry dubious assumptions about what the church is, what its public role should be, and what its voice should sound like."[7] The missional nature of the church is found in its recovery of an eschatological understanding of its relation to the coming of the kingdom of God. John Franke speaks of this as "eschatological realism." "This eschatological future is anticipated in the present through the work of the Spirit, who leads the church into truth (1 John 2:27)."[8]

Paul viewed the kingdom of God as moving toward its redemptive conclusion in stages. The resurrection of Christ was the "first fruits" of those who die and await their resurrection. Each has its own order:

> Christ the first fruits, then at his coming those who belong to Christ. Then comes the end, when he hands over the kingdom to God the Father, after he has destroyed every ruler and every au-

---

[5]Tony Jones, *Postmodern Youth Ministry* (Grand Rapids: Zondervan, 2001), p. 51.
[6]John R. Franke, *The Character of Theology* (Grand Rapids: Baker, 2005), p. 70.
[7]Guder, *Missional Church*, p. 109.
[8]John Franke, "The Nature of Theology: Culture, Language, and Truth," in *Christianity and the Postmodern Turn*, ed. Myron B. Penner (Grand Rapids: Brazos, 2005), p. 213. See also Franke, *Character of Theology*, p. 197.

thority and power. . . . When all things are subjected to him, then the Son himself will also be subjected to the one who put all things in subjection under him, so that God may be all in all. (1 Corinthians 15:23-24, 28)

It is worth noting here that it is not the church that is handed over to God the Father, but the kingdom. Christ is the head of the church but also the Lord of the kingdom. It is not a completed church but a fulfilled kingdom that Paul envisions as being finally accomplished through Christ.

KINGDOM LIVING IN THE CREATED ORDER

The emerging church at Antioch did not seem to spend much time and energy on a building program as their first priority. They were not so much interested in kingdom building as they were in living on the growing edge of the kingdom of God, where the dynamic presence and power of the Holy Spirit was found in a community of the Spirit rather than in a sanctuary of stone and glass. The temple was in Jerusalem. But do not feel left out, said Paul, you are "a holy temple in the Lord" and the very "dwelling place of God" (Ephesians 2:21-22). Perhaps Paul reminded them that it was not God's idea in the beginning to have a temple built, but David's, for which David received no permission (2 Samuel 7)!

Paul's theology of the kingdom of God was an eschatological vision of Christ's role and rule in restoring God's original reign over all creation, reaching back to the very beginning and moving toward the final consummation. Christ

is the image of the invisible God, the firstborn of all creation; for in him all things in heaven and on earth were created, things visible and invisible, whether thrones or dominions or rulers or powers—all things have been created through him and for him. He himself is before all things, and in him all things hold together. (Colossians 1:15-17)

This is kingdom language. An emergent theology with less than this cosmic vision lacks as much depth as it does height.

Would there have been a church in the Garden of Eden before the Fall? Or is the existence of the church a consequence of sin—belonging to the redemptive order and not the created order? What is the relation of church to the kingdom? These are not easy questions to answer. Although Paul thought backward from Christ to Adam and Eve (Romans 5:12-17), he did not tell us what his vision of the prefallen state of humans in the Garden of Eden might have been. Did Adam and Eve experience the kingdom of God?

I could well imagine that Paul would agree that the kingdom of God was the very realm in which the first humans were created as stewards of the earth and in which they lived their daily lives. The redemptive aspect of the kingdom of God is presupposed by this original "order" of creation that fell into disorder and became subject to the spiritual powers that were in rebellion to God's kingdom.

The prefallen creation should not be understood as a myth but as part of the historical, linear account of the story of creation and redemption. While the language and setting is more of a theological narrative than a historical matter-of-fact description, the story tells us of the realm in which the original humans, Adam and Eve, were taken from the dust of the ground, placed on earth, endowed with the image of the Creator by a divine inbreathing. They are placed there to till the ground, tend the animals and to be fruitful and multiply. These are tasks that occupied the first humans before the Fall. This was kingdom living!

Let's assume that the Fall did not occur immediately. By implication, these tasks (tilling, tending and multiplying) involved physical labor (water did not run uphill!), some elementary tool making, division of labor, domestic and family life. In this sense, the first humans' total environment was a workplace. If they did not work, they could not eat. If they did not manage their lives so that physical labor did not crowd out social and domestic life, not to mention personal growth and development, there would be consequences. In the original creation the whole of human life can be considered to be the workplace.

My point is this: In the original workplace—the habitat of humans—there was no polarity or tension between the sacred and the profane but only between God and the created order. The workplace where humans lived before the Fall was a secular place; that is, the created world is contingent on God the Creator for its existence, but as a created order it is other than God; only God the Creator is holy. Even though humans bear the divine image, the polarity between God the Creator and the created order includes humans. The divine image, endowed by the inbreathing of God's Spirit, is experienced both as a material and spiritual reality. Every aspect of human life before the Fall is the workplace in which humans experience simultaneously their spiritual and material existence. Their spiritual life does not divide the workplace into secular and sacred spheres, as though Adam and Eve had to withdraw from their material existence into some separate place in order to have a spiritual relation to the Creator. What we call the created order as differentiated yet contingent on God is secular, having both material and spiritual dimensions. The secular workplace is a kingdom realm.

Human nature is both material and spiritual. As originally created, humans experience their spiritual life as freely and fully as they do their material life, along with other creatures placed on the earth. Human beings are amphibious creatures! Not that they are equally at home on land and water, but they were created to move as freely in the spiritual dimension as in the material dimension of life. What constitutes spiritual life for Adam and Eve is not in contrast to or separate from their material life. Rather, their material, or creaturely, existence is spiritual at the very core. As distinct from all other creatures, however, humans might be said to have a sacramental relation with the earth and with each other due to the spiritual dimension of their human nature.

THE SACRAMENTAL ASPECT OF KINGDOM LIVING

A theology of sacrament can be expressed as a twofold movement: a gracious invitation to participate in the community of God's inner life as spiritual beings, and a gracious impartation of divine blessing on our life as human beings. Human life therefore might be considered as a secular sacrament through which gracious access to the Creator enables humans to serve as priests of creation, offering up praise and thanksgiving to him. At the same time, humans represent a gracious blessing from the Creator on the secular workplace, thus fulfilling the very nature of sacrament itself.

In Psalm 8 the writer expresses this thought in a theological hymn of praise.

> O LORD, our Sovereign,
>   how majestic is your name in all the earth! . . .
> When I look at your heavens, the work of your fingers,
>   the moon and the stars that you have established;
> what are human beings that you are mindful of them,
>   mortals that you care for them?
> Yet you have made them a little lower than God,
>   and crowned them with glory and honor.
> You have given them dominion over the works of your hands;
>   you have put all things under their feet. (Psalm 8:1, 3-6)

Humans are intrinsically spiritual beings, not religious beings. Spiritual life is to be manifested in every aspect of the workplace as the domain of human life. It is in this sense that we might begin to answer our initial question. It was through the grace of God that creation came into existence, and it was by the grace of God that humans were created and endowed with the divine image through the gift of spirit. Human life is a sacrament of grace by which the whole of life as distinguished from God becomes a blessing to God and receives the blessing from God.

This is kingdom living in the created order, where daily life and work constitute a secular sacrament of the kingdom of God. That is, every aspect of life in the workplace was secular in the sense that Adam and Eve were created from the dust of the ground, but at the same time their very existence was a sacramental expression of the divine image. The kingdom of God was both the realm and the reign of God of which they were the sacramental expression. Sacrament here, of course, means a visible sign of an invisible reality. The realm is of the earth and is temporal; the reign is of God and is eternal.

The spiritual nature of the human experience includes both our bond with the earth and with other humans. Respect for the earth from which human life came in a material sense entails both the social and spiritual nature of the image of God. There is solidarity with the earth but also differentiation from the earth.[9]

Was there a sabbath before the Fall? The second creation account begins with the statement, "Thus the heavens and the earth were finished, and all their multitude. And on the seventh day God finished the work that he had done, and he rested on the seventh day from all the work that he had done" (Genesis 2:1-2). It is noteworthy that the text does not say that God finished his work on the sixth day, but "on the seventh day God finished the work that he had done." The seventh day is the day of completing the work. The sixth day represents the culmination of crea-

---

[9]This is pointed out in the lovely meditation by Dietrich Bonhoeffer on Psalm 119:19: "I am a stranger on earth. Therefore, I confess that I cannot remain here, that my given time is brief. Nor do I have any claim here to houses and possessions. The good things which I enjoy I must thankfully receive, but I must also endure injustice and violence with no one to intercede for me. I have no firm hold on either persons or things. As a stranger, I am subject to the laws of the place where I sojourn. The earth, which nourishes me, has a right to my work and my strength. I have no right to despise the earth on which I live. I owe it loyalty and gratitude. It is my lot to be a stranger and a sojourner, but this cannot become a reason for evading God's call so that I dream away my earthly life with thoughts of heaven. There is a very godless homesickness for the other world which is not consistent with really finding one's home there. I ought to behave myself like a guest here, with all that entails. I should not stay aloof and refuse to participate in the tasks, joys and sorrows of earth, while I am waiting patiently for the redemption of the divine promise. I am really to wait for the promise and not try to steal it in advance in wishes and dreams" (Dietrich Bonhoeffer, *Meditating on the Word* [Cambridge, Mass.: Cowley, 1986], p. 139).

turely possibility while the seventh day represents the spiritual creativity imbedded in the secular workplace as the temporal habitat of humanity.

While the sabbath was not given specific content in the prefallen life of humans, as bearers of the divine image humans would also experience the sabbath as part of their existence in the workplace. Sabbath has to do with rhythm, not religion. As such the sabbath was itself a part of the secular sacrament meant to renew and refresh the life of humans in the workplace, not in a separate, detached sphere. Even under the later Mosaic law the sabbath was a secular observance, not a religious one. The emphasis was on domestic and social relationships centered around a common meal and release from normal duties. Nor was the sabbath different from the other days in its secular nature—it is still part of the workplace. The seventh day was originally part of the secular sacrament that consecrated the entire workplace (all seven days) as contingent on divine favor and grace.

THE BROKEN SACRAMENT

The original sin of Adam and Eve not only broke the law of God, but it broke the sacrament that bound humans to the workplace and the workplace to God. The consequence was an ecological disaster, rupturing the sacramental bond between God, the workplace and one human with another. What was originally a daily sacrament of divine partnership and human fellowship was fractured at the core, leaving humans estranged from God, alienated from the earth from which came their sustenance, and living in fear of one another. Contrary to conventional thinking, the humans were never cursed, only their relation to the earth was:

> Cursed is the ground because of you;
>   in toil you shall eat of it all the days of your life;
> thorns and thistles it shall bring forth for you;
>   and you shall eat the plants of the field.
> By the sweat of your face

> you shall eat bread
> until you return to the ground,
>> for out of it you were taken;
> you are dust,
>> and to dust you shall return. (Genesis 3:17-19).

What was originally a creative and sacramental union of the spiritual and the material nature of human life became split into two spheres with the material aspect of life bereft of spiritual purpose and blessing. The fact that God, in his grace, created a sacramental repair did not remove entirely the consequences for the human workplace. What was once creative work now was accompanied by burdensome toil. The symbiotic relation between humans and the earth was altered so that from the soil that provided sweet nourishment also came the thorns that brought bitter disappointment. As a result the spiritual sacrament of secular life was replaced by a redemptive sacrament of religious life. The origin of religion as something distinct from human life in the workplace can be traced back to the broken sacrament of the Fall. Redemption from guilt brought immediate release to the soul, but held in escrow the restoration of the workplace.

Creation itself, wrote Paul, "waits with eager longing for the revealing of the children of God; for the creation was subjected to futility, not of its own will but by the will of the one who subjected it, in hope that the creation itself will be set free from its bondage to decay and will obtain the freedom of the glory of God" (Romans 8:19-21).

While the redemptive sacrament of grace also implied healing and hope for those in the workplace, the separation of the sacred place from the profane people brought forth a new cult of the priesthood. The religious order and those who administered and manipulated the sacramental elements perpetuated a division between the sacred and the secular by the very nature of their calling. The entire narrative from the third chapter of Genesis to the end of the Old Testament labors under the consequence of the broken sacrament even while implementing its repair in a provisional way. The prophets occasionally broke through with a vision of a restored ecology of grace where "The wilderness and the dry land shall be glad, / the desert shall rejoice and blossom. . . . For waters shall break forth in the wilderness / and streams in the desert" (Isaiah 35:1, 6). Yet, there remained a poignant longing for the restoration of the sacrament of everyday life.

"I like the development of an emergent theology of the kingdom based on the creation narrative," one of my readers said, "but how does this fit with your thesis that Antioch is a better model of an emerging church than Jerusalem? Didn't Jesus say a lot about the kingdom, as well as John the Baptist, and would not the disciples have understood their own messianic community as kingdom living?"

Good question. The problem is that as I have indicated earlier in this chapter, as to how kingdom language can be used to interpret the risen Christ's lordship over creation we must look to Paul for a vision of the kingdom as an eschatological vision of the significance of Christ's death and resurrection. Furthermore, it was Paul's emergent theology of the kingdom that applied the meaning of Jesus' own words about the kingdom as a spiritual temple and a spiritual reign specifically to the new messianic community. When Jesus claimed to be "greater than the temple" and "lord of the sabbath" (Matthew 12:6-8), he pointed to a spiritual reality of God's redemptive order that took precedence over the temporal and physical. Thus Paul can say, "The kingdom of God is not food and drink but righteousness and peace and joy in the Holy Spirit" (Romans 14:17).

We do not find this kind of theological hermeneutic coming out of the Jerusalem community, where the physical temple loomed over their daily lives. Luke makes the point that their early assembly was ordinarily at the temple (Acts 2:46). For the church emerging at Jerusalem the temple, with its orientation to the past, had a powerful grip on their spiritual lives. The emerging church at Antioch was not merely separated geographically but theologically from the temple, as I pointed out in chapter one. Paul's emergent theology of Christ as Lord of the kingdom enabled him to define the people of God filled with the Spirit of Christ as the living temple of God (Ephesians 2:13-22). An emergent theology of the kingdom is of necessity a central core of Paul's theology.

KINGDOM LIVING IN THE REDEEMED ORDER

The kingdom of God cannot be equated with the church; it is instead the rule of Christ that includes the church but is larger than the church. The kingdom of God is the invisible sphere of Christ's power and reign into which we enter through the Holy Spirit and faith. In this way Paul viewed the kingdom of God as not primarily concerned with material things and political realms but rather as a personal and social reality—righteousness and peace and joy—the fruits of the indwelling Spirit. Kingdom living in the present time, according to Paul, begins with our reception of the Holy Spirit as the "down payment" *(arrabōn)* of our inheritance (Ephesians 1:14). The word signifies the promise of what lies in the future, not merely a promise but the present reality of living in that promise. Life in the Spirit is both a historical reality and a future realization, it is both experience and hope; the kingdom of God is both present and future; the blessings of the age to come have reached from the future into the present and have become immediate realities for us in Christ. For those in Christ, says Paul, the "end of the ages" have overlapped, the first part of the age to come reaches back into the last part of this present age so that the time between the resurrection of Christ and his coming again *(parousia)* is a time "between the times" (1 Corinthians 10:11).[10]

The church does not drive the kingdom into the world through its own institutional and pragmatic strategies. Rather, it is drawn into the

---

[10]For an insightful discussion of this point, see George Ladd's *Theology of the New Testament,* p. 409.

world as it follows the mission of the Spirit. The church is constantly being re-created through the mission of the Spirit. At the same time it has historical and ecclesial continuity and universality through its participation in the person and mission of Christ Jesus through the Spirit.

For Paul the messianic reign of Christ was not that of an earthly monarch over a territorial sphere but as the resurrected and exalted Lord at the right hand of the Father (Romans 8:34; Colossians 3:1), who now reigns as king. The enemies of the kingdom of God are no longer political and earthly powers but invisible, spiritual powers (Matthew 12:28). The object of this reign of Christ as Lord of the kingdom is to subdue these spiritual powers, until all rebellious enemies of the kingdom are placed under his feet, with death the last enemy to be destroyed (1 Corinthians 15:25-26). This corresponds to the fact that Jesus himself refused an earthly kingdom (John 6:15) and claimed that his sovereign rule came from a higher order than some earthly power (John 18:36).

The kingdom will become visible at the final appearing of Jesus Christ (2 Timothy 4:1). The sufferings that God's people endure in this world are for the sake of the kingdom of God (2 Thessalonians 1:5). This includes laboring for the kingdom of God (Colossians 4:11). Because of the resurrection and presence of Christ through the Spirit, those baptized into Christ have been transferred from the power of darkness into the kingdom of Christ (Colossians 1:13).

As the incarnation of God, Jesus not only repaired the sacrament broken by the Fall but restored the original sacrament of humanity in his own person. In him, wrote Paul, "the whole fullness of deity dwells bodily" (Colossians 2:9). Jesus is thus the primary sacrament by which all other sacramental relations and actions have their source.[11] The expansion of the New Testament church after Pentecost came about largely

---

[11]Karl Barth says that in the person of Jesus "A sacramental continuity stretches backwards into the existence of the people of Israel, whose Messiah he is, and forwards into the existence of the apostolate and the church founded upon the apostolate" (Barth, *Church Dogmatics* 2/1, p. 54).

as a result of the apostle Paul's ministry and teaching. While Jesus himself did not create the church, the Spirit of Christ following Pentecost brought forth the church as the leading edge of the kingdom of God in the world. What later became sacraments of the church—baptism and the Lord's Supper, in the Protestant tradition—have their origin in the person of Jesus as the primary sacrament and the effectual grace of all sacramental life.

The incarnation of God in the person of Jesus Christ was a sacrament of divine grace intended to repair the ecological rupture between the spiritual and material workplace of the human habitat. In this view of sacrament the division between the holy place and the profane workplace that resulted from the Fall was overcome. Through the redemptive sacrament of the incarnation the created order was restored as a unity of material and spiritual life.

Jesus was not a religious person when viewed from the perspective of the religion of his day. He had no right to the priestly office nor access to the holy place. Instead, he was the holy One in the midst of a secular place. He grew up in his own workplace, an apprentice in a carpenter's shop. While he called a select few to be his followers in his calling to be the Messiah, he called the rest to work out their salvation for the sake of the kingdom of God in their own workplace. His gospel was a gospel of the kingdom of God, not of the church. The writers of the Gospels only mention the church twice, with no suggestion that it was the purpose of Jesus to create it as a separate and sacred place. Indeed, he pronounced judgment on the temple as a place that now was abandoned, and pointed to his own person and life as the temple of God in their midst. He did not come to build a kingdom here on earth, but to empower others to kingdom living. While the church tends to differentiate itself from the world by its religious nature, the kingdom of God penetrates and transforms the world by its secular nature. This is why the Spirit of Christ calls us to be disciples of the kingdom rather than of the church. Discipleship is not a religious vocation.

LIVING AS KINGDOM-MINDED DISCIPLES

I have taken the term "kingdom-minded disciples" (which I like very much), from Dan Kimball, who wrote, "We must redefine how we measure success: by the characteristics of a kingdom-minded disciple of Jesus produced by the Spirit, rather than by our methodologies, numbers, strategies, the cool and innovative things we are doing."[12] To be kingdom-minded is to have the Spirit that impelled the emerging church at Antioch to send out Paul and Barnabas to expand the kingdom. To be kingdom-minded is to practice kingdom living (see pp. 101-4). To be a disciple of the kingdom is to have the Spirit of Jesus and the practical insight of John the Baptist with regard to the everyday aspect of kingdom living.

The gospel of the kingdom of God as announced by John and pronounced through the ministry of Jesus restored the workplace of human life under the reign of God's kingdom to be authentically human and deeply spiritual as a secular sacrament. There is, of course, a "now but not yet" aspect to the kingdom of God. Thus the secular sacrament of the kingdom exists in tension with the yet-unredeemed workplace. Those who live as disciples of the kingdom of God in the workplace have full assurance that the kingdom of God is at work through them even though they work alongside of those for whom the sacrament remains broken.

This is evident in the response given by John the Baptist to his disciples when they asked, "What should we do?" John replied, "Whoever has two coats must share with anyone who has none; and whoever has food must do likewise." When tax collectors came to be baptized, and asked, "What should we do?" John replied, "Collect no more than the amount prescribed for you." Soldiers also asked him, "what should we do?" John told them, "Do not exhort money from anyone by threats or false accusation, and be content with your wages" (Luke 3:10-14). In

---

[12]Dan Kimball, *The Emerging Church* (Grand Rapids: Zondervan, 2003), p. 15.

this way, no matter how a person finds a secular vocation and calling in the workplace, he or she can experience the workplace as a secular sacrament of the kingdom of God.

Jesus amplified the sacrament of the kingdom in his Sermon on the Mount (Matthew 5—7): "Strive first for the kingdom of God and his righteousness, and all these things will be given to you as well" (Matthew 6:33). What the Gentiles strive for—" 'What will we eat?' or 'What will we drink?' "—are things that are staples of the workplace. The kingdom of God does not demand that holy things be done but that secular things be done righteously—that is, sacramentally. The apostle Paul understood this perfectly. His own exhortations to believers at the end of most of his letters were directed toward their experience in the workplace, economically, socially and domestically (e.g. Romans 12:9-21; Ephesians 4:25-32; 2 Thessalonians 3:6-13).

From the perspective of the kingdom of God, there is only one workplace. It is where humans live as material and spiritual beings. The workplace was originally intended to be a secular sacrament by which human life was a daily sacrament, of which the sabbath was a reminder. God completed his work on the seventh day and rested. Humans were sacramental partners of God in their daily life and work. Humans too "complete their work" on the sabbath. Humans were not made just to keep the sabbath, as Jesus reminded us, but the sabbath is made to "keep humans" (Mark 2:27). That is, to make the human workplace both a redemptive and creative task in partnership with God.

CONCLUDING NONTHEOLOGICAL POSTSCRIPT

Early in my pastoral and preaching ministry I stressed the imperative of Christian discipleship by citing the words of Jesus when he called those to follow him: "Sell what you own, and give the money to the poor, and you will have treasure in heaven; then come, follow me" (Mark 10:21). After hearing this for some time, a member of my church came to me and said, "Pastor, you tell us that in order to be disciples of Christ we need to do as he did, by abandoning all, taking up our own cross and follow him." He went on. "But this is impossible. Nobody is doing this. You are not doing this, and yet you tell us that this is what we must do to be his disciples."

Ouch!

In attempting to save face and defend the biblical text, I replied: "But what Jesus said must be understood in a spiritual sense. We must be willing to sell everything in order to follow him, and if we are willing then we have fulfilled his commandment."

"But this is not what he said," the man replied. And while it ended the conversation, it was also the beginning of my own reflection on what it meant to understand discipleship in a larger context of the kingdom of God.

The fact is, Jesus only called very few to actually leave their families and their vocation to follow him. Even many of those who wanted to follow him he sent back to their families and to their work. Jesus himself is the disciple of the Father, and his mission was to do the Father's will, even to the point of death on the cross (John 12:27). To take the words of Jesus and tear them out of the larger picture of kingdom living is to end up with only a piece of a puzzle that does not fit the other pieces. Suppose that Jesus came to Bethany, near the end of his ministry, thinking of the comfort he had often received in the home of Mary, Martha and Lazarus, only to find that their home was occupied by someone else. When he inquired he was told, "Oh, Lazarus and his sisters sold all that they had and gave to the poor after hearing what you said about being disciples, and now they are somewhere in Jerusalem living on the street and begging for their own food."

I can imagine Jesus replying, "Oh no! I didn't mean it for everybody!"

I think that it is a mistake to take the words of Jesus out of context where he exhorted his would-be disciple to "Sell what you own, and give the money to the poor, and you will have treasure in heaven; then come, follow me" (Mark 10:21). Nor did Jesus expect his own disciples to do that; after all, he participated in their life in the workplace by going fishing with them. Jesus' strong words are given in the context of the demand of God on his own life, and any who sought to enter into that mission with him must be prepared to take up their own cross and follow him.

Too often, I fear, when the church attempts to make disciples out of Christians by urging them to follow Christ what is really intended is to mobilize the members of the church to take up church-related ministries and to develop their own interior religious life. A disciple of Christ is not intended to be a little messiah but to participate in the messianic mission to extend the kingdom into every crevice and corner of the world. For the most part, Jesus expected people to live sacramentally in the workplace as disciples of the kingdom rather than become messiahs in their own right.

If we were to ask the question, Where should a disciple of the kingdom of God be expected to live out that discipleship, in the church or in the workplace? the answer is obvious—in the workplace. Yet the temptation for the church is to continue to partialize and divide the workplace from its own place in the world by creating disciples whose primary task is to serve the church's existence and mission, not that of the kingdom. Filled with the Spirit of Christ, we are to live as disciples of the kingdom, partners with God, in the secular workplace. The church often seems to be in another place. The church may even appear to be in opposition to our kingdom discipleship in the workplace as it sets forth its own agenda and mission.

The church may think of itself as having its own place and space outside of the workplace, but this is not so. As part of the workplace, the church has its own calling and mission to serve the workplace and to empower disciples of the kingdom in their partnership with God. This is why the workplace, as it was originally intended, is still today for Christians a secular sacrament of the kingdom of God. For disciples of the kingdom in the workplace, the church is the way that we outsource our need for communion with other believers and our instruction and guidance from the Word of God, and recharge our spiritual batteries for our daily life in the secular workplace.

Would there have been a church in the Garden of Eden if there not been a Fall? No. For the church is part of the fallen world. As such, the church needs to live as a religious institution with a spirit of repentance toward God and with the fire of the kingdom burning in its bones as a human institution. There will be no church in heaven. It will be kingdom living, first class!

6

IT'S ABOUT THE WORK OF GOD, NOT JUST THE WORD OF GOD

When Barnabas came to Antioch and discovered that the church had already assimilated uncircumcised Gentile believers into the community on the evidence that they had received the Holy Spirit, he must have thought, *I'm over my head! I am a pastoral counselor not a theologian!* Indeed, he was given the name Barnabas—which means "son of encouragement"—by the apostles at Jerusalem because he had the gift of empowering and supporting others (Acts 4:36).

Barnabas was well aware of the fact that the church at Jerusalem was resistant to this accommodation made to Gentile believers. He also knew that their theological hermeneutic of the Word of God—the Law of Moses—made it impossible for them to accept the Gentiles if they were to remain faithful to the Scriptures as they knew them. Even Peter's brief foray into Gentile territory was tolerated but certainly not affirmed. While they could allow for an exception, the principle of Scripture was normative for the practice of ministry. Barnabas suspected that if he went back with mere anecdotal evidence, they would assign him to the ministry division of the theological faculty that, as we all know, is the Siberia of academia!

I need the A team, he thought. He remembered that Saul (Paul) was in nearby Tarsus. By that time he had become rather well-known, not only because of his scholarly study of the Scriptures under Gamaliel but more recently due to his zeal for the gospel of Christ in that region (Acts 22:3). He went to Tarsus to look for him, and when he had found him he brought Paul back to Antioch. Barnabas, true to his name, encouraged Paul to become the resident theologian for the first emerging church. For an entire year Paul stayed in Antioch where the church flourished and he "taught a great many people" (Acts 11:25-26).

Paul was also familiar with the "Word of God theology" held by the apostles at Jerusalem. His former teacher, Gamaliel, was a member of the council of the Pharisees (Acts 5:34). He was not about to confront his former mentor in the law because, since being his student, Paul had a personal encounter with the risen Messiah and had received direct revelation from him concerning his gospel of grace and freedom from the law. Christ had revealed to Paul that the law achieved its purpose and was no longer binding on either Jew or Gentile. Even as the written Gospels later recorded Jesus' claim to be the "lord . . . of the sabbath," Paul could say that the risen Christ is the "lord of the law" (Mark 2:28; Romans 10:4).

For Paul, the coming of the Holy Spirit on the Gentiles was an objective reality of Christ's continuing redemptive work, just as objective as his own encounter with Christ on the Damascus road. He would never allow for that event to be labeled merely a subjective experience with no evidentiary value. In his letter to the Corinthians, whose faith was being upset by the leaders of the church in Jerusalem who were using the text of Moses in demanding circumcision of the Gentiles, Paul wrote: "Have I not seen Jesus our Lord? Are you not my work in the Lord? . . . [F]or you are the seal of my apostleship in the Lord" (1 Corinthians 9:1-2). Again Paul made the same point when he wrote, "You yourselves are our letter, written on our hearts, to be known and read by all; and you show that you are a letter of Christ, prepared by us, written not with ink but with the Spirit of the living God, not on tablets of stone but on tablets of human hearts" (2 Corinthians 3:2-3).

Paul was later called to defend his position before the heads of the church in Jerusalem who argued against him from the text of Scripture; "It is necessary for them to be circumcised and ordered to keep the law of Moses" (Acts 15:5). In response, Paul argued that his text was actually the lives of the Gentile Christians who had been filled with the Spirit of Christ. "And God, who knows the human heart, testified to them by giving them the Holy Spirit, just as he did to us; and in cleansing their hearts by faith he has made no distinction between them and us." Indeed, Paul said, "we believe that we will be saved through the grace of the Lord Jesus Christ, just as they will" (Acts 15:8-9, 11). Paul said, we Jews will be saved just as those Gentiles are. The Jerusalem leaders are not going to like that!

There it is—emergent theology coming out of the first emerging church. When emerging churches set out to expand the kingdom of God in the world, they need to have a resident theologian on board. Kingdom work is not just mission work, it is God's work. The work of God must be read and interpreted along with the Word of God. Both are gospel narratives and each interprets the other. The Holy Spirit is the bond between them.

Narrative texts must always be read as contemporary even though they often emerge out of a historical context. For example, when someone begins a story "Once upon a time," a listener is not supposed to interrupt with questions like "Well, when exactly did it happen?" or "Who told you this story?" The truth of the narrative is in the narrative itself and in its affect on the listener or reader. When my youngest daughter was around seven or eight, her Sunday school teacher read the story of Moses and the plagues that were brought on Pharaoh. After hearing the story and all of the weird things that took place, my daughter confronted the teacher with the demanding question, "Is that really true?" Needless to say, the narrative text was deflated like a balloon from which all of the air was let out in a single whoosh!

A THEOLOGY OF THE WORK AND WORD OF GOD

Emerging churches in our generation are in need of a theology that emerges out of the work of God through the kingdom of God in local congregations. These congregations have their own narratives of God's work through the Holy Spirit. Rather than viewing these as merely anecdotal stories, we need to examine them for evidences of the work of Christ through the Spirit of Christ. As a basis for developing this emergent theology, I have begun with the emerging church at Antioch where Paul brought to bear the revelation received directly from the risen and ascended Christ as a hermeneutical criterion. He did this both with respect to the written Scriptures in which he was schooled in the law of Moses and the oral narratives of the work of the Spirit of Christ in bringing Gentiles into the kingdom of God.

In developing this emergent theology I will attempt to enter into the situation that Paul faces with respect to the active opposition by the elders of the church at Jerusalem to the practice of including Gentile believers. I want to examine how Paul is able to respond to their criticism by remaining faithful to the narrative of Scripture while, at the same time, affirming the work of the Spirit in the congregation at Antioch. This was not a philosophical problem with respect to competing or even obsolete worldviews (such as the modern and postmodern debate in our generation), but rather an exercise in practical theology by one who is on the fireline of gospel ministry.[1] What follows is partly Spirit-inspired (I hope!) theological imagination along with biblical exposition.

If we consider the Scriptures of both the Old and New Testaments to be narratives of God's self-revelation through word and deed as experienced and recorded by those who had the original encounter, then Scripture may be considered to be a narrative text transmitted first by oral tradition and then by Spirit-inspired written form. This narrative text is what we have come to call the Word of God, Holy Scripture, the Bible.

---

[1]See my book *Ministry on the Fireline* (Downers Grove, Ill.: InterVarsity Press, 1993), particularly chap. 8, "An Emerging Church," pp. 135-48.

Within this narrative text, however, there is evidence of another text at work that constitutes an interpretive or hermeneutical criterion. For example, the narrative text of the law of Moses had become the authoritative Word of God concerning sabbath keeping. Jesus as the contemporary, incarnate Word of God (John 1:14) experienced the work of God in his life and ministry in such a way that another narrative text emerged. The sabbath healing of the man who was born blind constituted just such a text of God's work that revealed a deeper truth concerning the sabbath than the narrative text of the law was understood to contain. Faced with the fact that the man had been healed (which by now has become a narrative text), those who opposed Jesus reviled the man, saying, "You are his disciple, but we are disciples of Moses" (John 9:28). Jesus did not claim to break or destroy the law of Moses but to fulfill it in accordance with God's purpose for the restoration of broken and estranged humanity (Matthew 5:17; Luke 24:44).

Contrary to this traditional understanding of the sabbath, Jesus interpreted the law of the sabbath in accordance with God's work on the sabbath to mean that "the sabbath was made for humankind, and not humankind for the sabbath" (Mark 2:27). There was no text that literally said this in the Old Testament Scriptures. However, the narrative text of the healing on the sabbath became a lens through which we can see the actual purpose of the sabbath that lay behind the law of the sabbath. Those who only knew the sabbath as a law perceived only the surface of the original text and so failed to perceive the truth of the sabbath as the word of God now revealed in the work of God. The saying of Jesus thus became a new text of the Word of God, but only as a result of the narrative text of the work of God. Even so, this new text that became the word of God must still be read in such a way that it does not hammer a contemporary work of God into submission to the letter of the law, destroying the Spirit. "The words that I have spoken to you are spirit and life" (John 6:63). "For the letter kills, but the Spirit gives life" (2 Corinthians 3:6).

I view Paul as having the same problem as did Jesus when it came to facing those who challenged his ministry on the basis of the Scripture text. Healing the blind man on the sabbath (John 9) was, in the minds of the Pharisees, a clear violation of the commandment of Scripture. The story of the healing, however, constituted a narrative text of the work of God that Jesus appealed to as fulfillment, not a violation, of the sabbath. In the same way, when confronted with the woman who had committed adultery, the Pharisees demanded that Jesus impose the punishment prescribed by the Scripture text (John 8). When Jesus sent her away without condemning her, he appeared to be in violation of the law of Moses. However, Jesus revealed mercy itself to be a work of God.

In Paul's case, his accusers had the Scripture text that commanded circumcision on their side. The coming of the Holy Spirit to the Gentiles, however, constituted for Paul a narrative text that must be understood as the work of God through the Spirit of Christ. Paul is well aware that circumcision is a commandment of God given to Abraham and reiterated by Moses to the effect that no uncircumcised Gentile should be counted as righteous before God in the same way as a Jew. Following Paul's dramatic encounter with the resurrected and ascended Jesus and after being "filled with the Holy Spirit" (Acts 9:17), he encountered the coming of the Spirit to the Gentiles. Paul interpreted this as the work of God through the Spirit of Christ. This became a contemporary narrative of the work of God requiring Paul to find in the Scripture narrative a basis for affirming the experience as truly of God. Paul's theology of the work of God is a narrative theology that he places alongside the text of Scripture as Word of God. To use the Word of God to forbid the work of God was to misread the Scripture text. Paul then had to go back deeper into the narrative of the Scripture text to find a basis for affirming the narrative text of the work of God.

SCRIPTURE AS LIVING WORD

Paul appears to view the Scripture texts as the living, contemporary

Word of God that recounts the work of God. Though at one time he might have treated the texts as archeological stones, to be viewed in their historical context and treated as ancient relics to be revered, he could no longer do this. When read through the lens of Christ's revelation, they come alive. He can tell the story of Abraham as though it were written yesterday, with the four hundred years of history separating Abraham from Moses as thin as the parchment on which the text is inscribed. The contemporary narrative of the Holy Spirit's coming to the Gentile believers is laid alongside the narrative of Scripture so that the work of God through the Spirit becomes the lens through which he reads the Word of God. As a result, he hears what he had never heard before. It was there all the time. Abraham was a Gentile and was declared righteous before being circumcised. The scribes and the lawyers of the Judaic tradition used the texts as building blocks in their theology of law. They were no longer storytellers but technicians who crafted a legal case for their religion silencing the voice of the storyteller.

While Paul does not view the narrative text of the work of God through the Spirit as superior to or replacing the narrative text of the Word of God, neither is the work of the Spirit crushed beneath the hammer of tradition on the anvil of Scripture text. When both Word and work are lighted by the Spirit, one (the Word) from behind and the other (the work) from the future, both come alive as revelation. In somewhat the same way as Jesus held himself to be contemporary with Abraham—"before Abraham was, I am" (John 8:58)—the narrative text of the Spirit's work is contemporary with the narrative text of Word of God.

THE TWO HORIZONS

Modern theories of biblical interpretation have largely concentrated on the biblical narrative as a text to be studied and understood primarily as a structure of language that contains truth. This has been pictured by Anthony Thistelton as a modern horizon that needs to be correlated with the first-century horizon in which the text was first created.[2] These two horizons then are seen to bracket the biblical text with the task of the interpreter to discern the original intent of the author of the text or, as in some cases, the way that the text emerged through a process involving more than one author and in some cases an unknown author. This approach, while attempting to extract truthful content from the Scripture text, does not really get to the depth of the Word of God as living Word with a contemporary voice, but merely extends the surface of the text backward as a conceptual act—for there is no way actually to recover the historical moment in which the text emerged. Rather than the text emerging with a voice that speaks to the contemporary situation, this voice is silenced under the anesthesia of the science of textual criticism. I do not intend to disparage the work of textual criticism as a way of understanding more accurately the sense of the text and its larger context. This work can be of valuable to the teacher and preacher of Scripture. But when that work has been done, the Word of God has not yet been heard with regard to its purpose and effect.

The truth of Word of God does not lie between the two horizons bracketed by the same Scripture text, but between the two narratives. One narrative is the Scripture text that confronts us in the same way that a story does—we listen rather than probe and dissect. The other narrative is the work of God through the Holy Spirit. Emerging churches are where this narrative is being told. The two narratives are both contemporary, in a sense, assuming that the contemporary text of Scripture is a faithful rendering of the original. Along with the contemporary Scripture narrative text is the narrative text of the work of the Holy Spirit. By saying that the work of God interprets the Word of God, I am speaking of these two narratives, distinguished as a canonical and inspired text of Word of God and a noncanonical narrative of the contemporary work of Christ through the Holy Spirit. The first narrative presents itself to us in

---

[2]Anthony Thistelton, *New Horizons in Hermeneutics* (Glasgow: Harper Collins, 1992).

Scripture as the Word of God written. The Scripture is the authoritative narrative with regard to inspired Word of God and revelation. The second narrative is a contemporary account of the work of the Holy Spirit as the contemporary presence and power of the resurrected Christ, who is already coming into the world through the eschatological reality of Holy Spirit. This second narrative presents us with the hermeneutical significance of the Holy Spirit as the work of Christ interprets the Word of Christ.

To this point I have attempted to show that the work of God can be understood not only as the source of Word of God, but that the work of God, as the work of Christ in the power and presence of the Holy Spirit, can also become a narrative text along with the existing narrative text of Scripture. The fact that Scripture itself forces us to this conclusion can be demonstrated, as I have attempted to do in the first half of this book. Paul's emergent theology assumes that the risen and ascended Christ is his contemporary in the form of the present work of the Holy Spirit in such a way that where the Spirit is, there is the Lord. "Now the Lord is the Spirit, and where the Spirit of the Lord is, there is freedom" (2 Corinthians 3:17). If that is true for Paul, it can also be true for us. The same Holy Spirit that brought about the work of God in the church at Antioch, and those that emerged out of Antioch, is at work today as the Spirit of the risen and coming Christ.

THE BIBLICAL ANTECEDENT FOR THE WORK OF GOD

Does every claim to be led of the Spirit of Christ have equal merit as a hermeneutical criterion? The answer is no. Returning again to the way that the two narratives are correlated within the biblical text, we find that for the apostle Paul and for Jesus there is always a biblical antecedent for what presents itself as a creative and liberating work of the Spirit. For example, regarding circumcision, Paul does not simply replace the law of circumcision (nor the law of Moses, for that matter) with a new law of the Spirit. It is not the Holy Spirit that made an end of the law, but Christ brought the law to its conclusion (Romans 10:4). Paul has the narrative text of the Holy Spirit as the Spirit of Christ coming upon uncircumcised Gentiles. Now he looks back into the Scripture narrative for an antecedent to which he can link the narrative of the Spirit's work. He finds it in Abraham, who is declared righteous by God before he is circumcised (Romans 4). Consequently, Paul views the Scriptural narrative of the law given by Moses as a temporary expedient when he argues his case to the Galatian Christians. "The law [of Moses] was our disciplinarian [pedagogue] until Christ came" (Galatians 3:24). Remember, the pedagogue was not the teacher but the slave who took the child to the teacher (see p. 53). At that point, the role of the pedagogue was completed. So too if Jesus is the teacher, then the law has served its purpose and has come to an end. Paul does not grasp this clearly until the narrative of Christ's Spirit coming upon the uncircumcised forces him to see it.

Circumcision, as a legal requirement of the law, has a historical precedent in the Scriptural narrative. It was the concept of Scriptural precedent that determined to a large degree the opposition of the religious leaders to the ministry of Jesus as well as to that of the apostle Paul. Without consideration of the narrative of the work of God, the narrative of Word of God takes precedence. However, when the narrative of the work of God's Spirit through Jesus Christ is taken into account, we now discover what I have called an "eschatological preference." I have coined this phrase to capture the difference between the historical precedent by which the eleven disciples following the resurrection chose Matthias as a replacement for Judas (Acts 1:21-26), and the choice of Saul of Tarsus by (the Spirit of the resurrected and ascended) Christ (Acts 9). The disciples assumed that because there were originally twelve disciples, the number twelve was a principle that carried over after the resurrection. The "eschatological preference" refers to the work of Christ that comes out of the future into the present by the Holy Spirit. In defending his own apostolic authority Paul cannot appeal to historical precedence as did the others at Jerusalem. His call to be an apostle comes from the risen Lord Jesus, not the historical Jesus.[3]

The Holy Spirit is a contemporary work of the coming Christ. Thus, the Spirit of the coming Christ already at work in the contemporary narrative provides a hermeneutical clue to the antecedent for such a work in the Scriptural narrative. However, I need to note that in addition to the historical precedent that comes out of the past and the eschatological preference that comes out of the future, Paul required a biblical antecedent as a verification for the eschatological preference. Without such an antecedent, we cannot allow for what might be claimed as a new work of the Spirit to become a hermeneutical criterion. The antecedent, in the case of circumcision, was the case of Abraham, whom God declared righteous before being circumcised. In this way, the historical precedent of circumcision was viewed by Paul to have been completed in Christ so that the antecedent of God's gracious work in blessing Abraham (and the Gentiles) could be seen as a scriptural basis for affirming the blessing of God on the Gentile believers at Antioch without circumcision.[4]

Where a New Testament teaching appears unanimous and consistent in every pastoral situation, I am not suggesting that the presence of the living Lord in the church can be understood in such a way that this single voice can be silenced or made to sing a different tune. But where apostolic teaching and practice is clearly governed by the readiness or openness of the situation to experience full freedom in Christ, the hermeneutical criterion of the resurrected Christ as a continuing presence in the church is, in my judgment, indispensable. For it is here that the tension between the *now* and the *not yet* is most evident. This is not to suggest that we have here a kind of God of the exegetical gaps! All exe-

---

[3]What I call "eschatological preference" may be somewhat like saying that a text of Scripture has a prophetic trajectory, a concept suggested by Old Testament scholar Walter Brueggemann and picked up and used by J. Richard Middleton and Brian J. Walsh in their book *Truth Is Stranger Than It Used to Be* (Downers Grove, Ill.: InterVarsity Press, 1995), p. 94.

[4]For a discussion of historical precedent, eschatological preference and biblical antecedent, see my book *The Soul of Ministry* (Louisville: Westminster John Knox, 1997), pp. 14-15, 21-23.

gesis of Scripture must finally be accountable to the resurrected, always present and already coming Lord. For the purpose of this discussion, I am focusing on those areas that are most clearly in this eschatological tension and that require unusual sensitivity to the hermeneutical criterion I am advocating.

SOME CONTEMPORARY EXAMPLES

My preparation for ministry took place between 1956 and 1959 in a seminary consisting of approximately 300 students of which 292 were male and 8 were female. The female students were not allowed to earn the bachelor of divinity degree but had to enroll in the master of religious education degree. Assuming that they could not be ordained and serve as pastors but only as teachers and educators, they were not permitted to take courses in biblical languages or in exegetical study of Scripture. My recollection is that the female students did not complain but had enrolled with the understanding that the seminary faculty was convinced that Scripture did not permit the ordination of women for pastoral ministry.

But something happened in the 1960s. A larger number of female students came to the seminary with the expectation that they should be allowed to take courses leading to ordination in their respective churches. Their argument was not based on ideological feminism or on the cultural changes regarding the role of women in society. Rather, they simply said that their churches had affirmed their calling and anointing by the Holy Spirit for pastoral ministry, and had sent them to be prepared for ordination to this ministry. The church was emerging!

The faculty was in somewhat of a quandary. The first response was to create a new degree especially for the female students enabling them to take courses in biblical exegesis, but to retain the B.D. degree exclusively for men. The absurdity of this soon became apparent, and certain of the faculty took seriously the fact that all the churches that were sending these women to be prepared for ordination may not be disobedient to

Scripture. As a result, when the theologians went back to read the text of Scripture from this perspective, they exclaimed in effect, "What do you know! We now see ways of exegeting the text to allow women to be prepared for ordination in the church." The seminary was becoming an emerging seminary!

In retrospect, I have concluded that if the number of female students had not increased and had not challenged the faculty's view of these women as led by the Spirit, the seminary to this day would still hold that only males should be given pastoral leadership in the church, a view that some seminary faculties still hold.

I have two comments regarding this narrative. First, the response of the theologians on the faculty was to find a new exegetical basis for the their decision to allow female students to receive the B.D. (now M.Div.) degree in preparation for ordination. This resulted in some tortured exegetical maneuvers that, at least in the case of one of my former teachers and later a colleague on the faculty, led to the conclusion that the apostle Paul was simply wrong in what he wrote to Timothy forbidding women to teach and have authority over men in the church (1 Timothy 2:11-15). After publishing his conclusions he was censored by the seminary's trustees but allowed to continue teaching. And, as it turned out, the faculty continued to accept women into the B.D. degree program based, at least in part, on his position. Having become an emerging seminary, the faculty had not yet begun to articulate an emergent theology.

My second comment on this case is that the faculty basically failed to grasp the hermeneutical implications of the narrative text provided by the women who came under the authority and sponsorship of their churches to prepare for ministry. They did not view the work of the Holy Spirit in anointing these women for ordained pastoral ministry as a text to be read alongside of their reading of the biblical text. Instead, the faculty turned back toward new and creative exegetical devices in order to find in Scripture the basis for what was, in fact, a rather pragmatic solution to their dilemma, even at the risk of playing one Scripture text against another.[5]

My point is this: Confronted with the narrative text represented by the presence and testimony of these women students, backed up by the discernment of the church that the Spirit of Christ indeed was at work, the hermeneutical significance of this narrative text was ignored. The resurrection of Christ as a contemporary reality of the Spirit constitutes a hermeneutical criterion equivalent to that recognized by Peter when he gave his narrative account of the baptism of Cornelius.[6] After recounting the incident before the leaders of the church at Jerusalem, Peter said, "And as I began to speak, the Holy Spirit fell upon them just as it had upon us at the beginning. . . . If then God gave them the same gift that he gave us when we believed in the Lord Jesus Christ, who was I that could hinder God" (Acts 11:15, 17)?

Indeed, if the work of Christ on earth is the work of God and the work of the Spirit of Christ through the Holy Spirit, who can hinder God? If the same Holy Spirit that anoints males for leadership and pastoral ministry also anoints and sets apart females for the same leadership, who can hinder God? I argue that to refuse to recognize the work of Christ through the contemporary operation of the Holy Spirit might well be hindering the work of God. The biblical antecedent for this work of God is not hard to find.

While the New Testament speaks with an emphatic voice concerning a restriction on the role of women in certain teaching and ministry situations, in other situations the emphasis is as clearly on the side of full participation and full parity. We only have to compare the insistent commands issued by the apostle Paul that women be "silent in the churches" (1 Corinthians 14:34) and not be permitted "to teach or to have author-

---

[5]For a discussion of the role of women students at Fuller Theological Seminary, see George Marsden, *Reforming Fundamentalism* (Grand Rapids: Eerdmans, 1987), pp. 123-28, 280-82.
[6]See my chapter "The Resurrection of Jesus as Hermeneutical Criterion," in *The Shape of Practical Theology* (Downers Grove, Ill.: InterVarsity Press, 2001), pp. 77-101.

ity over a man" (1 Timothy 2:11) with the rather matter-of-fact instruction that a woman who prophesies (in public worship) should keep her head covered (1 Corinthians 11:5).

Even more significant is the same apostle's practice of identifying women as coworkers *(synergoi)* along with men (Philippians 4:2-3), and his commendation of Phoebe in the church at Rome as a "deacon" (Romans 16:1-2).[7] The apostle's overt recognition of the role of women serving as coworkers alongside other apostles is worthy of note. There is a strong possibility, according to many scholars, that the Junias mentioned along with Andronicus as being "among the apostles" was actually a woman—Julia, changed by early biblical translators to Junia, a masculine name (Romans 16:7)![8]

Let me give another example. Early in my pastoral experience, a woman who was a member of the church and who had been divorced for many years came to me with this question: "I was not the innocent party to the divorce, but I have confessed my sin and have received assurance of Christ's forgiveness and presence in my life. Pastor, you know the man with whom I am now in love, as he attends this church and is part of our fellowship. He is a man who has also been divorced but along with me has experienced the forgiveness and healing of Christ. We feel that Christ is present in our lives and in our love for each other. But I also know what the Bible says, and from this I have been taught that I can never remarry because this would constitute adultery. But Pastor, on which side is God? Is God on the side of the Bible, or is God on our side in our new relationship in Christ?"

Her story and her life as a part of our congregation was a narrative of the work of Christ, as it also was in the case of the man that she loved. I

---

[7]Some versions of the Bible translate the masculine noun *diakonos* as "deaconess," which is dubious.

[8]See Bernadette Brooten, "Junia . . . Outstanding Among the Apostles," in *Women Priests,* ed. Leonard Swidler and Arlene Swidler (New York: Paulist Press, 1977), pp. 141-44. Also Scott Bartchy, "Power, Submission, and Sexual Identity Among the Early Christians," in *Essays on New Testament Christianity,* ed. C. Robert Wetzel (Cincinnati: Standard Publishing, 1978).

reviewed this narrative of Christ's work in her life and looked into the Scripture, and I found that Christ's provision of mercy and forgiveness for sinners constituted an antecedent for my decision in this case. Faced with that question, I could only respond by saying that God was indeed present in their lives as the Spirit of Christ was clearly at work in renewing their lives in grace. When Jesus said that humans were not made for the sabbath but that the sabbath was made for humans (Mark 2:27-28), I took that also to apply to marriage. Humans were not made just to live under the law of marriage with no mercy for failure, but marriage was made for the benefit of humans. Jesus is not only the Lord of the sabbath, he is the Lord of marriage. The words of Jesus concerning divorce cannot be lifted out the context of his debate with the religious authorities in such a way as to counteract his basic teaching concerning the power of God's grace to heal and forgive what the law condemned. On that basis I performed their marriage. I could not and would not use the words of Jesus to cancel out the work of Jesus in his redemption of those who were not able to live by the law.

Some years later I participated in a debate with another faculty member sponsored by students over the issue of divorce and remarriage. My counterpart in the debate argued his position strongly. It was absolutely impossible to permit the remarriage of a divorced person on the grounds that Jesus forbad it by his teaching. Even the so-called exception clause in Matthew 19:9—"except for unchastity"—he argued was a later addition to the teachings of Jesus. There could be no exception, he stated, because the word of Jesus was final. I recounted the narrative of the woman in my church as a text of God's work and as a criterion for interpreting the Word of God so as to release her from the judgment of the law in order to receive the grace of Christ. This only served to confirm his opinion that my position was questionable if not heretical, and he firmly restated his own view—no remarriage according to biblical principle.

At that point a student raised his hand and asked, "Professor, you say that the sin of divorce, while it can be forgiven, allows for no remarriage; is that correct?" The answer was yes. "Then is it not also true that in the case of the death of one's spouse the surviving spouse could remarry, as that would not violate the teaching of Jesus?" Again, the response was affirmative. I quickly saw where the good professor was being led, and remained silent as the lamb was led to slaughter!

"Then what about this?" the student asked. "In our city there was a pastor who became angry with his wife and shot and killed her. When he gets out of prison, is he now free to remarry, seeing that instead of divorcing his wife he killed her?"

It was too late. The branch had been sawed off, and the professor, consistent with his formal logic to the end, had to admit that, "yes, this man could remarry!" The laughter of the students over the absurdity of this case reduced his argument to folly in their eyes. He, of course, while expressing deep discomfort over the logical outcome of his position, remained unmoved.

I have suggested two narratives: (1) the case of the role of women in pastoral leadership in the church and (2) the case of pastoral ministry to those who have experienced divorce and seek God's grace for remarriage. The second narrative comes into play as we seek to discern the purpose of Word of God through the work of God in specific situations that require us to make decisions in the context of emerging churches. This is in accord with the teaching of Word of God itself, which urges us to discern not only the nature of Word of God as divine revelation but also the purpose of Word of God as it is proclaimed and taught (Isaiah 55:11).

In the same way, while Paul adhered to the scriptural narrative so far as it was useful in evangelizing both Jews and Gentiles, and in pastoral care of the churches, he left several pointers to the narrative of the anointing of women for leadership in the church. While he permitted the circumcision of Timothy out of expediency (Acts 16:3), he refused to have Titus circumcised as a sign of liberation from this historical and physical sign of membership in the covenant community (Galatians 2:3). While he apparently restricted the role of women in the church at Ephesus (1 Timothy 2), he openly acknowledged the ministry of Lydia in the church at Philippi, of Phoebe as *diakonos* (Romans 16:1), and Julia, who was "prominent among the apostles" (Romans 16:7).

SUMMARY

I can summarize my case for a theology of emerging churches in this way. First, the work of God through Christ became a narrative text that served as a critical criterion for interpreting and applying the narrative Scripture text. Second, Christ's work as the work of God took place through the power of the Spirit of God. "But if it is by the Spirit of God that I cast out demons, then the kingdom of God has come to you" (Matthew 12:28). Third, following the resurrection Jesus breathed the Spirit upon his disciples with the promise that through the Spirit his own authority to minister the work of God on earth would continue (John 20:22). Fourth, the presence and power of the Holy Spirit following Pentecost was assumed by the emerging church to be equal to the words of Jesus prior to his crucifixion. Thus, Paul virtually equates the words of the historical Jesus carried forward by his disciples with Paul's own teaching as having the "mind of Christ" (1 Corinthians 2:16). This led to the practical application that Paul's teaching contained both. For example, "To the married I give this command—not I but the Lord" (1 Corinthians 7:10). "To the rest I say—I and not the Lord" (1 Corinthians 7:12). "Now concerning virgins, I have no command of the Lord, but I give my opinion as one who by the Lord's mercy is trustworthy" (1 Corinthians 7:25). Paul's confidence in placing his own teaching alongside that of the historical Jesus is that the same Jesus is now guiding him through the Spirit. This is an example of Paul's emergent theology for emerging churches. The Holy Spirit is the Spirit of the same Jesus, who spoke when he was on earth and now speaks through the Spirit.

Finally, I assume that the Holy Spirit is not only the Spirit of the histor-

ical Jesus as a contemporary Christ but is the Spirit of the coming, eschatological Christ. Thus the Holy Spirit makes contemporary the Christ who
is to come and who will give the final verdict as to what constitutes the will
of Christ through the life and ministry of the church as the body of Christ.
Paul is quite clear about this regarding his own teaching and ministry.

> Think of us in this way, as servants of Christ and stewards of God's
> mysteries. Moreover, it is required of stewards that they be found
> trustworthy. But with me it is a very small thing that I should be
> judged by you or by any human court. I do not even judge myself.
> I am not aware of anything against myself, but I am not thereby ac-
> quitted. It is the Lord who judges me. Therefore do not pronounce
> judgment before the time, before the Lord comes, who will bring
> to light the things now hidden in darkness and will disclose the
> purposes of the heart. Then each one will receive commendation
> from God. (1 Corinthians 4:1-5)

From this I assume that the resurrected and coming Christ enters now
into the present time as our contemporary, creating new narratives of
Christ's work by the Spirit through which we are to read and interpret the
textual narrative of holy Scripture. These contemporary narratives of the
work of the Spirit do not become holy Scripture, nor do they become revelation in the same way that Scripture itself is. However, the contemporary
narratives as evidence of the work of Christ serve as hermeneutical criteria
in reading and applying the Scripture narratives as Word of God.

A word of caution. What I am saying is not to be construed as arguing
for equal revelatory status of the two narratives. I hold the Scripture narrative to be the infallible and only source of revelation as the Word of
God. At the same time, the Scripture text says that Word of God has a
purpose and an effect that must be recognized and read so as to receive
the Word of God. I then hold that the contemporary narrative text of the
work of Christ through the Holy Spirit must be interpreted as at least one
form of the "purpose" for which Word of God is sent (Isaiah 55:11).

CONCLUDING NONTHEOLOGICAL POSTSCRIPT

"Does Jesus think about things today?" I posed this question to a group of pastors enrolled in our doctor of ministry degree program. They were somewhat amused by the question and waited to see where I was going with it. I engaged them in this dialogue.

"Can I assume that all of you would give assent to the statement that the resurrection of Jesus from the dead included his body and not just his spirit?" They all nodded in agreement. Some, anxious to reinforce their evangelical credentials even raised their hand, thinking that we were voting on the issue. "How many of you," I then asked, "have considered that if Jesus was raised bodily from the grave that his brain was reconstituted as well so that he could have new ideas, thoughts and intentions? In other words, does Jesus think about things today?"

"I hadn't thought about that," one pastor said.

"Then think about it," I responded. "If the body of Jesus was raised, and his brain also, then do you think that Jesus has ever had a new idea or thought concerning God's purpose for the past two millennia? If so, how do you think that he would communicate that to us?"

There was a moment of stunned silence. "Or," I suggested, "do you think that he is just sitting at the right hand of the Father leaving us with the Bible and the words he spoke to us before he ascended to heaven without having anything new to say?" This is not the same thing, I assured them, as asking "What would Jesus do?" For that assumes his absence. When the Spirit of Christ speaks (always consistent with Scripture), this assumes the presence of Jesus.

The discussion that ensued revealed a great deal of concern as to what this would mean with regard to the Bible as our sole source of revelation. Some protested that it would be very dangerous to think that "new revelation" could occur after the closing of the biblical canon as a final authority. "Sola scriptura," one pastor suggested was the formula undergirding Luther's stance against the claims of the medieval church for an authority alongside of or beyond the Bible.

"What then is the role of the Holy Spirit as the continuing witness to the presence of Jesus in our midst?" The responses generally went in two directions. Those who considered themselves in the Reformed theological tradition argued that the Holy Spirit's role was to illuminate the text of Scripture, guiding the reader into the true intent and purpose of Word of God. Others, more in line with the Pentecostal tradition, suggested that the Holy Spirit's role was that of a personal filling or baptism of the Spirit resulting in the charismata, or gifts of the Spirit, enriching the devotional life and empowering the ministry of the church. When pressed, those in the Pentecostal tradition admitted that even such phenomena of the Spirit's presence and work must be strictly in line with biblical teaching. In the end, we agreed to think about it!

The criterion for the work of the Spirit as discerned in the ministry context is not determined by cultural relevance or pragmatic expediency. It is the work of the risen Jesus Christ in the power of the Holy Spirit that becomes normative and calls the church into repentance where it has imposed its own normative and binding rules. The emerging theologian is a theologian of the Holy Spirit (not just of the church), of the work of God (not just of the Word of God), of revelational theology (not just historical theology). Emergent theology takes place in the context of emerging churches.

Does Jesus think about things today? I think so! But Jesus thinks theologically, not merely pragmatically. Jesus speaks the truth in love (Ephesians 4:15). Our neighbors can show us how to do this.

7   IT'S ABOUT THE LAW OF LOVE, NOT THE LETTER OF THE LAW

The emerging church at Antioch under Paul's leadership came to birth in a pluralistic and relativistic culture, not unlike what in our day is called postmodernity. There were at least three predominant language/cultures, Jewish (Hebrew), Greek and Roman (Latin), all found within the church at Antioch. Cultural, ethnic, social and religious pluralism constitute the world in which the emerging church exists. Paul dealt with philosophers at Athens, dockworkers at Corinth, business women in Macedonia, Roman government officials at Cypress, spiritual counterfeits at Philippi, demonic spirits at Ephesus and Jewish zealots who sought to murder him at Jerusalem. With the absolute principles established by the law of Moses no longer binding, as Paul taught, the church swam in the unfamiliar currents of a postlaw environment that some exploited as virtual antinomianism (no law) or autonomy (self law). "All things are lawful for me" and "food is meant for the stomach and the stomach for food" were some of the self-indulgent slogans of the Corinthians that Paul repeated in order to dismiss them as senseless (1 Corinthians 6:12-13).

What all of these facets of human society have in common is some form of religion. Most forms of religion have to do with fear and anxiety over judgment, death and sin, along with rituals to overcome negative visions and versions of life, and to affirm and achieve the positive. While the concept of sin has many variations in each culture, death is an unavoidable reality. All humans in every culture face the inevitability and reality of death. Sin is a theological concept; death is an empirical fact.

In this culture of pluralism, diversity is as much the problem as the solution. In an attempt to be inclusive by affirming everyone, no one is happy. Rather than unity through diversity, mutual suspicion, charges of unfairness and conflict result. Syncretism (a little of each) is as dangerous as is absolutism (my way or the highway). In an attempt to find a common denominator in every religion and culture, a new religion and a new culture emerges, often more intolerant and demanding. Political correctness becomes the mantra of oppression in the name of liberation. Even a secular culture has its own theologians!

In such a context Jesus chose Saul of Tarsus to become the lead theologian of the emerging church, expanding the kingdom of God beyond the boundaries of insular Judaism. The dispersion of the Jews only resulted in scattered cells, not an emerging church. It was a stunning and at the same time strategic choice. For deep in his soul Saul, a cosmopolitan world citizen, was "a Hebrew born of Hebrews" and "a Pharisee, a son of Pharisees" (Philippians 3:5; Acts 23:6). So zealous was he in his persecution of the early believers that he hunted them down like wild animals to be delivered to prison, and in some cases to death. That this man, so filled with hostility and arrogance, should become the apostle of love (before John ever wrote of love!) and a humble bond slave of the very Jesus that he hated, is more than stunning. It is so extraordinary that it appears to be madness, as Festus, the governor exclaimed, "You are out of your mind, Paul! Too much learning is driving you insane" (Acts 26:24).

Jesus' choice of Saul was also a strategic choice, however. Saul, despite his deep immersion in Judaism, was really an outsider to the Jerusalem community. Even after his conversion he was viewed with suspicion by the apostles, and it took the intervention of Barnabas for him to gain access to the inner circle (Acts 9:26-27). It was Saul (Paul) who drew a line in the sand when the Jerusalem community almost succeeded in extending its tentacles as far as Antioch to draw the church back under its authority. As Paul reports the incident when Peter—and even Barnabas—were caught like insects in the web of legalism, leaving Paul alone to cut the church free for the sake of the gospel (Galatians 2:11-14). Except for Paul, who severed the ties that bound the emerging church at Antioch to the temple-centered and Moses-driven Jewish messianic community at Jerusalem, there may well have been no Christian church such as we know it today. The law-centered religion of Jerusalem sought to contain the new messianic communities of believers within the traditions of Moses. As with all other cultures in the first century, the Jews defined their identity in world culture by virtue of their religious heritage and practice. How is it possible for Paul, who had lived by the letter of the religious law, to become an ambassador for a God of love without promoting a new religion? The emerging church at Antioch, under Paul's leadership, had to find a way to advance the kingdom of God in what might be called a nonreligious way.

In his day, where religion had become irrelevant, Dietrich Bonhoeffer asked the question "How can we speak of God without religion in a world come of age?"[1] Bonhoeffer's solution was to speak of Christ as the very incarnation of God without using religious language and without presenting Christ to the world as a religious person. The key to his approach was that Christ, as the very presence and reality of God, could be proclaimed in a gospel of salvation, reconciliation and hope as a theological theme and practice even if religion no longer was viewed by the world as either true or relevant. His view that the world was rapidly moving toward a time when religion would no longer concern humans was premature and, as it turned out, mistaken. The contemporary

---

[1]"What do a church, a community, a sermon, a liturgy, a Christian life mean in a religionless world? How do we speak . . . in a secular way about God?" (Dietrich Bonhoeffer, *Letters and Papers from Prison,* enlarged ed. [New York: Macmillan, 1971], p. 280).

world, like the city of Athens in Paul's time, is "extremely religious . . .
in every way" (Acts 17:22). Emerging churches today, like the emerging
church at Antioch in the first century, encounter religious pluralism at
every turn, not the absence of religion. However, Bonhoeffer's concept
still holds good—Christ represents not only the "fullness of God" but
also the core of humanity. In the midst of cultural, ethnic and religious
pluralism, the human side of God in Christ speaks to that which is human in every society.

The emergent theology of Paul was not based on a new religion but
new life through resurrection. To the philosophers at Athens he did not
proclaim religion but resurrection (Acts 17:31-32). To the Corinthians
he preached Christ crucified and risen from the dead. In fact, he asserted
that even death on the cross did not achieve forgiveness of sin apart from
resurrection. "If Christ has not been raised, your faith is futile and you
are still in your sins" (1 Corinthians 15:17). Religion binds humans to
the letter of the law. Resurrection is liberation from religion that enslaves.
The resurrection of Christ produced an outpouring of the love of God
through the Spirit of Christ. If the gospel of Christ is to advance the kingdom of God in the face of world religions, it cannot succeed by competing on the basis of offering a better religion but rather a new way of living—by the law of love.

THE HUMANITY OF LOVE

There is no love where law is the rule of conscience and the custodian of
the Spirit. "For the letter kills, but the Spirit gives life" (2 Corinthians
3:6). Finding his own spirit crushed by the law but healed and empowered by the Spirit of Christ, Paul turned to the law of love and the law of
the Spirit as the polity and practice of the emerging church. Paul had experienced the love of Christ even in the very act of persecuting him and
knew, therefore, that the message of God could be communicated in the
language of love. The very commandments of God were now to be interpreted by the presence and ministry of the resurrected Christ. It is not

human love by itself but God's love that empowers human love to fulfill the law of God. "God's love has been poured into our hearts through the Holy Spirit that has been given to us" (Romans 5:5). "Through love become slaves to one another," wrote Paul (Galatians 5:13). Thus one who fulfills God's law of love through love of the neighbor has fulfilled the commandments.

Love is the single criterion for that which upholds the dignity, integrity and essential value of the other person in the concreteness of every social relation and every culture. The commandments of God as well as the ethical principles that bind humans one to another are contained in the command of love: "Owe no one anything, except to love one another; for he who loves his neighbor has fulfilled the law. . . . Love does no wrong to a neighbor; therefore love is the fulfilling of the law" (Romans 13:8, 10). Love seeks the empowerment of others as a positive effect, not power over them. As the Christian ethicist Stanley Hauerwas once said, "No one rules more tyrannously than those who claim not to rule at all because they only want to love us."[2]

When we take on someone as a project in order that we become their savior, we contribute to their weakness as a way of gaining power. In Arthur Miller's play *After the Fall* the lead character, Quentin, struggles to understand why his love could not save his wife from her own willful self-destruction. In the end, he realizes that his love was really an attempt to exercise power, to be the savior of others. "God's power is love without limit. But when a man dares reach for that, . . . he is only reaching for the power. Whoever goes to save another person with the lie of limitless love throws a shadow on the face of God."[3] *Mere human love does not fulfill God's commandments, but God's love through Jesus Christ. God's love became human through the incarnation of Jesus Christ, and the Spirit of Christ within us that empowers our love for others.*

---

[2]Stanley Hauerwas, *A Community of Character* (Notre Dame, Ind.: University of Notre Dame Press, 1981), p. 172.
[3]Arthur Miller, *After the Fall* (New York: Viking Press, 1972), pp. 106-7.

A social bond lies within every form of humanity. It follows then that the social structure of humanity contains elements of a common denominator or essential core that is recognizable to some extent in every culture, race and ethnic community. Concepts of human rights, justice and concern for the unborn and the aged are not ethical self-perceptions subject to cultural modification but demands on individual and collective actions that seek to uphold the very structure of humanity itself. When Jesus healed on the sabbath, ate with publicans and sinners, and asked a Samaritan women to minister to his thirst, he penetrated through all racial, sexual, social, and cultural barriers to restore true humanity to others. Indeed, his own humanity could hardly have been the true humanity that it was if he had drawn back from the real humanity of others.

The particular, concrete humanity of Jesus of Nazareth is real humanity. The humanity of this man, this circumcised Jew, this member of a particular family and particular culture exists as the real form of humanity. Yet it was also this man who recognized and affirmed the humanity of the non-Jew, the uncircumcised, the despised Samaritan, the lowly slave, the "invisible" women and the Greek with the foreign language and culture, and even the hated Roman soldier, who represented the oppressive power of the quasi-divine claim of Caesar. Jesus penetrated through these social and cultural forms of humanity and addressed the true humanity of each person, and so revealed his own humanity as the touchstone of divine grace. In the real humanity of Jesus we see the humanization as well as the socialization of humanity.

In his person and in his actions Jesus embodied both grace and truth (John 1:17). His moral presence was both convicting and empowering. He drew to his side the fugitive from the law as well as the furtive Pharisee, without shaming either. He ignored the categories established within his own society. For him the despised Samaritan was a woman who could give him a drink; the self-righteous Pharisee was a man who wanted to talk; the leper was a person who needed to be touched. While people came to him in droves, needs came with a human face. A gathering was not a mob to be sent home to eat but individuals to be fed with bread broken with his own hands. In a crowd he was never simply pushed by people, but touched by someone who hurt. Within the shouting sounds of a multitude he heard the cry of the blind man, the sigh of a sinner, the murmur of a skeptic. He permitted people to be who they were and offered to help them become who they could be. He had no uniforms for his disciples and no masks for his friends. He did not ask for conformity but for commitment. In the person of Jesus there was a spiritual integrity that revitalized the spirit of the human person amid the dead weight of tradition and legalism—where Jesus was there was life. In the life of Jesus was a moral integrity that brought an absolute sense of right to specific human situations. In the truth of Jesus there was a personal integrity that spoke with authority against the enslaving influences of religious formalism and demonic delusion.

Nor did Jesus institute some new ethical concept of what is good as a kind of Christian ethic. He merely reinstated the criterion of goodness that belongs to true humanity as the ethical foundation for all of the laws and commandments. This same criterion was quite clear to the prophet Micah:

> He has told you, O mortal, what is good;
>> and what does the LORD require of you
> but to do justice, and to love kindness,
>> and to walk humbly with your God. (Micah 6:8)

Confronted with the breakdown of traditional orders, and with the secularizing of sacred myths and concepts that were used to provide stability for the Gentile world, Paul provided a criterion of Christian community that is grounded in the identification of Christ himself with those in whom his Holy Spirit dwells. Here too both Jew and Gentile must learn to shift their obedience and loyalty from traditional concepts of authority, by which they sought stability and order, to the structure of social life regulated by the community as the body of Christ (Ephesians

2:11-22). The foundational social structures of family, marriage, parents and children, and the existing political and economic structures, are basically affirmed as good and necessary. Yet all of these structures are radically qualified by the humanization of humanity that occurred through Jesus Christ.

The core identity of true humanity is thus bound up with this shifting of the criterion from seeking our own good to that of the other person. This shows that the single commandment of love—to love God and to love the neighbor as yourself—is grounded in social humanity, not merely in individual humanity. But we cannot know this love fully apart from the gracious love of God addressed to us in Jesus Christ. Thus when we encounter the true humanity of Jesus Christ, a revelation of that humanity is also communicated through the gospel of Christ. For any attempt to define humanity on our own terms incorporates the fallacy of self-preservation into our social and ethical structures. As a result, change produced by social revolution alone cannot lead to the discovery and form of authentic human existence. The constant factor through social and cultural changes in human self-perception is the structure of humanity as a social reality of love. This love is experienced as a reciprocity of relations in which Jesus Christ is present as the objective reality of grace, freedom and responsibility. The law of God in Jesus Christ, while liberating us from the letter of the moral law, binds us to the moral responsibility of living by the law of love.

THE MORAL LAW OF LOVE

In his letter to the Ephesians Paul addressed the question of human moral life. In the face of the abolishing of the law of commandments and ordinances as well as the tearing down of the racial, social, and cultural boundaries between Jew and Gentile (Ephesians 2:14-15), the norm for determining what is the good is consistent with the humanization of humanity through Christ. No longer are human beings under the power and spell of their natural passions and natural religion. No longer are they "strangers and foreigners" one to another. No longer are they "tossed to and fro and blown about by every wind of doctrine" (Ephesians 4:14). No longer are they subjected to the inhumanity of personal egos bent on destructive and malicious behavior; no longer are they caught in the humiliating and demeaning roles that are defined by economic, sexual or political status.

Paul does not ground his appeal to moral life on the basis of the Jewish laws and ordinances; neither does he attempt to find some cultural principle in his own society as a dynamic equivalent to the law of God. Rather, he reminds Christians that having "learned Christ" (Ephesians 4:20) they are to "speak the truth to [their] neighbors," not let anger carry over into grudges and grievances against the other, and not to steal from one another, but rather do "work honestly with their own hands" so that they may be able to give to those in need (Ephesians 4:25-28). Paul drew out the implications of the gospel of Christ in such a way that the basic structures of that society were to be humanized through the activation of the Spirit and law of Christ. Paul did not seek to replace their culture with a concept of Christian culture. Rather, he called for the liberation of authentic human life within the culture as a freedom from the magical as well as from the mythical.

In Ephesus Paul created something of an uproar when it was discovered that the profitable business of those who practiced the magical arts was threatened by the Ephesians' conversion to Christ (Acts 19:23-41). The power struggle is not between the gospel and culture but between the gospel and the powers within any culture that dehumanizes and enslaves persons. Paul views the human mind and the human spirit to be enslaved and in need of conversion. The criterion for moral action cannot be the conscience alone, as Paul clearly saw. The conscience is the center of moral ambivalence, not moral authority. True, the conscience "bears witness," as Paul wrote, but it also is the center of "conflicting thoughts" that both "accuse or perhaps excuse them" (Romans 2:15). What conscience points to are the criteria for moral responsibility sunk deep into the structures of created human goodness experienced as fellow-humanity.

Therefore he appeals to the Christians in Ephesus to abandon the "futility of their minds," which are darkened, and to be "renewed in the spirit of your minds" as well as in their emotions and passions (Ephesians 4:17-24). Paul sought the renewal of the social structures and the humanization of culture, not the replacing of these structures and culture with the illusion of freedom that dissolves into moral anarchy and social chaos. The continuity of order and stability through social change and cultural pluralism is thus grounded in human nature as that which produces and lives by culture. In this respect, only when culture is open to change is it able to remain in continuity with the development of true humanity and those social structures that uphold humanity.[4] *When a culture becomes rigid, it usually also dehumanizes its adherents. Humans are more than cultural artifacts, though all humans express their humanity through culture. Freedom and dignity are human virtues, not only cultural values.*

Ethical norms remain constant when grounded in the true humanity of the other person rather than in culturally conditioned self-perceptions of individuals or the collective cultural mass. The moral good of the other person constitutes an ethical criterion from which no one is exempt by virtue of doctrinal, ideological, ecclesiological or political commitments. When understood in this way, the meaning of that which is good is not first of all an abstract principle mediated through one's own perception of the good, but it is first of all a moral event that takes place

---

[4]Jürgen Moltmann makes this point very well when he writes: " 'Every culture is a way of the soul to itself' (Georg Simmel), and all cultures can be understood as fragments of and routes to that human humanity which still lies hidden in the bosom of the future. In every culture man makes a form for himself and acquires an image of himself. But all historical forms and images which he has given or now gives himself, are transitory and open to change. This permits the conclusion that it is only the bare fact that from out of his inner amorphousness man always expresses himself in cultural forms that are lastingly and everywhere basically human" (*Man: Christian Anthropology in the Conflicts of the Present,* trans. John Sturdy [Philadelphia: Fortress, 1974], p. 11).

between persons created in the image of God.

Here we see how emerging churches do not fall away from the absolute moral principles of modernity into the relativism of postmodernity. Rather, the foundation for human morality is grounded in the social being of humanity as God intended it. Immoral acts are not primarily violations of an abstract moral law but are violations of the moral structure of human life itself. In his emergent theology, Paul has laid the groundwork for contemporary emerging churches to live in a postmodern world without succumbing to postmodernist relativism.

The poor, the hungry, the dispossessed, the oppressed as well as the oppressor constitute the criteria for responsible moral action. Poverty is not itself the criterion, nor is oppression, for this would leave the rich and the oppressor without a criterion for moral self-reflection and repentance. The criteria are lodged within the relation of the one to the other.

As a result, the impoverishment of one is immediately a matter of moral concern to the other. In the same way, the act of oppression is of moral concern to the oppressed ones. It is not enough to be liberated from the oppressor. The oppressed must also seek reconciliation with the oppressor for the sake of the humanity of the oppressor. Being oppressed does not free anyone from the moral demand of fellow humanity. Nor does being hungry free someone from the moral responsibility to seek the good of those who have plenty. I might only suggest here in passing that a theology of liberation cuts both ways. The theological basis for liberation is a theology of reconciliation. To harm the oppressor, to diminish or no longer to uphold his or her humanity, is also to destroy the basis for reconciliation. The law of love is never an abstract principle, but always acting in a concrete situation where one becomes the neighbor of the other.

IT'S ABOUT LOVING YOUR NEIGHBOR

No doubt Paul first heard the parable of the good Samaritan as reported to him orally before the Gospels were written. The parable was too good a story not to have been told a hundred times. He would have recognized immediately the scriptural basis for the commandment to love your neighbor as yourself (Leviticus 19:18). In this parable Jesus made the point that it was the Samaritan, not the man injured by the side of the road, who was the neighbor. "Which of these three, do you think, was a neighbor to the man who fell into the hands of robbers?" The man who was first asked the question replied, "The one who showed him mercy." Jesus replied, "Go and do likewise" (Luke 10:36-37). Jesus had already restated the first two great commandments as: " 'You shall love the Lord your God with all your heart, and with all your soul, and with all your mind.' This is the greatest and first commandment. And a second is like it: 'You shall love your neighbor as yourself' " (Matthew 22:37-39).

This Scripture command, reiterated and applied by Jesus, became the basis for Paul's own summary of what the law requires: "Owe no one anything, except to love one another; for he who loves his neighbor has fulfilled the law. . . . Love does no wrong to a neighbor; therefore, love is the fulfilling of the law" (Romans 13:8, 10). To make sure that his readers understood the sweeping nature of this law of love, Paul added, "The commandments, 'You shall not commit adultery; You shall not murder; You shall not steal; You shall not covet'; and any other commandment, are summed up in this word, 'Love your neighbor as yourself' " (Romans 13:9).

The implications of this are staggering! Not only does this go beyond the law of Moses as enshrined in the tablets of the law, it is the ultimate nonreligious expression of the command of God. Love is neither a religious demand nor a religious act. For Paul, the command to love your neighbor was extracted by Jesus from the law of Moses to become the law of love around which the emerging church formed its own inner life as well as the way that the ethical content of the gospel of Christ could be shared with people in every culture without imposing some religious demand on them. It also provided a way that Paul could expose the need of humanity for the saving grace of Christ without using a religious concept of sin in order to create a sense of guilt. For Paul, grace, not guilt, motivates us to live by the law of love. That which is contrary to the kingdom of God is not the wrong practice of religion but the inhumanity of core social relations found in every culture where love is not practiced. "The whole law is summed up in a single commandment," says Paul, "You shall love your neighbor as yourself." Then he adds, "If, however, you bite and devour one another, take care that you are not consumed by one another" (Galatians 5:14-15). Sin is living inhumanly, not just ungodly. Paul does not begin by making people feel like sinners according to God's law, but turns the microscope of love directly on what humans become when failing to live by the law of love.

In his vivid contemporary paraphrase of Paul's litany of human self-destructive behavior, Eugene Peterson puts it this way:

> It is obvious what kind of life develops out of trying to get your own way all the time: repetitive, loveless, cheap sex; a stinking accumulation of mental and emotional garbage; frenzied and joyless grabs for happiness; trinket gods; magic-show religion; paranoid loneliness; cutthroat competition; all-consuming-yet-never-satisfied wants; a brutal temper; an impotence to love or be loved; divided homes and divided lives; small-minded and lopsided pursuits; the vicious habits of depersonalizing everyone into a rival; uncontrolled and uncontrollable addictions; ugly parodies of community, I could go on. (Galatians 5:19-21 *The Message*)

In light of the disastrous consequences of living out self-interest rather than having regard for the other as neighbor, it is somewhat surprising that the command is to love the neighbor "as yourself." There is a negative aspect of self-love, to be sure. Paul warns Timothy that in the last days there will be times when love for the neighbor breaks down and love of self turns inward and becomes destructive. "For people will be lovers of themselves, lovers of money, boasters, arrogant, abusive, disobedient to their parents, ungrateful, unholy, inhuman, implacable, slanders, profligates, brutes, haters of good, treacherous, reckless, swollen with conceit, lovers of pleasure rather than lovers of God, holding the outward form of religion but denying its power" (2 Timothy 3:2-5).

While there is no explicit command that we should love ourselves, the motive power to love God and others includes regard for ourselves. God, the neighbor and ourselves are bound together in the one command of love. We cannot love God without also loving our neighbor, and we cannot love our neighbor without also loving ourselves. From this we could say: affirming the worth of our neighbor is simultaneously affirming the value of ourselves. We cannot esteem ourselves without also esteeming God and our neighbor as of ultimate and essential value to the self. This seems to lie behind Paul's admonition "In the same way, husbands should love their wives as they do their own bodies. He who loves his wife loves himself. For no one ever hates his own body, but he nourishes and tenderly cares for it, just as Christ does for the church, because we are members of his body" (Ephesians 5:28-30).

In this basic form of humanity as social being grounded in love, our neighbor emerges in our line of vision. The neighbor has become real humanity through the incarnation. No new ethical criterion has been introduced through the humanity of Jesus. The original and basic form of humanity as fellow humanity has been renewed and brought under the saving determination of God. The neighbor is not first of all an ethical construct based on some general ethical or legal principle of duty. The neighbor is both Christ and the other. To deny the other as neighbor is to deny Christ. To recognize the other as neighbor is to recognize the good and the right as what the law of love requires.

The use of the word *neighbor* in Scripture obviously refers to persons who are living in some form of civil and social community rather than to individuals who are engaged in unlawful or criminal activities destructive to the community. For example, in our own society, we consider neighbors as those who uphold the life of persons in community rather than seek to abuse or destroy life. In the case of child abuse, the child is the neighbor and the abuser is to be restrained or incarcerated to prevent further harm. A rapist or murderer should be apprehended, convicted and punished (humanely); it is the victim who is the neighbor. Therefore, love of the neighbor does not mean excusing or ignoring wrong done to a neighbor. Rather, love requires that an offender is held responsible for violence, abuse or exploitation of a neighbor. Love also expects that the one who is a witness to harm done to another is responsible for reporting that and securing help. It is in this sense that the church includes the neighbor while at the same time requiring that the neighbor respect and contribute to the welfare and good of the community.

Christ exists for me as the neighbor, said Dietrich Bonhoeffer. The reality of God in Christ is not an abstract concept but the concrete reality of the other person, whether Christian or not, who makes the same demand on me as does Christ to be the neighbor.[5] The neighbor is not a form of humanity accessible only to the private sphere of Christian ethics but is the person available to me, making an absolute claim on me through the concreteness and factuality of fellow humanity. "Christ, reality and the good," said Bonhoeffer, comprise a single sphere of moral and spiritual unity.[6] This is also a point made by Karl Barth. The neighbor is a criterion of Christ for me.

He who was God's eternal Word, but was a fellowman and not an angel or a star, having assumed our humanity, our human nature, fundamentally reveals—whether we see and hear it or not is another question—each of our fellows to be a question, a promise, a

---

[5]"The You of the other person is the divine You. Thus the way to the other person's You is the same as the way to the divine You, either through acknowledgment or rejection. The individual becomes a person ever and again through the other, in the 'moment.' The other person presents us with the same challenge to our knowing as does God" (Dietrich Bonhoeffer, *Sanctorum Communio* [Minneapolis: Fortress, 1998], pp. 55-56).

[6]Dietrich Bonhoeffer, *Ethics* (New York: Macmillan. 1955), p. 188.

supremely living reminder of his humanity . . . as they confront me, so also the man Jesus confronts me.[7]

The neighbor as criterion of Christ for me cannot be identified only as a fellow member of the church. It may be that the one who stands outside of the church is precisely the neighbor of the church and therefore the criterion of Christ for the church as well. If I refuse to meet this neighbor, even though he or she may appear to be ungodly to me, says Barth, I may deny the Christ living in me.

Emerging churches find their true humanity in the relation between Jesus Christ and all humanity. The church finds its true ministry in the upholding, healing and transformation of the humanity of others as already grasped and reconciled to God through the incarnation and atoning life, death, and resurrection of Jesus Christ. The church cannot be truly human when it denies and dehumanizes the humanity of others. Nor is the command to love our neighbor invalid because of the failure of our neighbor to love in return. We are to view others created in the image of God, and one sign of the image of God in us is to love God's image in our neighbor. No human relation can be exempt from the form of the command of God that comes in the form of the neighbor. The neighbor presents us with the only absolute ethical demand, other than God himself. God and neighbor constitute the concrete situation in which the law of love occurs as an ethical event. The law of love cuts across but does not obliterate the responsibilities that we have to others in terms of sexuality and kinship. It is my neighbor who breaks through the egocentricity of my self by his or her own concrete existence in fellow humanity that demands my conduct be such that the command to love is heard and obeyed.

If there are irreversible forms of human relations (sexual or parent-child relations) as well as differentiations of a more subtle character

---

[7]Karl Barth, *Ethics,* ed. Dietrich Braun, trans. Geoffrey W. Bromiley (New York: Seabury Press, 1981), p. 335; cf. also pp. 432-34.

(color of skin and national origin), these all must be brought under the demand the neighbor places on us through the law of love. In other words, the law of love takes priority over specific doctrinal, ideological, ecclesiological and political commitments.

Our "near neighbors" are defined in terms of those who stand close to us through bonds of kinship, marriage and family as well as those who comprise the immediate social community of our historical existence. But beyond this circle of nearness, there is a larger circle of the "distant neighbors" that includes those who may live in proximity to us but who do not share with us cultural, ethnic or even religious patterns and styles of life. We have no choice but to live out the law of love with both those who are near as well as the distant neighbors we share our human existence with. I cannot evade the demand of love that comes to me through the neighbor who shares my space and whose life I am bound up in common personal and social identity. The law of love accepts diversity but does not make diversity a moral virtue. Rather, all that divides and differentiates us finds its unity and wholeness in our common humanity. It is this form of humanity that has been assumed by God in Christ and, for Paul, became the human form of emerging churches.

Emerging churches are a community of love offering healing, hope and salvation to humans. The life of community in Jesus Christ must be shaped by the structure of a social community that enhances the participation and belonging of each person. A theology of emerging churches must be developed that embodies an authentic human culture in terms of the existing culture and social structures. The church must develop strategies that uphold the dignity and value of persons as members of the body of Christ rather than practices that exploit the weaknesses and insecurities of individuals. The church can often be guilty of drawing persons into the work of the church who are emotionally insecure or without adequate time and resources to care for their lives. It is not enough to seek volunteers to maintain the church programs without also sensing the effect this has on those who respond. The unity of the church will be found in the diversity of the gifts of the Spirit that seek to uphold the unity of the Spirit and uplifts the humanity of the church as the body of Christ in each particular culture.

If there is a culture that belongs to the kingdom of God and transcends all other cultures, it is a culture of true humanity as the gracious power and presence of Christ in a structure of human social and personal relations. This culture of the kingdom of God has no other language and no other custom other than that of the particular people and society who become its manifestation. Yet these existing social and cultural forms are relativized to the real humanity of Jesus Christ as expressed through the embodiment of the gospel in the lives of those in whom Christ dwells. Emerging churches do not export their own culture in their mission outreach but seek to expand God's kingdom so that every culture can bear in its own social structures the reality of the kingdom of God and make manifest the humanity of the kingdom through its own forms.

CONCLUDING NONTHEOLOGICAL POSTSCRIPT

I must confess that I find it hard to retain the spirit of love toward those who proclaim, often with a posture of moral smugness (and usually on television!), "I love the sinner but hate the sin." I wonder if people who say that have any idea how destructive and downright ungracious that concept is! Whatever my sins and failures may be, that is who I am! You cannot love me without accepting the whole of me, painful and threatening as that may be. And when you say that you hate my sin, I find it difficult to believe that you really love me! I suspect that those who utter such platitudes mean well. They apparently want to claim the virtue of love in order to make them immune from the criticism of being judgmental, but at the same time they need to be viewed as against sin. What makes me wince in hearing such pronouncements is that it does not pass the smell test—it has the odor of arrogance. We can hardly claim love as a moral virtue while holding the object of love at a distance. We know that Jesus did not seem to find this possible.

For example, some label homosexuality sinful and a perversion, but at the same time they claim the higher moral ground of love for the sinner. The distinction between moral and immoral behavior does not lead to arrogance; we expect such moral discernment of all persons who possess moral character. The self-certainty of being right without being loving causes us to see only the sin and not the sinner at all. Jesus' harshest words were directed toward the sin of arrogance clothed in self-righteousness. For those caught in moral contradictions and spiritual contrariness, he expressed compassion and provided access to divine love and empowering grace as a means of healing, hope, and repentance. The spiritual responsibility of repentance is also a work of grace rather than of mere guilt. And if grace is to be the mark of emerging churches, it must be an amazing grace, grace that embraces moral and spiritual ambiguity for the sake of bringing persons to a greater dimension of human wholeness. This will not be easy. The boundary of emerging churches will of necessity need to be porous and somewhat ambiguous even as the center is clear and truthful. Jesus had a high degree of tolerance for those who pressed in close to him. At the same time, he held them to a high standard of love and truth in becoming his followers.

A lack of a sense of the tragic in dealing with moral complexity as a human condition can lead to moral smugness. To be prolife in principle and hold that the death of a fetus at any stage of development is a tragic loss is based on the principle that human life at every level is of value. We can hold this as a moral principle without moral smugness as long as it does not become a claim to moral virtue by labeling all who disagree as "baby-killers." The moral context of life is often layered and complex, with "bad" competing with "worse," not simply "good" versus "evil." This is the essence of the tragic moral choice. Failure to recognize this can lead to the arrogant assertion of my own good as a moral right even if it means violence against the rights if not the persons of others.

We could wish that good and evil could always be separated with surgical precision, and that moral virtue could be achieved by making absolute moral judgments. But in many cases it is not so. We who make moral judgments suffer from moral ambiguity if not also moral fault. In an effort to earn the right to wear the label "evangelical," I fear that many seek issues on which to make absolute moral pronouncements. Responsible moral discernment and action bears a sense of the tragic. Where good and evil are inextricably bound up in the fabric of our own existence, responsibility to act on behalf of the victim of injustice, oppression and abuse is a moral responsibility. But in such actions we may not be able to claim moral innocence as measured by abstract moral principles. Jesus himself entered into the realm of moral ambiguity and finally bore the legal penalty of moral guilt in order to redeem those without moral standing. If this is what we mean by evangelical witness to the truth, it is less likely to leave behind the odor of arrogance or reek of moral smugness.

Paul's prayer for the emerging church was that "he may grant that you may be strengthened in your inner being with power through his Spirit, and that Christ may dwell in your hearts through faith, as you are being rooted and grounded in love" (Ephesians 3:16-17). We cannot be a community of love without being a community filled with the Spirit. Emerging churches are to be known by the "fragrance that comes from knowing him. For we are the aroma of Christ; . . . a fragrance from life to life" (2 Corinthians 2:15-16). If the church cannot pass this smell test, it needs to pray "Come Holy Spirit!"

8 IT'S ABOUT THE COMMUNITY OF THE SPIRIT, NOT JUST THE GIFTS OF THE SPIRIT

I have fantasized about what it would have been like to be a member of the early Christian community following Pentecost. I linger over Luke's description of their sense of joy and mutual sharing in communal living while experiencing the miracles of healing and praising the Lord in the power of the Spirit. I am not sure that it lasted very long, however. The incident with Ananias and his wife, Sapphira, must have sent shock waves through the community (Acts 5:1-11). And before long they experienced serious division over the issue of leadership (Acts 6:1-6). While Paul's view of the community was no doubt skewed by the attacks on him and the churches he planted by representatives of the Jerusalem community, it is clear that he had no sympathy for their legalistic concerns for the continued observance of many of the laws of Moses (including circumcision). While Paul must have appreciated their generous response to his appeal for acceptance of the Gentile churches as a result of the Acts 15 conference, the relation was steadily eroded, it seems, by their continual sniping at his authority.

The emerging church at Antioch no doubt had their own problems, but when we look for a profile of a community led and empowered by the Spirit, we turn to Antioch, not Jerusalem. Luke tells us that it was while worshiping the Lord that "the Holy Spirit said, 'Set apart for me

Barnabas and Saul for the work to which I have called them.' . . . So being sent out by the Holy Spirit, they went" on their way (Acts 13:2, 4). There must be something special about this community of faith—the Holy Spirit speaks to them! Consequently, for this chapter, we will look to Antioch and Paul's emergent theology of the Spirit for our guidance. There was something in the air up there!

"The Spirit becomes for the believing community more the environment in which it lives than an object of its consciousness."[1] I wish that every emerging church would post this as the first PowerPoint slide for every service! I could not live without the oxygen in the air that surrounds me, but I don't think much about it—I just breathe, and usually I am not even aware of that! The health of emerging churches is in the air that they breathe, not in the activities that consume their energy. The word used for "spirit" in both Hebrew (*ruach*) and Greek (*pneuma*) is also used for "air," "breath" and "wind" The Holy Spirit is not merely an "air freshener" but the oxygen in the air that the emerging church breathes—air without oxygen is not good for one's health!

There are churches whose environment is stale and sterile, with hardly a breath of the Spirit's presence. In such churches one is reminded of a wax museum, where the living and the dead mingle cautiously and circumspectly, so as not to disturb each other. When the church appears to lack spiritual vigor and vitality, a new infusion of the Spirit may be necessary—someone who knows how to do spiritual CPR! In CPR one person actually breathes air into the lungs of another, which restores the function of the body. Spiritual renewal is more than a stirring up of en-

---

[1]The full context of this quote is "The dynamic force within this eschatological community is the Spirit, which creates that community and sustains it and at the same time gives to each person within the community his [or her] own individual personhood. . . . Thus the Spirit becomes for the believing community more the environment in which it lives than an object of its consciousness. In particular, the importance of the Spirit as an eschatological phenomenon reminds us that its relation is both to the risen Christ and to the community which is oriented towards God" (Wesley Carr, "Towards a Contemporary Theology of the Holy Spirit," *Scottish Journal of Theology*, 28, no. 7 [1975]: 506, 507-8).

thusiasm but actually receiving the Holy Spirit on the part of the members. What Paul found when first arriving in Ephesus may be true for many churches today. "Did you receive the Holy Spirit when you became believers," he asked? "No," they replied, "we have not even heard that there is a Holy Spirit." "When Paul had laid his hands on them, the Holy Spirit came upon them, and they spoke in tongues and prophesied" (Acts 19:2, 6). It was not just the gift of speaking in tongues that they lacked, but the gift of the Holy Spirit.

Churches can be so preoccupied with the Spirit's activity that environmental chaos and confusion reigns, with members competing with one another for spiritual space in which to exercise their own gifts. We are reminded of the chaos and competition at Christmas when several youngsters open their presents and play with their toys at the same time! Gifts of the Spirit are not for the purpose of making the Spirit visible but to make the body healthy and fully functioning.

Spiritual health is not evidenced by possessing spiritual gifts but rather being possessed by the Spirit in such a way that each member is a gift to the health of the body. One of the marks of spiritual maturity is that we find our spiritual identity in what we contribute to the life of the body even when it means sacrificing our own needs and pleasure. Body life, in this sense, is not what follows a gift but what precedes the gift. When the free gift (charism) of the Spirit of Jesus Christ experienced by the church as a community of persons, the church then functions as the body of Christ.

In the Corinthian church, where gifts of the Spirit were sought and exercised for their own sake, Paul encouraged the members to synchronize their gifts in order that they could function more effectively and freely. Using the metaphor of the human body, Paul wrote, "But God has so arranged the body, giving the greater honor to the inferior member, that there may be no dissension within the body, but the members may have the same care for one another. If one member suffers, all suffer together with it; if one member is honored, all rejoice together with it"

(1 Corinthians 12:24-26). Paul's magnificent chapter on love follows immediately, demonstrating what this mutual life in the Spirit means. Without love, the gifts themselves are noisy, empty and futile. When he was a child, Paul concludes, he acted in immature and childish ways. In growing up in Christ, he no longer practices such self-indulgence (1 Corinthians 13:11).

Paul liked to use analogies, let me try one of my own. In order to demonstrate how spiritual gifts relate to the overall function of the church, consider an automobile and its optional accessories. The gifts are like the accessories while the Spirit is like the power source, the engine, including its electrical system. The air conditioner has a different function than the heater, though both draw on the same power source. A car can even have a computerized location system that connects to a satellite that plots its exact position and gives audible directions.[2]

Each accessory has its own specific function, but should not become so obvious as to be annoying. "Turn that radio down so we can hear ourselves think!" Or "Turn off the air conditioner, we're freezing back here!" Have you ever wanted to say something like that in a church where someone's spiritual gift was more of a distraction than a blessing? We must be careful, for each accessory draws on the same power supply. Some have discovered that when they start their vehicle, the accessories have drained the battery and there is not enough power to start the engine! Some churches are loaded with accessories—but never get out of the parking lot. Gifts and ministries are multiplied, facilities expanded, energy consumed and power dissipated, but the kingdom remains stalled.

I think that I have driven that analogy into the ground!

The empowerment of the Spirit began at Pentecost, where the 120 in the upper room were "filled with the Holy Spirit" (Acts 2:4). Subse-

---

[2]I could get carried away here and suggest that the apostle Paul seemed to have this very accessory when he heard the voice of an angel giving him directions (Acts 27:23-24)!

quently, other people were said to be "filled with the Holy Spirit" (Peter [Acts 4:8], the believers [Acts 4:31], Stephen [Acts 7:55], Saul of Tarsus [Acts 9:17; 13:9], the disciples [Acts 13:52]). While these are quite specific instances of being filled with the Spirit, they are relatively few considering the importance Luke gives to the Holy Spirit in the book of Acts.

Jesus promised that the Spirit would come as a comforter (*paraclete*). Luke stresses the fact that the Holy Spirit is to bring power, not merely fullness of the Spirit. "But you will receive power when the Holy Spirit has come upon you; and you will be my witnesses in Jerusalem, in all Judea and Samaria, and to the ends of the earth" (Acts 1:8). Prior to Luke's description of Stephen's being "filled with the Spirit," Stephen was "full of grace and power" and did great signs and wonders (Acts 6:8; 7:55). Overall, Luke's emphasis is on what I would call empowerment rather than simply an experience of being filled with the Spirit (cf. Acts 2:11, 22; 4:7, 33; 8:10, 19; 10:38).

In a study of Paul's writings it also becomes clear that his emphasis was not so much on the *filling* of the Spirit, as such, but on "the *power* of the Spirit." In only one place does Paul explicitly speak of the filling of the Spirit: "Do not get drunk with wine, for that is debauchery; but be filled with the Spirit" (Ephesians 5:18). A better translation of the Greek verb (*plēroō*) translated as "be filled" in this verse might be "*seek the fullness* that the Spirit gives." The Greek word *plērōma* conveys more the idea of moving into fullness rather than a container being filled to capacity. Paul's letters have more than two dozen references to power and the power of the Spirit. For example, "I pray that, according to the riches of his glory, he may grant that you may be strengthened in your inner being with power through his Spirit" (Ephesians 3:16); "for God did not give us a spirit of cowardice, but rather a spirit of power and of love and of self-discipline" (2 Timothy 1:7; cf. also Romans 15:13, 19; 1 Corinthians 2:4; 1 Thessalonians 1:5).

"The Spirit produces and exists in koinonia [fellowship in the body], but perishes in an institution," wrote theologian Emil Brunner. He says that the key to the first-century church is not historical memory but the fellowship of the Spirit. The extraordinary power of this charismatic manifestation is dramatically captured by his description of how the church emerged:

> The Spirit operates with overwhelming revolutionary, transforming results. It manifests itself in such a way as to leave one wondering why and how, and in such a way as to demolish the walls of partition separating individuals from each other. . . . People draw near to the Christian community because they are irresistibly attracted by its supernatural power. . . . There is a sort of fascination that is exercised mostly without any reference to the Word, comparable rather to the attractive force of a magnet or the spread of an infectious disease. Without knowing how it happened, one is already a carrier of the infection."[3]

Allowing for a good bit of hyperbole in Brunner's comment, there *is* something contagious about a community in which the Spirit of Jesus becomes the dynamic that not only binds the members into a fellowship of common love but also touches all who come in contact with these members so as to awaken in them a spiritual response. Even though this infectious and contagious life in the Spirit led to a certain amount of craziness among the Corinthians, Paul did not call for less of the Spirit but for more responsibility in their experience of the power and gifts of the Spirit. The human spirit can easily get tangled up in the Spirit of Christ producing some crossed circuits within the self and a chaotic circus within the community.

THE HUMAN SPIRIT AND THE HOLY SPIRIT

One source of confusion regarding the Holy Spirit as a subjective aspect

---

[3]Emil Brunner, *The Misunderstanding of the Church* (London: Lutterworth, 1952), pp. 24, 49, 52. See also his *Dogmatics,* vol. 3, *The Christian Doctrine of the Church, Faith and the Consummation* (London: Lutterworth, 1962), p. 45.

of our experience of God is the inner, psychological ambiguity as to what we experience when the Spirit of God enters into our lives. What we may take as the conviction of the Spirit may well be a psychological feeling. On the other hand, we may miss the actual conviction of the Spirit by explaining it as a mere psychological need.

Each one of us has spirit as the "breath of life" that inspires us to thought, will and action. The story of creation tells us that God formed the first human from the dust of the earth and "breathed into his nostrils the breath of life" (Gen 2:7). Humans thus have a spirit that has some affinity with the Spirit of God; though its source is God, it is differentiated from the Spirit of God. After his resurrection Jesus met with his disciples and breathed on them and said, "Receive the Holy Spirit" (John 20:22). How were they to understand this? Did the Holy Spirit replace their human spirit or come alongside their human spirit, or was the Holy Spirit dissolved into the human spirit, producing a new kind of spirit? They really had no idea, although it quickly became apparent that their human spirits were still operating in full force as evidenced by some of their later actions!

There really is no way that we can discover through introspection the difference between the Holy Spirit and our own human spirit. It is not as though we can say to ourselves with certainty, Well now, this emotion, this feeling, this impulse, this idea is clearly prompted by the Holy Spirit within me, while this other feeling and urge is my own spirit. It does not work that way, and if we think it does, we may end up like Peter, who thought that he was giving Jesus some spiritual wisdom only to be told, "Get behind me, Satan! You are a stumbling-block to me; for you are setting your mind not on divine things but on human things" (Matthew 16:23). Lest we explain that by saying that this incident took place before Jesus breathed on him and gave him the Holy Spirit, we only need to remember that Paul later confronted and rebuked Peter for not acting in accord with the truth of the gospel (Galatians 2:14). Having received the Holy Spirit is no assurance that our own spirit will always defer to the Holy Spirit. Acting as though our human spirit is actually the Holy Spirit is even worse. I think that I have met some of these people!

If we cannot be sure whether it is our human spirit or the Holy Spirit prompting us to some thought or action, what can we do? Can we discern the difference? First, we need to remember that the inner actions of the Holy Spirit are not of primary concern in the New Testament. Rather, what is noted is what the Spirit produces through us, not merely in us. Thomas Torrance writes:

> We have become accustomed to think of the coming of the Holy Spirit far too much as the interiorizing in our hearts of the divine salvation, with the result that the presence of the Spirit is so often identified with inward moral and religious states. Creator Spirit and our own creative spirituality tend to become confused. . . . Certainly the Holy Spirit is sent into our hearts where he begets enlightenment and conviction, and bears witness with our spirit that we are the children of God, but the psychologizing and subjectivizing of this is entirely, or almost entirely, absent from the New Testament.[4]

The fruit of the Spirit, for example, as Paul describes it, is to be found in attitudes and actions that mainly affect our social relationships rather than merely our inner life (Galatians 5:22-23).

There is one objective test for the presence of the Holy Spirit, that which affirms and builds up Christ within the community (1 Corinthians 12:7; 14:12). I want you to understand, Paul writes, "no one speaking by the Spirit of God ever says 'Let Jesus be cursed!' and no one can say 'Jesus is Lord' except by the Holy Spirit" (1 Corinthians 12:3). Another criterion we can use to discern the presence of the Holy Spirit in our lives is the fruit of the Spirit. Those fruits that Paul lists are characteristics of healthy human personal and social relationships: for exam-

---

[4]Thomas F. Torrance, *Theology in Reconstruction* (Grand Rapids: Eerdmans, 1965), p. 242.

ple, love, joy, peace, patience, kindness, gentleness (Galatians 5:22). In contrast, the "works of the flesh" lead to the dehumanizing of ourselves and others: for example, strife, jealousy, anger, quarrels, envy (Galatians 5:19-21). Paul's point is that those who claim to be filled with the Spirit and led by the Spirit of Christ can be identified by the humane quality of their lives as contrasted with dehumanizing behavior. "For as long as there is jealousy and quarreling among you, are you not of the flesh, and behaving according to human inclinations?" (1 Corinthians 3:3).

One aspect of the incarnation of the divine Logos in Jesus of Nazareth may be helpful in our exploration of the relation of the human spirit and the Holy Spirit. Jesus was not only conceived by the Spirit of God, he was anointed by the Spirit, and in him the Spirit of God and the human spirit became "one spirit." So in receiving the Holy Spirit we also receive the Spirit of Jesus of Nazareth. When the Spirit comes, Jesus said, "He will glorify me, because he will take what is mine and declare to you" (John 16:14). Jesus assured his disciples that when the Spirit came to abide in them, that he would also be with them. "I will not leave you orphaned; I am coming to you" (John 14:18).

Irenaeus, a second century theologian, pictures the coming of the Spirit into Jesus as a way that the Spirit of God can become "accustomed to dwell" in and with humans.

> For God promised, that in the last times He would pour Him [the Spirit] upon His servants and handmaids, that they might prophesy; wherefore He did also descend upon the Son of God, made the Son of man, becoming accustomed in fellowship with Him to dwell in the human race, to rest with human beings, and to dwell in the workmanship of God, working the will of the Father in them, and renewing them from their old habits into the newness of Christ.[5]

---

[5]Irenaeus *Irenaeus Against Heresies* 3.17.1 (Edinburgh: T & T Clark, 1868), 1:334.

I tell my students that the Spirit of God that was experienced as wild and untamed in the Old Testament became domesticated and fully compatible with humanity in Jesus. As a result, the Holy Spirit that comes to us comes already clothed in humanity, conformed to the human spirit in such a way that the effect of the Spirit on and through our lives is not merely supernatural but natural. Thus the Holy Spirit is the Spirit of healing, health and wholeness, bearing the humanity of Christ as well as his divine nature, including the gift of eternal life.

Thomas Torrance puts it eloquently when he writes:

> He came as the Spirit who in Jesus has penetrated into a new intimacy with our human nature, for he came as the Spirit in whom Jesus lived through our human life from end to end, birth to death, and beyond into the resurrection. And therefore he came not as isolated and naked Spirit, but as Spirit charged with all the experience of Jesus as he shared to the full our mortal nature and weakness, and endured its temptation and grief and suffering and death, and with the experience of Jesus as he struggled and prayed, and worshipped and obeyed, and poured out his life in compassion for mankind.[6]

The community of the Spirit is formed by the charism, or gift, of the Holy Spirit and thus can be called a charismatic community. The body of Christ becomes the corporate manifestation of this life in Christ; the fruit of the Spirit becomes our personal manifestation of this life in Christ. The koinonia (fellowship) of the Holy Spirit has an objective basis in which our subjective experience of the Spirit is grounded.

---

[6]Torrance, *Theology in Reconstruction,* p. 247. Michael Green reinforces what Torrance says: "No longer is the Holy Spirit encountered as naked power; he is clothed with the personality and character of Jesus. . . . This power given to individuals by the Spirit is not the naked *ruach* that we sometimes met with in the Old Testament days in men like Saul and Samson. It is the powerful application to believers of the character of Christ" (Michael Green, *I Believe in the Holy Spirit,* rev. ed. [Grand Rapids: Eerdmans, 2004], pp. 50, 110-11).

THE CHARISMATIC COMMUNITY OF THE SPIRIT

According to the apostle Paul, every Christian is "charismatic," in the sense of being born into the family of God through the charism of the Spirit. The charism of the Spirit is the birth gift of every Christian. It is by the Spirit of God that we are given the free gift (charism) of eternal life: "For the wages of sin is death, but the free gift [charism] of God is eternal life in Christ Jesus our Lord" (Romans 6:23; cf. Romans 5:15-17). This birth gift of the Spirit is common to all in the beginning, for each Christian is born into the body of Christ by the same Spirit. "For just as the body is one and has many members, and all the members of the body, though many, are one body, so it is with Christ. For in the one Spirit we were all baptized into one body—Jews or Greeks, slaves or free—and we were all made to drink of one Spirit" (1 Corinthians 12:12-13).

But we are born as spiritual infants, and many do not develop this birth gift of the Spirit and do not mature as intended. The gift of the Spirit, as it brings us to maturity, produces gifts of ministry that are not only necessary for the growth and well-being of the body of Christ but for the extension of Christ's ministry through each member. It is the Christ of Pentecost who ascended on high and "gave gifts to his people" (Ephesians 4:8). These gifts, Paul went on to say, were to "equip the saints for the work of ministry, for building up the body of Christ, until all of us come to the unity of the faith and of the knowledge of the Son of God, to maturity, to the measure of the full stature of Christ" (Ephesians 4:12-13).

Two aspects of emerging churches become apparent when we read the account of the spread of the gospel in the book of Acts. The early Christians were always proclaiming Jesus Christ as the Messiah, crucified and risen from the dead (kerygma), and the commonality of life in the Spirit (koinonia). These two—kerygma and koinonia—are both aspects of a Spirit-filled community. Paul insists that he is never ashamed to proclaim the gospel for "it is the power of God for salvation" (Romans 1:16). He reminds the Corinthians that "my speech and my proclamation [kerygma] were not with plausible words of wisdom, but with a demonstration of the Spirit and of power" (1 Corinthians 2:4).

Wesley Carr says that the very structure of the church needs to be formed by the charism of the Spirit that comes to the church from the future, not from the past.

> If the Church is to witness to this constant relevance of the future for its existence and to the breaking in of that future to the present in the act of God in Christ, then that witness must be substantiated in the structures of the Church. These structures need to be charismatic, i.e., they must reflect the Spirit both as formative force in the community and as representing the judgment of the end upon that community.[7]

Roman Catholic theologian Hans Küng says that "the rediscovery of the charisms is a rediscovery of specifically Pauline ecclesiology, the importance of which for the problems of Catholicism and ecumenism cannot be overstated. . . . Hence one can speak of a charismatic structure of the Church."[8]

What united the emerging churches in their various local and geographical forms was neither a hierarchy of leadership nor a common polity. Their unity was experienced as a community of persons bound to each other and to Christ by a common baptism of the Spirit. This was put succinctly by Paul when he wrote "For just as the body is one and has many members, and all the members of the body, though many, are one body, so it is with Christ. For in the one Spirit we were all baptized

---

[7]Wesley Carr, "Towards a Contemporary Theology of the Holy Spirit," *Scottish Journal of Theology*, 28, no. 7 (1975): 513. "Christians hope to be one with Christ in the final resurrection and their experience in the Christian community is a partial and anticipatory experience of that end. Their place in this eschatologically oriented community has been brought about by the achievement of Christ (hence the significance of the images of the body and of suffering), and it is realised constantly by the agency of the Spirit which is present as a guarantee or first-fruits of the end" (ibid., p. 506).

[8]Hans Küng, *The Church* (London: Sheed & Ward, 1967), pp. 180-81, 188; reprinted in *Theological Foundations for Ministry*, ed. Ray S. Anderson (Grand Rapids: Eerdmans, 1979), p. 478.

into one body—Jews or Greeks, slaves or free—and we were all made to drink of one Spirit" (1 Corinthians 12:12-13). In the emerging church that came out of Antioch, Paul developed the basic model of what we call the charismatic community as the form of the church in the first century. In each of the churches that came into being through his ministry, he left certain individuals as overseers through the gift of the Holy Spirit. This is made explicit in the charge he gave to the elders of the church at Ephesus when he made his last visit on the way back to Jerusalem: "Keep watch over yourselves and over all the flock, of which the Holy Spirit has made you overseers, to shepherd the church of God that he obtained with the blood of his own Son" (Acts 20:28).

The role of spiritual leader is one fraught with risk, both to the leader as well as to those who are subject to the leader. James warned: "Not many of you should become teachers, my brothers and sisters, for you know that we who teach will be judged with greater strictness. For all of us make many mistakes. Anyone who makes no mistakes in speaking is perfect, able to keep the whole body in check with a bridle" (James 3:1-2). The apostle Paul was well aware of the danger of spiritual leadership when he spoke of his own role as "the aroma of Christ to God among those who are being saved and those who are perishing." As he considered the implications of this, he cried out, "Who is sufficient for these things" (2 Corinthians 2:15-16)?

As if to answer his own question, Paul wrote:

But we have this treasure in clay jars, so that it may be made clear that this extraordinary power belongs to God and does not come from us. We are afflicted in every way, but not crushed; perplexed, but not driven to despair; persecuted, but not forsaken; struck down, but not destroyed; always carrying in the body the death of Jesus, so that the life of Jesus may also be made visible in our bodies. For while we live, we are always being given up to death for Jesus' sake, so that the life of Jesus may be made visible

in our mortal flesh. So death is at work in us, but life in you. (2
Corinthians 4:7-12)

In this early charismatic community the Spirit does not create offices
but rather ministries. The need for ministry results in the creation of the
office. This is apparently what took place when the early church experienced contention and division over the distribution of food to the widows. The apostles solved the problem by setting aside seven men "full of
the Spirit" to attend to this ministry. The apostles laid their hands on
them, which does not imply ordination to an office but the communication of the Holy Spirit as empowerment to fulfill the ministry (Acts 6:1-
6). Their position with the community became more official, as it were.
But, in this case, the office of ministry was grounded in the charism for
this ministry. This became the model for establishing the charismatic
(Spirit anointed) order of leadership and ministry for the early church.
Every community needs leadership. But leadership is more of a function
of community than an externally applied authority.[9]

THE CHARISMATIC GIFTS OF THE COMMUNITY

Earlier in this chapter I used the analogy of auto accessories as a way of
explaining how the gifts of the Spirit function in relation to the Spirit as
the main power source for the community. I still like the analogy, but I
agree that Paul's analogy of the human body with its various parts and
functions serves better to demonstrate the dynamic and indispensable

---

[9]"Leadership is a function of the Christian community, and not a status over against it. That the
Christian community needs some form of leadership nobody doubts. . . . That the Christian
community needs an ordained ministry, however, cannot be taken for granted, but needs to
be discussed with reference to both the theological demands of the Christian faith and the or-
ganisational demands of a contemporary human association. Given these requirements it
seems rather odd that in some Churches the particular understanding of the ordained ministry
is still focused on the now obsolete metaphysical understanding of past times and on the or-
ganisational needs of medieval congregations. Most urgently needed is a reassessment of the
relationship between the ordained minister and the ordained community" (Werner Jeanrond,
"Community and Authority," in On Being the Church, ed. Colin E. Gunton and Daniel W. Hardy
[Edinburgh: T & T Clark, 1989], pp. 96, 98).

relation of the gift to the body. My analogy is mechanical rather than organic and leaves the impression that an accessory is more of a luxurious add-on item than a component of a living community of the Spirit. In the ancient emerging churches the gifts of the Spirit worked somewhat like a democracy—it may be the most inefficient way for a people to govern themselves, but it is better than all the other ways!

In several of Paul's letters to the churches he reminds them of the importance of developing and exercising their gifts (cf. Romans 12; 1 Corinthians 12; Ephesians 4). Paul is fond of using the analogy of the human body to describe the way that each member of the church relates to another and all to the whole. "Now there are varieties of gifts, but the same Spirit; and there are varieties of services, but the same Lord; and there are varieties of activities, but it is the same God who activates all of them in everyone. To each is given the manifestation of the Spirit for the common good" (1 Corinthians 12:4-7). The gifts of the Spirit (charismata) may be understood as the shaping of the birth gift of ministry as applied in a particular context and to meet a particular need.

In the various places that Paul lists some of the gifts, we find some duplication and some additions. The consensus among scholars today is that we cannot develop an official list of gifts by merging the various listings given by Paul. There appear to be as many gifts available to the community as there are needs, with some highlighted in each community according to the ministry focus. The gifts of the Spirit are often interpreted as the means by which members of the church can be equipped to carry out their ministries, and as part of this equipping process they are encouraged to take an inventory of what gifts might be sought or already in use. This kind of shopping for gifts as a way of mobilizing lay persons for ministry often creates initial enthusiasm and bursts of energy, but just as often it can lead to personal frustration and spiritual fatigue.

Unless empowerment precedes equipping, many people who are encouraged to exercise a spiritual gift find that their enthusiasm and motivation wanes. The empowerment comes through the life of Christ that flows through us as the Holy Spirit touches the core of our own spirit. When we exercise a spiritual gift, others receive the blessing of that act. In the same way we are touched by the spirit of the other and so are moved to respond in friendship and love. And so the Spirit of God moves with the body and fills us with the very Spirit of Christ. This is what being filled with the Spirit means, not merely power but presence, not only competence to speak in other tongues but a compelling urge to communicate the good news in our own tongue.

The authentic charism that liberates is not the spirit of power but the Spirit of Christ. An authentic charismatic theology is one that empowers blacks in South Africa to participate as full members of the human race—socially, politically and spiritually. Charismatic theology empowers women to have full parity in every structure of society, especially the church and its ministry. It empowers the poor, the marginalized, the weak and the homeless to live meaningful and comfortable lives as human beings created in God's image. An authentic charismatic theology is one that disarms the church of its pride and privilege, causing it to repent and to enact repentance toward God through responsible service toward the world that God loves. Thomas Smail says it well:

> The charismatic Christian with his world-affirming approach and his awareness of both the demonic and the prophetic should be among those who can catch the vision. God wants to give in local churches structures of relationship that have their roots in the central relationship to himself, but that express themselves horizontally and practically in such a way as to challenge the oppressive structures of society in which the church lives.[10]

Charismatic Christians, Smail continues, should be as much concerned for the socially demonic in the form of oppressive structures as for the personally demonic.

---

[10]Thomas Smail, *The Forgotten Father* (Grand Rapids: Eerdmans, 1980), p. 179.

Despite all of the craziness that some profess and act out in the name of the Holy Spirit, it is well to be reminded that, as one theologian said, "What is divine is never weird!"[11] The reports of people possessed by the Spirit making animal noises or bursting out in holy laughter make me hope that God has a sense of humor! When we consider that Jesus was filled with the Holy Spirit "without measure," we see that this experience did not make him less human but more human. The proper form of a spirit-filled human being is that of Jesus of Nazareth, and the evidence is not in some form of temporary derangement of mind, emotion or tongue, but in his inner stability of peace under great stress and his outer life of compassion and ministry toward the weak and the wounded in the world. When I pray to receive the Holy Spirit, it is the Spirit of Jesus that I seek as a counselor and advocate of my own spirit. The evidences, as the apostle Paul said, are quite clear, to have the same mind that was in Christ Jesus (Philippians 2:5-8).

In writing to the Corinthians Paul warns those who were hyperactive with regard to manifestations of the spiritual gifts but still infants with regard to their spiritual life and growth. With all of their religious activity they were in effect still living on baby food, and this accounted for their lack of spiritual maturity (1 Corinthians 3:1-4). In contrasting the works of the flesh with the fruit of the Spirit, Paul points out a nutritional guide that provides nourishment in our search for the body of Christ where our spiritual needs are fulfilled (Galatians 5:16-26).

The Holy Spirit adds no content to our spiritual life other than that of Jesus Christ. Being filled with the Spirit is being conformed to Christ, and the Spirit is a good mentor and teacher! "When the Spirit of truth comes, . . . he will not speak on his own, but will speak whatever he hears, and he will declare to you the things that are to come. He will glo-

---

[11]Old Testament theologian Abraham Heschel said, "What is divine is never weird. This is the greatness of the prophet: he is able to convert terror into a song. For when the Lord smites the Egyptians, he is both 'smiting and healing' (Isa. 19:22)" (Abraham Heschel, *The Prophets* [New York: Harper & Row, 1962], 2:63).

rify me, because he will take what is mine and declare it to you. All that the Father has is mine. For this reason I said that he will take what is mine and declare to you" (John 16:13-15).

CONCLUDING NONTHEOLOGICAL POSTSCRIPT

I know that my own spirit is too tame when it should be adventurous. My spirit can be too impulsive and sometimes brash when it should be measured and modest. My spirit can waver in doubt and uncertainty when I should be brave and bold. This is why I ask for the Holy Spirit to come beside my spirit, not to take my place but to make my place more resemble a home where Jesus lives than a college dormitory. This is the Spirit I seek when I pray "Spirit of God, descend on my heart."

I don't want the Spirit of God to startle me in the middle of the night when I need my rest. I don't want the Spirit of God to make me anxious in order to seek first the kingdom of God. I don't want the Spirit of God to make me bark like a dog or laugh like a hyena in order to fulfill a craving for more of God. On the other hand, there is something I desire in being filled with the Spirit, and that is captured in the poignant words of the psalmist:

I have calmed and quieted my soul,
   like a weaned child with its mother;
   my soul is like a weaned child that is within me. (Psalm 131:2-3)

I am not sure that I want to go through the weaning process—nor am I sure that God wants to go through it with me! The parent suffers more than the child, I suspect. To be weaned from the kind of relationship with God where my needs for gratification demand his immediate response is to walk alone, it seems. But Jesus went through that process, first in being weaned from the breast of his mother, and then from the power of God as a form of temptation. It was, after all, the Spirit that led Jesus into the wilderness (Matthew 4:1).

The Spirit of Jesus is a weaned Spirit, no longer demanding to be fed but returning once more to the Father. My spirit is still too restless. I want every prayer to be answered. I want to keep praying even when there is no answer. In the end, I want to be able to trust God to hold my unanswered prayers like letters from a separated lover, close to his bosom. This is the Spirit of my prayer.

I do not expect the church to meet my every need. The church can and should provide the kind of body life where the Spirit can reveal to each of us our own particular needs. If I am weak in faith, I need to be in a church where I am not required to profess more faith than I have. Rather, I need the freedom and security to express my faith deficiency with the expectation that I can draw on the faith of others as a stimulus for my own growth in faith. If I am starved for love, it may indicate that I have a love deficiency in myself rather than lack of others to love me. The Holy Spirit knows what I need, and he will, through the loving care and concern of others, prompt me to grow more in love through a body life where love is expressed generously and openly.

Nutritionists remind us that there are essential ingredients in our daily diet that are necessary to maintain good health. Consumer protection laws have been enacted that require labels on food products that help the purchaser make good decisions about his or her food purchases. Here, rather than a prescription that offers a remedy for some distress or dysfunction (though that is still a good idea!), we should each develop our own nutritional guideline that contains the essential ingredients for our spiritual life and growth. It is not the quantity but the quality of food intake that is necessary for our health. A person can suffer serious malnutrition with a full stomach! I have known people who have been so preoccupied with church activities that they are literally full of religion but starving themselves spiritually.

I have come to the conclusion that an individual is not given a gift of the Spirit because he or she needs it but because the community of the Spirit needs that individual. I do not seek a spiritual gift because I need one to be more spiritual. I need to belong to a community that needs me and needs the gifts that I can bring to the service of Christ within that community. I need to belong to a community that needs me.

A spiritual gift is not an honorary title but a subpoena of the Holy Spirit issued by the body of Christ to fulfill a task or responsibility. Just because it is a gift I should not assume that it will not cost me something to use it. The exercise of a spiritual gift will require my time and energy that could otherwise be used for my own benefit or for the welfare of family and friends who look to me for support. This is why the community of the Spirit needs to have the Spirit's wisdom in distribution of the gifts. The gifts of the Spirit are not burdens placed on our already burdened lives. Gifts of the Spirit yoke us to Christ, whose yoke is easy and whose burden is light (Matthew 11:29-30). When we become burdened in our exercising of a spiritual gift, it is no longer a gift that brings a blessing to ourselves but a duty that bruises our spirit.

When the body of Christ of which I am a part reaches out for someone to fill a need, I respond by saying "I can do that." It's that simple. And I am convinced it was that simple for Paul. His analogy of the human body works very well here. If I need to taste something to determine if it is ready eat, my tongue says "I can do that." If I need to look at a page in a book in order to read it, my eyes say "We can do that." If I have some toxic waste in my blood that needs to be filtered out, my kidneys say "We can do that." I won't press the analogy any further!

The point is, the community of the Spirit, not just the gifts of the Spirit, is what emerging churches are about. If the community is alive in the Spirit and the members are allowing the Spirit that birthed them into Christ to flow into every nook and cranny of their lives, and to conform their human spirits to the Spirit of Christ within them, there will be as many gifts as the body needs, no more, no less.

■ ■ ■ ■ ■ ■ ■ ■ ■ ■ ■ ■ ■ ■ ■

9   IT'S ABOUT MISSION, NOT JUST MINISTRY

Christians are not the end users of the gospel. This is how Brian McLaren's opened a discussion of the need for emerging churches to be a community driven by a sense of mission to the world in order to avoid becoming a community seeking to gratify its own self-interest at the expense of the world.[1] The "what's in it for me" syndrome, McLaren claims, turns the church into a purveyor of religious goods and services designed to keep its own members from shopping around for a church that "meets my needs better."[2]

The narrow focus on individual salvation as the primary mission of

---

[1]Brian McLaren, *A Generous Orthodoxy* (Grand Rapids: Zondervan, 2004), p. 107. In an earlier book I said somewhat the same thing: "The church is not the end result of the gospel by virtue of its own existence; it exists so that the gospel can be carried out in mission to the world. The church is an agent of the work of the gospel, not the final form of the gospel itself as an organization or institution. Nor is mission capable of sustaining itself as an activity or organization except as it is grounded in the life of the church through the power and authority of the gospel" (Ray S. Anderson, *Minding God's Business* [Grand Rapids: Eerdmans, 1986], p. 6).

[2]"Occasionally, after 'winning' people based on personal self-interest, churches can entice people to care a little about the church—but is it any surprise that people 'won to Christ' by self-interest come to the church asking, 'What's in it for me?' Is it any surprise that with this understanding of salvation, churches tend to become gatherings of self-interested people who gather for mutual self-interest—constantly treating the church as a purveyor of religious goods and services, constantly shopping and 'trading up' for churches that can 'meet my needs' better? Is it any surprise that it's stinking hard to convince churches that they have a mission to the world when most Christians equate 'personal salvation' of individual 'souls' with the ultimate aim of Jesus?" (McLaren, *Generous Orthodoxy*, p. 107).

the gospel can be a form of reductionism, argues Darrell Guder.

> Reductionism is our understanding of the gospel and of salvation,
> linked with old and continuing shifts in eschatology and Christol-
> ogy, has wide-reaching missional implications. The gospel has
> been reduced to a message focused on the individual's salvation:
> the fundamental evangelistic question is assumed to be "Are you
> saved?" The process of evangelization and "discipling" has thus be-
> come the program of spiritual and religious exercises that deals
> with that salvation.[3]

Guder does not discount the importance of individual salvation—it is
not a matter of either-or but of both-and. What he questions is the narrow focus on the personal benefits of the gospel at the expense of the
mission of the gospel.

I suspect that the word *mission* has become politically incorrect in a
postmodern world that has an excessive horror for words and phrases
that suggest ideological or epistemological hegemony. Or to put it more
candidly is afraid of a "my truth must become your truth" attitude. And
if you do not agree me, I will seek to convert you either by coercion or
by exploitation.

In a postmodern way of thinking, absolutist claims to reality (meta-
narratives) are nothing but power grabs and conspiracies to legitimize
the dominant power structures and to marginalize, trivialize and oppress
those whose stories and experiences do not fit. In the words of one ad-
herent, such universal claims have a "secretly terroristic function."[4] The
modernist presumption of totality, of universality, and of rational truth

[3]Darrell L. Guder, *The Continuing Conversion of the Church* (Grand Rapids: Eerdmans, 2000), p. 120.
[4]Gary John Percesepe, himself sympathetic to postmodernism, writes: "The totalization of truth is what we have learned to fear most. The friendly face of fascism, one must remember, was announced to Italians and Germans as truth. Stalin effectively marshaled a Truth Industry to justify his purges; Orwell's Winston Smith—do not miss the irony—worked in the Ministry of Truth" (Gary John Percesepe, "The Unbearable Lightness of Being Postmodern," *Christian Scholar's Review* 20, no. 2 [1990]: 128).

about the world is labeled a mere power play. For the postmodernist there are no overarching, grand stories that explain reality. Such meta-narratives are considered modernist ploys to legitimize the power of those in authority; they are nothing more than propaganda meant to impose particular preferences on others. The antidote to such terror is tolerance, which often requires the surgical removal of words that convey, at best, arrogance and, at worst, imperialist invasions of other cultures and communities.

In 1983 the faculty of Fuller Seminary endorsed the president's proposal for "The Mission Beyond the Mission." The mission of the seminary had been stated as the nurture and training of men and women for the manifold ministries of Christ. While this was still considered to be the central purpose of the institution, it was felt to be too narrowly focused on the church. The mission beyond the mission attempted to enlarge the mission statement to include a broader vision of the mandate of Christ for the world. At the same time it also meant to include segments of the seminary's own faculty, such as the graduate School of Psychology and the School of World Mission, whose students were being prepared to serve Christ beyond the local church. The mission beyond the mission statement added these specific items:

- Go and make disciples.
- Call the church of Christ to renewal.
- Work for the moral health of society.
- Seek peace and justice in the world.
- Uphold the truth of God's revelation.

Twenty-one years later, in 2004, that same faculty, while holding to the language of the mission beyond the mission, voted to change the name of the School of World Mission to the School of Intercultural Studies. By dropping "world mission" from its name and from the diploma awarded to its graduates, the school argued that it provided easier access into other cultures that might view missionaries as invaders who are out to undermine the structure of autonomous political societies and nations. "Intercultural studies" was chosen because it suggests an academic discipline rather than religious imperialism.

Did a tsunami of postmodernity hit our seminary, wiping out a cherished truth of the gospel? Not likely. I know these people. The gospel message is the same, even though the nametag has been changed. The apostle Paul, not having read our postmodern authors (though quite familiar with the classical Greek philosophers!), had his own way of putting it: "I have become all things to all people, that I might by all means save some" (1 Corinthians 9:22). Karl Barth said it less eloquently but just as pointedly, "The true church may sometimes engage in tactical withdrawal, but never in strategic. It can never cease wholly or basically from activity in the world."[5]

"What's in a name?" Shakespeare once asked. "That which we call a rose, by any other name would smell as sweet."[6] Hubert H. Humphrey, former U.S. senator and vice president added his own qualification when he said, "In real life, unlike in Shakespeare, the sweetness of the rose depends upon the name it bears. Things are not only what they are. They are, in very important respects, what they seem to be."[7] Is mission what it is or what it seems to be? If it is God's mission in the world and to the world through Christ, I would say that it must be what it is. And if calling it "mission" preserves the essence of what it is, emerging churches should at least speak the word out loud to their own members! Seminaries may wish to study human cultures; mission seeks to transform them. In the end, it is not so much about lexicology but theology. In the lexicon of the church, *emerging* is a synonym for *mission*.

The Holy Spirit in the emerging church at Antioch was experienced not only as a Spirit that created ministry but as a Spirit with a mission,

[5]Karl Barth, *Church Dogmatics* 4/3, trans. Geoffrey W. Bromiley (Edinburgh: T & T Clark, 1961), p. 780.
[6]William Shakespeare *Romeo and Juliet*, act 2, scene 2.1.
[7]Hubert H. Humphrey, in a speech given on March 26, 1966, Washington, D.C. <http://www.bartleby.com/66/57/29657.html>.

"Set apart for me Barnabas and Saul for the work to which I have called them" (Acts 13:2). Emerging churches are about mission, not just about ministry. Both issue from and are directed by the Spirit of Christ, but there is a priority of one over the other. Mission without ministry can lead to imperialism. Ministry without mission can become narcissism. Ministry keeps mission from grandiosity, triumphalism and kingdom-building. Ministry keeps mission close to humanity, even if it means building a hospital rather than a temple. But mission keeps ministry from becoming a mirror in which the church, like the mythical Narcissus, sees its own reflection and ends up withering away until it becomes a potted plant—a narcissus!

MISSION LEADS, MINISTRY FOLLOWS

Luke does not tell us that the emerging church at Antioch practiced the ministry of spiritual gifts such as Paul mentioned in writing to the other churches. But we can assume that he taught the same during the year that he ministered in Antioch before being sent out by the Holy Spirit to other people groups (Acts 11:26). For the most part the gifts of the Spirit that Paul enumerated in his letter to the churches were what we might call ministry gifts—prophets, evangelists, pastors, teachers, helpers, discernment of spirits, tongues (Romans 12:6-8; 1 Corinthians 12:8-10; Ephesians 4:11). The gift of apostleship is mentioned specifically in his letter to the church at Ephesus. An apostle is one who is sent out with a specific commission and task, with the responsibility of reporting back when the task is completed. When Paul and Barnabas were sent out by the church at Antioch they were sent out as apostles on a mission under the anointing and direction of the Holy Spirit. This is reflected not only in the authority that Paul claimed as an apostle commissioned directly by Christ (Galatians 1:1) but in reporting back to the church at Antioch following his first mission (Acts 14:26-28). Wherever mission led, ministry followed.

The church at Jerusalem was strong on ministry but weak on mission.

Following Pentecost the believers gathered regularly for worship, prayer and common meals. When there were some in need, especially widows, they made provision for their support. There were miraculous healings and amazing results from their evangelistic ministries. The gift of generosity spurred many of them to sell their property and give the money to the leaders for distribution to the poor (Acts 4:32-37). But there is no record of an extensive mission outreach by the Jerusalem church. Peter did go out as far as Lydda and Joppa (Acts 9:36-42) and Philip to Samaria and Gaza (Acts 8:4-40), but no record of churches planted. The Jerusalem community apparently went into a fortress mentality, fiercely defending their own version of being a messianic community in the tradition of Moses. Those who were sent out later on a mission were specifically sent to undermine and counteract the emerging churches under Paul's apostolic leadership. When we look for mission in the early church, we look to emerging churches; and when we look for the emerging church, we expect to find mission as well as ministry. Mission is the apostolic gift of the Spirit to the emerging church.

Paul's apostolic mission was anchored on the one end by the gospel that he had received directly from Christ by revelation through personal encounter (Galatians 1:12). It was anchored on the other end by the Spirit's mission of making Christ known in regions not already evangelized by this gospel. The strategic plan of the apostle Paul is laid out in Romans 15. Writing from Ephesus he told them that he planned to visit them for the sake of seeking their support for his mission to Spain (Romans 15:24-25).

> For I will not venture to speak of anything except what Christ has accomplished through me to win obedience from the Gentiles, by word and deed, by the power of signs and wonders, by the power of the Spirit of God, so that from Jerusalem and as far around as Illyricum I have fully proclaimed the good news of Christ. Thus I make it my ambition to proclaim the good news, not where Christ

has already been named, so that I do not build on someone else's foundation. (Romans 15:18-20)

Paul has already preached his gospel as a fulfillment of Isaiah's messianic prophecy: "I have set you to be a light for the Gentiles, so that you may bring salvation to the ends of the earth" (Acts 13:47; see Isaiah 49:6). This is Christ's apostolic and messianic mission that continues the trajectory of God's mission as revealed in the Old Testament. This is God's mission through the Spirit of the Messiah (Christ) by which the emerging church as a missionary people of God continue the purpose set forth in the calling and consecration of Israel in the Abrahamic blessing (Genesis 12). The gospel through which mission receives its mandate is truly Christ's gospel, and as such it is the continuation and fulfillment of God's gospel that was given by grace through Abraham as a promise to "all the families of the earth" (Genesis 12:3).

Emerging churches exist in the center of this continuum between gospel and world mission. In this way the church cannot be the church simply by encasing the gospel in its liturgical practice, nor can the church be the church by defining itself solely by mission, without accountability to the gospel.

This is the breakthrough that Jürgen Moltmann points to when he suggests that the messianic mission of Jesus is not entirely completed in his death and resurrection. Through the coming of the Spirit, Jesus' history becomes the church's gospel for the world. The church participates in his mission, becoming the messianic church of the coming kingdom. There is, says Moltmann, a "conversion to the future" through which the church enters into the messianic proclamation of the coming of the kingdom. He then suggests that the "sending of the Spirit" can be viewed as a "sacrament of the kingdom."

In so far as Jesus as the Messiah is the mystery of the rule of God, the signs of the messianic era are also part of his mystery. In so far as the crucified and risen Jesus manifests the salvation of the world determined on by God, proclamation and faith and the outpouring of the Holy Spirit on the Gentiles are also part of this salvation. . . . It also follows that a christological ecclesiological rendering of the term—Christ and the church as the primal and fundamental sacrament of salvation—certainly touches on a further sphere covered by the New Testament but does not go far enough, especially if the church of Christ is only understood in its sacraments and not at the same time in the context of the eschatology of world history.[8]

The mission of the church overrides its boundaries, spilling out into the world in fulfillment of the apostolic commission to "go into the world." The church's mission is not to build up an empire or kingdom but to disperse the mission of God through the lives of its members as well as the various groups and organizations that they form. The church finds its being in its mission, under the guidance and power of the Spirit. Its intention and direction is oriented to the world that God loves and to which it is sent.

By the ministry of the church, I mean its life, activities and programs by which it carries out its mission. Jesus had both a mission to fulfill as the apostle who was faithful to his calling (Hebrews 3:1-3) and a ministry by which he carried out this mission. The church carries out ministries and so participates in God's mission. The ministry of the church should always be understood as grounded in the mission of God in Christ to reconcile the world to himself (2 Corinthians 5:19). When mission leads, ministry follows. In this way the ministries and programs of the church are empowered by the presence of the Spirit in the life of the members of the community.

WHERE MISSION LEADS THE CHURCH EMERGES

The church does not exist other than in its life given to its members as

---

[8]Jürgen Moltmann, *The Church in the Power of the Spirit* (New York: Harper & Row, 1977), pp. 83, 80, 199, 204-5.

the visible and corporate manifestation of God's mission to the world. The church has no doctrine of God except its understanding of God as revealed in his mission to the world. The church has no theology of mission except that it articulates the theology of God's mission originating in the creative will of the Father, accomplished through the reconciling life, death and resurrection of Jesus Christ, his Son. The church has no theology of its own existence except as it participates in Christ's mission in the world through the redemptive power and presence of the Holy Spirit, of which the church is the servant and sign of this kingdom power.

The church emerges out of mission as it comes to understand its nature as grounded in God's own mission inaugurated through Israel and consummated in Christ. This means that there is a theological priority belonging to mission as determining the nature of the church and its relation to the mission of God for the world. The mission of the church is to embody in its corporate life and ministry the continuing messianic and incarnational nature of the Son of God through the indwelling of the Holy Spirit. The nature of the church is determined in its existence as the mission of God to the world. The church's nature as well as its mission and ministry have their source in the life of the triune God: Father, Son and Holy Spirit.

If the mission of Christ through the presence and power of the Spirit determines the nature and ministry of the church, then we should expect that mission itself becomes the source of the renewed vision and life of the church. This is why mission, rather than ministry, expands God's kingdom and renews the spiritual life of the church. Ministry expends Spirit in programs and body building; mission breathes in Spirit and promotes body movement. Ministry tends to become centripetal—drawing energy toward the center; mission tends to be centrifugal—impelling energy outward. Pentecost is the manifestation of incarnational mission, not merely an infusion of spiritual enthusiasm. For the church to be both incarnational and Pentecostal in its theology and praxis, it must recover the dynamic relation between its nature and mission.

When I speak of the nature and the mission of the church, I am making a somewhat artificial distinction between what the church is and what it does. In a sense the church becomes what it is (nature) by virtue of its existence as a witness to Christ's continued ministry of reconciliation in the world (mission). Mission and nature thus cannot be separated as though the church could exist without mission or that mission could take place without the existence of the church as the presence and power of Christ.

The Holy Spirit is the creative power and presence of Jesus Christ as the inner logos, or inner logic, of God's mission of redemption. The experience of the Holy Spirit at Pentecost was not only an event that Christ promised but an event in which the same Christ continues to be present as the goal or telos of history. The church is a continuing witness to the presence and power of the crucified and resurrected Messiah, Jesus Christ our Lord. The church is not an "extension of the incarnation" through its historical and institutional life alone. Jesus Christ himself is the continuing mission of God in the world and thus is the reality that constitutes the church as the body of Christ. Mission, thus understood, precedes and creates the church. Or, we could say, the nature of the church is revealed through its existence in the world as the mission of the people of God who receive the Spirit of Pentecost as their point of origin and means of empowerment.

The nature of the church as the continuing mission of God through Jesus Christ is determined by its relation to Pentecost, not only to the Great Commission, which was given by Jesus prior to his crucifixion and resurrection. The command "Go . . . and make disciples of all nations" (Matthew 28:19) anticipates the promise "you will receive power when the Holy Spirit has come upon you; and you will be my witnesses" (Acts 1:8). The Great Commission gives the church its instructions, Pentecost provides its initiation and power. "At the beginning of the history of the New Testament Church stands the Pentecost event," writes Harry Boer.

"It does not stand approximately at the beginning, or as a first among several significant factors, but it stands absolutely at the beginning. . . . It does not, however, stand in isolation from preceding and succeeding redemptive history."[9]

The Great Commission as recorded by Matthew, years after the emerging church came into being, was no doubt part of the oral tradition that became well known by Paul. At the same time it did not appear to be a conscious factor in the mission thinking of the early church. It was the Pentecost event that provided the impetus for mission outreach. This is set in contrast to much of modern mission emphasis that attempts to locate the mission imperative of the church on obedience to the Great Commission. This tendency has sometimes led to a dichotomy between the church and its mission program. If we view the nature of the church as a continuation of the mission of Christ through the power of the Spirit, then the Great Commission becomes a command that is to be heard by a church already empowered by the Holy Spirit to fulfill that command as its very nature. The missionary thrust and program of the church thus issues out if its own nature and not as an addendum or appendage.

Karl Barth points to the same priority of Pentecost when he says, "As the quickening power that accomplishes sanctification [the Holy Spirit] comes down with utter novelty and strangeness from above (as described in the story of Pentecost) and thus constitutes an absolute basis and starting point."[10] It is in this sense that one must speak of the nature of the church as revealed in its participation in the mission of God as empowered and directed by the Holy Spirit.

When we begin theological reflection on the nature of the church as an emerging community, we are led to a clearer understanding of the church in its incarnational form as the continued mission and ministry

---

[9]Harry R. Boer, *Pentecost and Missions* (Grand Rapids: Eerdmans, 1961), p. 98.
[10]Karl Barth, *Church Dogmatics* 4/2, trans. Geoffrey Bromiley and Thomas Torrance (Edinburgh: T & T Clark, 1962), p. 563.

of God in Christ. Without Pentecost as the beginning, the church can lose its connection with the mission and ministry of God. The church then becomes the incarnation of a human ideal rather than the continuing mission of the incarnate One, Jesus Christ.

If the church were to abandon the mission of Christ that now takes place in the humanity of the church's solidarity with the world, the church would forsake its share in the reconciliation of the world to God through Christ (2 Corinthians 5:18-21). If the church were to lose the presence and life of the Spirit as the source of its own existence and life, the church would sever its vital connection to Christ so that its ministry would become meager and its religion mere ritual.

When the nature of the church becomes the object of theological reflection in such a way that it is separated from the context of the mission of the church under the direction of the Spirit, the doctrine of the church becomes more of an academic enterprise than a mission event. This leaves the life and ministry of the church to be determined by pragmatic and often nontheological methods. When students who are preparing for ministry within the church leave seminary, they are often well prepared academically for their theological examinations, but ill equipped to examine critically the tactics and methods that they must use to be successful in leading the church in its mission.

Paul does not define the church as a theological treatise, but in the context of the gospel and mission as constitutive of its life and purpose. Jesus as the beloved Son, anointed by the Spirit, completes the messianic mission given to Israel in his own self-offering for the sins of the world. The Holy Spirit, as the contemporary presence and power of this messianic-kingdom promise of redemption, creates the missionary people of God out of every nation, tribe and culture. This is to fulfill Christ's mission of reconciliation of the world to God.

The church will always be tempted to make itself and its confession of faith the agenda and content of its theological reflection. If it does this, it loses its apostolic witness and authority. For the church to be apostolic it must also follow the Holy Spirit's leading through the apostolic mandate of mission. An apostolic church clearly understands the gospel as the mission of God originating in God's redemptive purpose for all humanity, fulfilled through Christ Jesus and released into the world through the Holy Spirit.

The church's nature and mission are bound together in the same way that incarnation and Pentecost are linked, with death and resurrection being the inner logic of atonement for sin and reconciliation to God. This led Paul to say that the church is the mystery (*mystērion*) of God now revealed through Christ, that "through the church" the manifold wisdom of God would become known throughout the entire cosmos (Ephesians 3:9-10). Because Jesus Christ himself is this mystery (Ephesians 3:4), Paul can say that there is "one body and one Spirit, just as you were called to the one hope of your calling, one Lord, one faith, one baptism, one God and Father of all" (Ephesians 4:4-6).

This is the mission of God himself to those in the world who are without God and thus whose own humanity is distorted and deformed. It is the mission of one who has already pledged his own humanity, and so it is a mission with no strings attached.[11] The gospel mission has as its goal the humanizing of humanity. Its criterion is not merely human need but divine love. Its justification is that it is a fulfillment of divine intentionality, not in the response it produces.

THE MISSION OF CHURCH AND WORLD

The church has never been comfortable with its relation to the world. At

---

[11]The comment by Dietrich Ritschl is apropos: "The goal of diaconia is not the attuning of those who receive the diaconia to the faith of those who perform it. The basis of diaconia should not be confused with its goal: diaconia in solidarity with the poor and those without rights can be practised without the secret aim of convincing the recipients of the basis of the diaconia. The conversion of the recipients of works of diaconia to the faith of those providing it is a particular and additional miracle of the presence of the Spirit of God. It is not the goal of the diaconal activity" (Dietrich Ritschl, *The Logic of Theology*, trans. John Bowden [Philadelphia: Fortress, 1987], pp. 270-71).

times it has taken the words of John quite literally, "Do not love the world or the things in the world. The love of the Father is not in those who love the world" (1 John 2:15). John also remembers the words of Jesus, "They do not belong to the world, just as I do not belong to the world" (John 17:16). John's emphasis could well have emerged out of the self-concept of the Jerusalem church with its fortress mentality. It is certainly not the basis of the emerging church's thinking or that of Paul's! "Everything created by God is good, and nothing is to be rejected, provided it is received with thanksgiving; for it is sanctified by God's word and by prayer" (1 Timothy 4:4-5). However, it is also true that Paul, while a world Christian with cosmopolitan temperament and tastes, knew well the hostility of the world against the kingdom of God. Emerging churches must not define themselves as a separate entity over and against the world but by their impact in the world. I often tell my students that the church that is merely different from the world makes no difference to the world.

At the other end of the continuum are those churches too comfortable in the world. They are like the proverbial frog in the pan on the stove unaware that it needs to get out while it is still alive! The church needs to find Christ in the world before it suffocates from the lack of spiritual oxygen behind walls with windows that were not made to open. Stained-glass windows remind me of heavenly images, when viewed from the inside. But they also prevent the world from seeing the church as it really is on the inside.

I like to use diagrams to make certain concepts more visible. When the church views itself as a self-contained custodian of Christ in the world, it defines its own boundary as an unbroken line while the world is viewed as essentially broken; only by entering into the sanctuary can the world be saved and made whole. Christ and the church are sheltered in the cross, with the world excluded. Note that the church appears whole and complete in this diagram (fig. 9.1), possessing Christ for itself. It wants to fill in the gaps in the broken world, but only on its own terms. The church attempts to place religious Band-Aids on the broken edges of a secular world in order to close the gap by making the world more religious.

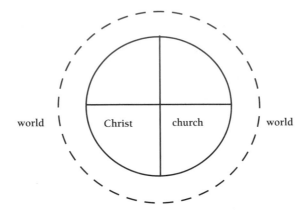

Figure 9.1. The church separated from the world

In figure 9.2 the outer circle represents the world as a solid line while the line that marks off the church within the world has openings. Through the incarnation of God in Christ the world has been reconciled to God (2 Corinthians 5:19). Humanity estranged from God constitutes the world that God loves (John 3:16). The church does not possess Christ for itself but finds Christ in the world. This is the model of the church in the world as Dietrich Bonhoeffer viewed it:

> In Christ we are offered the possibility of partaking in the reality of God and in the reality of the world, but not in the one without the other. The reality of God discloses itself only by setting me entirely in the reality of the world, and when I encounter the reality of the world it is always already sustained, accepted and reconciled in the reality of God. This is the inner meaning of the revelation of God in the man Jesus Christ. . . . One is denying the revelation of God in Jesus Christ if one tries to be "Christian" without seeing and recognizing the world in Christ.[12]

[12]Dietrich Bonhoeffer, *Ethics* (New York: Macmillan, 1955), pp. 193. Otto Weber echoes this theme: "Seen Christologically, every rejection of the world by the Community would have to

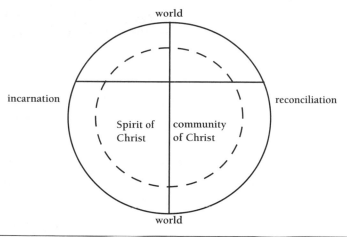

Figure 9.2. The church and the world reconciled to God

Viewing the world from this perspective, says Bonhoeffer, is what Paul meant when he said, "In Christ God was reconciling the world to himself, not counting their trespasses against them, and entrusting the message of reconciliation to us. So we are ambassadors for Christ, since God is making his appeal through us; we entreat you on behalf of Christ, be reconciled to God" (2 Corinthians 5:19-20). The church must never deprive the world of Christ, for Christ came to embrace the world in order to provide the possibility of its redemption in him through the Spirit. This is a mission gospel, in Bonhoeffer's mind.

Whoever sets eyes on the body of Jesus Christ in faith can never again speak of the world as though it were lost, as though it were separated from Christ; he can never with clerical arrogance set himself apart from the world. The world belongs to Christ, and it

place in question 'docetically' the incarnation of Jesus Christ. It would have to have been the case that God did not become 'true man' in Jesus Christ if the Community were intended not to be 'truly' in the world. But above all, the victory of the Resurrected One over the 'cosmos' (John 13:33) would have to be disregarded if the Community were supposedly to understand the 'world' solely as a confusing, alien reality, to be held at a distance and excluded" (Otto Weber, *Foundations of Dogmatics II* [Grand Rapids: Eerdmans, 1983], pp. 525-26).

is only in Christ that the world is what it is. . . . Everything would
be ruined if one were to try to reserve Christ for the Church and to
allow the world only some kind of law, even it were a Christian
law.[13]

Through the incarnation of God in Christ, Bonhoeffer asserted, "all
men are taken up, enclosed and borne within the body of Christ, and
that this is just what the congregation of the faithful are to make known
to the world by their words and by their lives."[14] However, Bonhoeffer
goes on to say that this testimony is foreign to the world and will actually
be a threat when announced. The world will reject this gospel because it
challenges the claim to autonomy and self-determination by which it
lives.

While the world defines the context of the mission of the church, it
does not determine the content of the mission. Being in the world determines the reality of mission—for mission is "being there," not simply going there. On the other hand, the world does not know why it is there
or the meaning of its own existence. Karl Barth makes this point clear
when he says:

The world does not know itself. It does not know God, nor man,
nor the relationship and covenant between God and man. Hence

---

[13]Bonhoeffer, *Ethics,* p. 203.

[14]Ibid., p. 203. Karl Barth adds a powerful commentary on the concept of solidarity with the
world. "Solidarity with the world means full commitment to it, unreserved participation in
its situation, in the promise given it by creation, in its responsibility for the arrogance, sloth
and falsehood which reign within it, in its suffering under the resultant distress, but primarily
and supremely in the free grace of God demonstrated and addressed to it in Jesus Christ, and
therefore in its hope. . . . Solidarity with the world means that those who are genuinely pious
approach the children of the world as such, that those who are genuinely righteous are not
ashamed to sit down with the unrighteous as friends, that those who are genuinely wise do
not hesitate to seem to be fools among fools, and that those who are genuinely holy are not
too good or irreproachable to go down into 'hell' in a very secular fashion . . . since Jesus
Christ is the Savior of the world, [the church] can exist in worldly fashion, not unwillingly
nor with a bad conscience, but willingly and with a good conscience. It consists in the recognition that its members also bear in themselves and in some way actualise all human pos-
sibilities" (Barth, *Church Dogmatics* 4/3, pp. 773-74).

it does not know its own origin, state nor goal. It does not know what divides nor what unites. It does not know either its life and salvation or its death and destruction. It is blind to its own reality. Its existence is a groping in the dark.[15]

To know the world through mission is to know it as affirmed by God, even in its fall away from God's original purpose (Genesis 1:31; 1 Timothy 4:4).

REDEFINING THE MISSION: IT'S ABOUT SEEKING JUSTICE, NOT ONLY SAVING SOULS

It is hard to convince the church to have a mission in the world, says Brian McLaren, "when most Christians equate 'personal salvation' of individual 'souls' with the ultimate aim of Jesus."[16] The gospel *is* also about personal salvation; it *is* about the transformation of those who are spiritually dead into the life of Christ; it *is* about being reconciled to God through new birth into the family of God. But, as McLaren says, humans are not just individuals who happen to have souls that need to be saved. Humans have physical and social being as well as a spiritual life of the soul. Sin effects the whole person, not just the soul. Being estranged from God as a consequence of sin threw the whole of humanity into personal disgrace, social disorder and moral deviance. From the beginning our first parents and their offspring suffer tragic consequences of their fall away from God. Adam and Eve seek to provide covering for their nakedness, their children treat others with contempt and disregard for their dignity and human rights. Cain murders his brother; fathers sacrifice their firstborn sons in an attempt to avert the wrath of impersonal and unknown gods. But Jesus came to right wrongs, not only to create righteous people. A mission gospel goes right to the heart of humanity

---

[15]Barth, *Church Dogmatics* 4/3, p. 769.
[16]McLaren, *Generous Orthodoxy*, p. 107. McLaren continues this theme in his latest book, *The Last Word and the Word After That* (San Francisco: Jossey-Bass, 2005), p. 155.

and takes up the cause of humans in their time of need and distress. Claiming that salvation has come to humans without seeking to correct injustice and restore dignity and value to human life is to defraud humanity of the gospel; it is cheap grace. Offering salvation for the soul alone and promising peace and justice only in the life to come is to abandon Christ in this world while hoping to be with him in the next.

Thomas Torrance was born of missionary parents in China. While he was both a world-class academic theologian and prominent leader in the Church of Scotland, the mission of Christ called him into the world; and the reality of Christ came to him clothed with the humanity of men and women in every culture. He was not so much a student of human culture but of human need as viewed through the transparent humanity of Christ.

> The Church cannot be in Christ without being in Him as He is proclaimed to men in their need and without being in Him as He encounters us in and behind the existence of every man in his need. Nor can the Church be recognized as His except in that meeting of Christ with Himself in the depth of human misery, where Christ clothed with His Gospel meets with Christ clothed with the desperate need and plight of men.[17]

If the church cannot see Christ in the eyes of those who suffer in this world, it will fail to discern the face of Christ when it kneels to receive the communion of Christ. Paul did not scold the Corinthian church for improper administration of the elements at the Lord's Supper, but for the injustice of serving themselves while ignoring the lack of bread in the hands of others.

RECALIBRATING THE AIM: IT'S ABOUT HAVING A CLEAR TARGET, NOT JUST LOADING AND FIRING

It is no use having a target if the sight is not properly calibrated. To

---

[17]Thomas F. Torrance, "Service in Jesus Christ," in *Theological Foundations for Ministry*, ed. Ray S. Anderson (Edinburgh: T & T Clark, 1999), p. 724.

launching a satellite into space you must have specific goals and objectives. And without sufficient launching power, the rocket will never get beyond the pull of gravity and will fall back to earth. But it is not enough to blast off into space; the onboard computers must be carefully calibrated to place the satellite in orbit at exactly the right speed and distance.

The metaphor is an apt one, for the mission of a church does not ride on rails, like a train, but moves on a trajectory that requires faith in calculations that take into account the invisible, the unexpected and the untried! Many churches make the mistake of launching a mission without carefully calibrating its computers. The role of the Holy Spirit is not to provide raw power for launching a mission but to provide a guidance system by which the church can recalibrate its aim. Paul had to recalibrate his aim several times when he sought to accomplish his mission in Asia. Twice the Holy Spirit told him to go back and to set his sights higher! Finally, in a vision during the night, he heard a man from calling out, "Come over to Macedonia and help us" (Acts 16:9).

Emerging churches must not be so quick to launch its missions. It must occasionally pause to "hear the Macedonian call." This requires all the more a consensus of the Spirit on the part of the members of the church. Renewal of mission comes about through listening for this call, not by launching new models based on obsolete data. This has to do with counting the cost before undertaking a mission as well as measuring the distance that can be reached given resources at hand (see Luke 14:28-30). Some, even among the emerging churches, have attempted to reach a "bridge too far," and end up looking foolish when they wished to appear fearless.

UNLEASHING THE PEOPLE FOR MISSION: IT'S ABOUT RELEASING, NOT JUST REACHING

In faithfulness to his apostolic mandate, Paul targets Spain as the next mission horizon for the gospel. He could have made his plans to go directly to Spain and bypass the church in Rome. But he does not have the resources to undertake the mission on his own. He invited the Roman church (that had not to this point shown much interest in being an emerging church) to partner with him. He is as much interested in having them become involved in their own mission as in tapping their resources for his mission to Spain. He wrote for the sake of inspiring them to think beyond ministry, perhaps even to unleash some of their own people to accompany him. As far as we know, Paul never did reach Spain, though he ended up in a prison in Rome. It is possible, however, that the church at Rome did in fact undertake the mission, not just to Spain but to what we know today as Europe and even the Scandinavian countries. The church at Rome apparently did become an emerging church; those released for mission followed the roads and the armies into northern Europe.

While emerging churches have a mission of reaching the lost, they must also have the spiritual wisdom to release those who are found. Those who are gathered around the meal of Christ at the altar must arise with the mission of Christ burning in their hearts. We sup with Christ in order to run with him. The church needs to unleash it members and become a sending church rather than a gathering one. If the only theme song of the church is "Blest Be the Tie That Binds," it could get all tangled up in its own apron strings. The Spirit of Christ cannot be tethered to institutional programs or contained in the straight jacket of ecclesial politics.

CONCLUDING NONTHEOLOGICAL POSTSCRIPT

Jim Rayburn, founder of Young Life, in a personal conversation before he died in 1970, recounted to me his experience as a youth pastor in a church in Texas. "I found out that the kids would only accept me when I met them on their turf and won the right to talk about Christ to them on their terms. I spent most of my time on the playground and in their backyards. Their response to Christ was thrilling and powerful."

The church, however, did not see much of the kids, nor of Rayburn, and became impatient with his ministry. "I was given an ultimatum," Rayburn told me. "Bring the kids back into the youth program of the church or find another job." It did not take long for him to make his decision, and as a result, Young Life emerged, while the church remained inside its walls.

Christians are not the end users of the gospel. Nor is the existence of the church an end in itself—it is merely a means to an end. Where the property line that separates the church from the world ends, the kingdom of God begins. When Mary Magdalene encountered Jesus at his resurrection, obviously she did not want to let him go. "Do not hold on to me," Jesus told her, "but go . . ." (John 20:17). What marks emerging churches as different is that they let go of what the church has been in order to become the church that will be. When the Spirit speaks, as at Antioch, it is time to let go—and go.

10 IT'S ABOUT THE CHURCH AHEAD OF US, NOT ONLY THE CHURCH BEHIND US

We celebrated Reformation Sunday last week, on October 30, in the Lutheran church where I attend and teach. In the liturgy and sermon we were reminded of the tradition that defines this Protestant Lutheran denomination going back almost five hundred years to Martin Luther himself. The Augsburg Confession was cited as an expression of our legacy of freedom in the form of worship as well as our foundation in *sola scriptura*—the Word alone. The heady air of tradition was exhilarating and the visual signs and symbols stimulating. But even then, five hundred years is not so far back!

In 2005 the death of Pope John Paul II brought forth a rich pageant of liturgical and ecclesial tradition viewed on television throughout the world. We were reminded that John Paul II represented an unbroken line of 264 predecessors going back to St. Peter himself in the year A.D. 67. The church behind us has a powerful attraction and offers a compelling sense of security in a world where disposability and displacement threatens the very foundations on which we stand.

I think that I understand why more than a billion people find satisfaction and security in being attached to something so permanent and so mystically powerful as religious ritual that draws them into the *mysterium tremendum* of divine reality. A venerable history is far more compelling than a vulnerable future. A historical Christ (even though wrapped in tradition) is more predictable than a Christ emerging out of the future in the breath of the Spirit.

Several years ago I knelt by the gravesite of my great grandparents behind a church building that continues to serve a congregation in Norway for more than eight hundred years. As at Antioch, so in Rome, the Holy Spirit spoke and the church set apart some of its own members on a gospel mission. On behalf of my Viking ancestors in Norway, I thank them! There was a felt connection with the communion of saints to be sure. But there was nothing there except what the human spirit longs to touch. The spirit of my ancestors as well as all those who passed through that church over the years lies ahead, not behind.

During my study in Scotland I walked amid the ruins of the old Glencorse Parish church a few miles south of Edinburgh located on the grounds of the country estate where I lived. I was told that a Christian church was built on that small hilltop in or around the eighth century A.D. It was a former Druid worship site. The Druid stones were simply rolled down the hill and the foundation for a church was set in their place. (I walked down the hill and saw some of the Druid stones still there!) The church built was, of course, a Roman Catholic Church planted by missionaries out of Rome. If the apostle Paul never got to Spain, as was his plan, he certainly got to Rome (even as a prisoner) and his emergent theology apparently stuck with that church!

During that same time, I attended St. Giles church in the center of Edinburgh, and sat amid the oldest walls built in the eleventh century, which still provide a place of worship. I preached on Good Friday in the fourteenth-century Roslyn Chapel in the village near where we lived. Still in use as an Anglican church, it remains one of the few churches in Scotland not destroyed by Oliver Cromwell (1599-1658) as he sought to purify the Scottish church of its Catholic symbols.

My purpose in this book is not to minimize the faith of the fathers (and mothers!) who carried the gospel from century to century by their own conviction and sometimes-stubborn faith. Emerging churches respect and value the congregations of the faithful who brought the gospel to our generation. It is not as though we can turn our back on history and tradition. After all, Joseph made his children promise that they would take his bones with them when the Lord brought them out of Egypt so that he could be buried with his father Jacob and grandfather Abraham, in the land of promise. Four hundred years later, Joshua took those very bones with him across the Jordan to bury them next to Abraham. There is something to be said for having an anchor to the past that holds firm against the fickle and often contrary winds of the present. But anchors, like tradition, only serve to hold us in place. No sailor will raise the sails to the wind until the anchor is pulled. I would like to lift anchor, raise the sail and test the wind of the Spirit in order to move toward that which lies ahead of us.

Recall the words of Brian McLaren cited in the preface: "You see, if we have a new world, we will need a new church. We won't need a new religion per se, but a new framework for our theology. Not a new Spirit, but a new spirituality. Not a new Christ, but a new Christian. Not a new denomination, but a new kind of church in every denomination."[1]

There is no need of creating another church or another denomination. The Roman Catholics are not the only ones with a church behind them. Some of us who are in the Protestant tradition can trace our own historical roots far enough back to stir our spirit every October on Reformation Sunday! The emerging church is not about turning our backs on the church behind us as though to deny its contribution to the church that embraces us today. It is not either-or but both/and. In the same way that we feel the power of the past to remind us of our heritage, we need to feel the pull of the future so that fascination with what has been does not become an altar at which we worship. Emerging is not achieved by turning away from the church we came from but turning our face toward where we are meant to

[1]Brian McLaren, *Reinventing Your Church* (Grand Rapids: Zondervan, 1998), p. 13.

be when Jesus comes. At the same time, if we are permitted occasionally to glance back, we should beware of the reason to do it.

"Remember Lot's wife," warned Jesus. Each time I read those three words I want to say, "Wait a minute, what is the context for that?" From what immediately followed, Jesus apparently was reminding his disciples that fascination with what lies behind could turn them into a frozen monument that keeps them from becoming a flowing movement. "Those who try to make their life secure will lose it, but those who lose their life will keep it" (Luke 17:32-33). When the church inhales too much of the incense of its ancestors, it tends to become either droopy or dopey. But when children have breathed only the air of a scientific and sterile environment since birth, the smell of incense and the smoky light of candles may offer a spiritual home for their anxious souls.

WHAT HAS ANTIOCH TO DO WITH JERUSALEM?

The church at Jerusalem could always look back, and they often did, in order to be assured that Moses and the Messiah were on the same track. They carried on what came to be known as the "tradition of the Twelve" (see Acts 6:2; 1 Corinthians 15:5). This assured them of continuity with Jesus the Messiah. At the same time, circumcision represented for them continuity with the law of Moses. Delegates from the church at Jerusalem were sent to Antioch with the demand "Unless you are circumcised according to the custom of Moses, you cannot be saved" (Acts 15:1). Circumcision, originally given to Abraham as a covenant sign, has now become for the church at Jerusalem the religious equivalent and requirement of the law of Moses.

For Paul and the emerging church at Antioch, composed largely of Gentiles, this was untenable and nonnegotiable. Paul argued that continuity with Jesus the Messiah could not be established backward through a historical connection but only forward through an eschatological conversion. His encounter with the risen and ascended Messiah occurred within history but was not historically conditioned. In other words, he came to know Jesus of Nazareth first of all as one coming to him from the future rather than from the past. Rather than looking to the Christ behind him he turned to the Christ ahead of him. He could and did allow for the fact that the church at Jerusalem was also a church that had Christ as its founder and head. He also reckoned the apostles at Jerusalem to be true apostles, acknowledging that they were commissioned by the same Lord Jesus as he was.

Here we see that the emerging church at Antioch, which came out of the future by virtue of the Spirit of Christ gathering and baptizing both Jew and Gentile into the body of Christ, accepted, affirmed and claimed to be part of the community of Christ at Jerusalem. The Jerusalem church did not reciprocate, however. Paul made a trip in order to convince those at Jerusalem that not only was the church at Antioch a true church but they were part of the church that had historical continuity as well (Acts 15). While he did secure some kind of tacit agreement that allowed the Antioch community to include uncircumcised Gentiles, that agreement was not honored when "certain people came from James" (Galatians 2:12) continued to undermine his apostolic credentials and the churches that were established through his ministry (e.g., Corinth, see 2 Corinthians 10—11). Paul's attempt to maintain good relations with the church at Jerusalem is indicated by his massive fundraising project conducted throughout the churches to raise money for the church at Jerusalem to feed those who suffered from the famine.

My point is this: emerging churches affirm their place within the history of the church of Jesus Christ from the very beginning—they are built on the foundation of the apostles and the prophets. The cornerstone, however, is the living Christ, who comes out of the future in the power of the Spirit, not just the historical Jesus. The emerging church does have a common denominator with the church at Jerusalem, but it is not the apostolic foundation; it is the cornerstone—Christ Jesus himself—"In him the whole structure is joined together and grows in a holy temple in the Lord; in whom you [Gentiles!] are built together spiritually into a dwelling place for God" (Ephesians 2:21-22). When Christ the living cornerstone comes, he brings the foundation with him. But a foundation without the cornerstone is just a pile of stones!

THE APOSTOLIC EMERGING CHURCH

In the days following the death of Pope John Paul II, a friend who is a member of the Roman Catholic Church asked me how a Protestant could say that the church had an apostolic foundation when it had separated from Rome at the time of the Reformation. He was not challenging me to a debate but was curious as to how a Protestant would answer the question.

I responded by saying that the dispute over apostolic authority did not begin with the Reformation in the sixteenth century when Luther broke with Rome, nor did it begin in the eleventh century when Rome broke with the Eastern Orthodox churches (A.D. 1054). Rather, the argument over apostolic authority began between Jerusalem and Antioch in the first century. Paul claimed to be a true apostle of Christ even though he was not part of the tradition of the Twelve at Jerusalem.

According to the letters in the New Testament attributed to Paul, he was never completely accepted by the leaders of the church at Jerusalem as an apostle. But neither did he yield control of the churches that emerged out of Antioch to Jerusalem's apostolic authority. In his letter to the Galatians he made quite explicit the separation between him and his ministry from the church at Jerusalem. He said, first of all, that his own knowledge of Christ came by revelation, not through any contact with the apostles at Jerusalem. Only three years after his conversion and ministry at Antioch did he go to Jerusalem to meet with Peter and James, the Lord's brother, and then only for fifteen days. Fourteen more years passed before he went back to Jerusalem again (perhaps the Acts 15 meeting), where he reports, "we did not submit to them even for a moment, so that the truth of the gospel might always remain with you [Galatians]. . . . [T]hose leaders contributed nothing to me" (Galatians 2:5-6). To the Corinthian church he wrote, "I am not at all inferior to these super-apostles. . . . The signs of a true apostle were performed among you" (2 Corinthians 12:11-12).

The emerging churches that came out of Antioch, though not considered part of the chain of apostolic succession claimed by the later church of Rome, had their own claim for apostolic authority through Paul's direct commission by the risen Christ to be an apostle. What is at dispute is not whether the Antioch churches were under the authority of Christ but whether it was the tradition of the Christ emerging out of history or the Christ emerging out of the future that constituted apostolic authority. This is an issue that goes back to the very beginning of the Christian church.

While Paul did not, by all accounts, personally found the church at Rome, many of those that he names in his letter to the Roman church were converts from the churches that resulted from his apostolic ministry in Asia Minor. (See the list of greetings to specific persons in Romans 16.) At the same time, it may be that some believers fled the church at Jerusalem during persecution and ended up in Rome. It was, however, under Paul's urging that the church at Rome was pointed to mission work in Spain and, by inference, into present-day Europe. The point is not to play Paul against Peter—both were recognized by the early church as apostles. Peter was actually one of the first to make a case for the baptism of uncircumcised Gentiles in the Jerusalem church. Luke gives considerable attention to this event (Acts 10—11). Why then did the Jerusalem community not follow through with this and be more open to Paul's ministry to the Gentiles? I can only speculate, but my feeling is that the emerging church at Jerusalem, even though it had apostolic authority and leadership, did not develop an emergent theology. It was Paul, at Antioch, who developed the theological basis for the emerging church.

The discussion over apostolic authority and continuity, as I pointed out to my friend, must begin with the question, What has Antioch to do with Jerusalem? Or to put the question more theologically, Which Jesus is the true Apostle? The Jesus of history represented by the "tradition of the Twelve," or the Jesus at the right hand of the Father and emerging in the church as the Lord who is the Spirit?

The church at Jerusalem and the tradition of the Twelve tied their apostleship to the Moses tradition, but Paul argued that it is Jesus himself—the true seed of Abraham—who gives apostolic authority. The fact is, the issue of apostolic authority does not rest on either Peter or Paul but on Jesus himself, who is the true Apostle of the kingdom of God, and thus of the church. The author of the book of Hebrews identifies Jesus as "the apostle and high priest of our confession. . . . [W]orthy of more glory than Moses" (Hebrews 3:1, 3). There it is! Too bad that Paul did not have this text to buttress his argument!

In the New Testament there appear to have been several levels of apostleship, with many more than the original Twelve called to be apostles. James, the brother of Jesus, was considered an apostle and one of the pillars of the church in Jerusalem (2 Corinthians 11:5; 12:11). Barnabas was called an apostle (Acts 14:1, 6, 14), as were Andronicus and Junias—a woman! (Romans 16:6).[2]

Greek Orthodox theologian John Zizioulas says, "Apostolicity comes to the Church from the side of the future. It is the anticipation of the end, the final nature of the Church that reveals her apostolic character."[3] Lutheran theologian Wolfhart Pannenberg stresses the eschatological nature of the apostolic character of the church based on the fact that the Holy Spirit is the presence of the Christ who is coming as well as of the historical Christ.

The only criterion of apostolic teaching in this sense is whether and to what degree it is able to set forth the final truth and comprehensive universality of the person and work of Christ in the transforming and saving significance of his resurrection and its

---

[2]"The complex historical event of crucifixion and resurrection shattered many possible kinds of continuity, but it could serve only to cement together the pattern of crucifixion and resurrection in the teaching, and in the life and death, of Jesus, and the same pattern in the theology and apostolic practice of Paul" (C. K Barrett, *The Signs of an Apostle* [New York: Harper & Row, 1970], p. 81).

[3]John Zizioulas, *Being as Communion* (Crestwood, N.Y.: St. Vladimir's Seminary Press, 1985), pp. 179-80.

power that gives light to the world. . . . The vita apostolica does not mean copying the way of life of the apostolic age or what we think that way of life was, and it certainly cannot be lived by borrowing this or that form of life from the regulations of the apostles. That which was apostolic then may be irrelevant today or may even be a hindrance to our apostolic tasks.[4]

There is a threefold apostolic ministry of Christ that provides the basis for the apostolic nature of the emerging church. The first form of Christ's apostolic ministry is that of the historical Jesus, who, as the first apostle, gathered the Twelve around him and invested in them his own apostolic authority. This is what I call Christ's incarnational apostolic ministry. The second is that of the resurrected Christ who gathered the eleven disciples and reconstituted them as his apostles. This is the gospel that Peter preached on the day of Pentecost and that Paul received directly from the risen Christ. This is what I call the Christ's empowering apostolic ministry. The third is the apostolic ministry of the Christ who will return and who is returning through the presence and power of the Holy Spirit. This is what I call Christ's transformational apostolic ministry. Figure 10.1 depicts the threefold form of Christ's apostolic ministry.

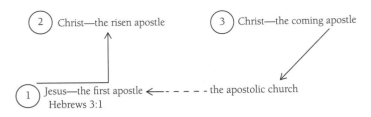

Figure 10.1. The threefold form of Christ's apostolic ministry

This threefold apostolic ministry is (1) that of the historical Christ (incarnational), (2) that of the risen and proclaimed Christ (kerygmatic),

---

[4]Wolfhart Pannenberg, *The Church* (Philadelphia: Westminster Press, 1983), pp. 56-57.

and (3) that of the coming Christ (eschatological). These three are simultaneous and always contemporary, for the apostolic life of the church is founded on Jesus Christ, the living cornerstone, the same, "yesterday and today and forever" (Hebrews 13:8).

Jesus' own life was marked by his self-conscious testimony to the fact that he had received his appointment and commission directly from the Father. As the "sent one" he bore in his own person the very personality of the Father (John 14:7). "Whoever welcomes one such child in my name welcomes me, and whoever welcomes me welcomes not me but the one who sent me" (Mark 9:37). The chosen ones (the Twelve) are brought within the circle of Jesus' own "sending and returning" and thus become bound to his own apostolic ministry as the Son of the Father. "You are those who have stood by me in my trials; and I confer on you, just as my Father has conferred on me, a kingdom, so that you may eat and drink at my table in my kingdom, and you will sit on thrones judging the twelve tribes of Israel" (Luke 22:28-30). The apostleship of Jesus continued after his death and resurrection, and will only come to an end when he "hands over the kingdom" to God the Father, having completed his commission as the Lord of the kingdom (1 Corinthians 15:23-28).

Following Pentecost, Paul considers Jesus to be the apostle through whom all apostolic ministry is released in the world by the Holy Spirit. "Now the Lord is the Spirit, and where the Spirit of the Lord is, there is freedom" (2 Corinthians 3:17). The Holy Spirit is the advance work of the coming Christ, leading the church in its mission into the world and equipping the church through all of its members for the apostolic ministry of Christ.

As the risen and ascended Lord who is coming, Christ's apostolic authority reaches toward us into the present time as the creative power for the church's apostolic ministry in every generation. Paul viewed the coming Christ as his apostolic authority who, by virtue of his Holy Spirit, was already at work in transforming the old into the new.

Think of us in this way, as servants of Christ and stewards of God's mysteries. Moreover, it is required of stewards that they be found trustworthy. But with me it is a very small thing that I should be judged by you or by any human court. I do not even judge myself. I am not aware of anything against myself, but I am not thereby acquitted. It is the Lord who judges me. Therefore do not pronounce judgment before the time, before the Lord comes, who will bring to light the things now hidden in darkness and will disclose the purposes of the heart. Then each one will receive commendation from God. (1 Corinthians 4:1-5)

Christ's threefold apostolic ministry will continue until his kingdom reign is completed. When that is accomplished, Christ will hand over the kingdom to the Father and his apostolic commission will be concluded. As Paul anticipates the end of the age, he envisions the apostolic ministry of Christ coming to a close. In the sequence of final events the coming of Christ will bring about the resurrection of all who belong to him. "Then comes the end, when he hands over the kingdom to God the Father, after he has destroyed every ruler and every authority and power. . . . When all things are subjected to him, then the Son himself will also be subjected to the one who put all things in subjection under him, so that God may be all in all" (1 Corinthians 15:24, 28).

The nature of the church, argued Paul, could not merely rest on a historical link with Jesus and the twelve disciples, but on the Spirit of the resurrected Christ who has "broken down the dividing wall [of] hostility" and created in himself "one new humanity in place of the two" (Ephesians 2:14-15). In regard to the nature of the church, the critical term for Paul is "new creation." This is "from God, who reconciled us to himself through Christ, and has given us the ministry of reconciliation" (2 Corinthians 5:17-18). The connection between the old covenant and the new covenant is a real one, but also one that is eschatological in nature. The relation is not predicated on historical necessity but on covenant faithfulness on the part of God.

With full assurance of Christ's continuing apostolic ministry, Paul welcomed the uncircumcised into the church on evidence of the Spirit's ministry, and set the church free from legalistic and crippling constraints where he saw the Spirit bringing gifts of grace to each member.

IT'S ABOUT THE FINAL CENTURY, NOT THE FIRST CENTURY

When Christ returns to bring to consummation his apostolic work now taking place by the gift of the Holy Spirit, it will be the final century. The Spirit is thus preparing the people of God for this "last century." While the first century of the church is normative for the revelation of Christ as the incarnation of God and the redemption of humans from sin and death, the return of the same Christ and the resurrection from the dead constitute the normative praxis of the Spirit.

Apostolic authority comes to the church out of the future, not from the past. The presence of the Spirit is the anticipation of the return of Christ as the chief apostle. Paul makes this clear when he wrote to the church at Ephesus reminding them that in receiving the Holy Spirit they were "marked with the seal of the promised Holy Spirit; this is the pledge of our inheritance toward redemption as God's own people, to the praise of his glory" (Ephesians 1:13-14). The "pledge" is literally the first installment or the "down payment" (*arrabōn*) on the inheritance promised as the eschatological fulfillment of God's promise.

Emerging churches become apostolic when they seek to define and make clear the apostolic work of Christ in the present century rather than the first century. Historical theology tends to look back to the first century of Christian experience as normative and apostolic. An emergent theology looks toward the "final century," or the century in which Christ can be expected to return, as normative and apostolic. Moving ever closer to this final century, the church expects the kingdom of God to be present in ever new and renewing ways.

The resurrection and ascension of Christ followed by Pentecost and the praxis of the Holy Spirit during the present age orients the church to the final century of historical life rather than merely to the first century. Apostolic authority thus comes into the present from the future rather than from the past. Paul anticipates the return of the Christ he has already encountered. The church ahead of him, not just the church behind him, produced his vision of what the church should look like when Jesus comes. The praxis of the ministry of the Holy Spirit can be understood as the church that God desires to behold at the end, not merely a replica of the church that struggled to come to birth in first century.

This is the perspective that Paul had during the first century. He looked toward the coming of Christ as the final word of approval on his own teaching and ministry. While the historical Jesus and the cross were central to Paul's theology of redemption and creation, the Spirit of the resurrected and coming Christ was normative for interpreting the past events in light of the coming ones. All of Paul's emergent theology was illumined from above and came to life below as "in a mirror dimly" (1 Corinthians 13:12).

In my early nears of pastoral ministry I discovered a book of poems by Sister Madeleva that nourished my soul. A member of the Sisters of the Holy Cross and former president of St. Mary's College for Catholic women, she has written and published over a dozen books of poetry. In the preface to this particular book, she said that she never published her poems until they had gone through the required waiting time. She heeded the advice of Saint John Baptist de La Salle who warned, "A good work divulged before its time is half destroyed." As a result, she wrote, "My words have had to work for their living." In the last poem in the book, she wrote, "I shall not forget the four last things."[5]

Unfortunately, I fear that *An Emergent Theology for Emerging Churches*

---

[5]M. Madeleva, "Ballade on Eschatology," in *The Four Last Things: Collected Poems* (New York: Macmillan, 1959), pp. 174-75.

is half-destroyed; I have not had the luxury of passing it through the sieve of time. I have always remembered, however, Sister Madeleva's poignant words, "I shall not forget the four last things." For over forty years I have tried to make these words that I have written work for their living. If they appear untried and untested, it is only due to the lack of a literary license, not to a sophomoric soul. And that I should be inspired by a Roman Catholic nun is all the more fitting in light of the shadow that the life and death of Pope John Paul II cast over this chapter.

THE FOUR LAST THINGS

What are the four last things?

Being in Christ, not just believing in Christ. The life of emerging churches is grounded in their conception and birth as the community of those who are children of God, whose lives are personally drawn into the very life and being of Christ. Those who are born anew by the Spirit of God are not merely Christians, or followers of Christ, but have been placed (adopted) into the personal relationship between the Son and the Father as children of God and "joint heirs with Christ" (Romans 8:17). The confession of faith that we recite in the form of a creed (*credo* = "I believe") can be recited from rote memory. The words are as old as the formation of the earliest Christian community. "I believe in God, the Father Almighty, Maker of heaven and earth. And in Jesus Christ." One could say the words and even believe that they are true, but not yet "be in Christ." Belief is confessional, belonging is communal. The philosopher Michael Polanyi wrote, "Our believing is conditioned at its source by our belonging."[6]

The apostle Paul experienced the reality of Christ before coming to believe in him. This became the creative edge of the emerging church's proclamation of the gospel. In every letter that Paul wrote there is an underlying theme of union with Christ. Participation in the life of Christ is

---

[6]Michael Polanyi, *Personal Knowledge* (London: Routledge & Kegan Paul, 1958), p. 322.

not an extracurricular option for Christians, it begins with being baptized into Christ by the Spirit (1 Corinthians 12:13). He reminded the Christians at Colossae of their experience of Christ, not just of their faith in Christ. He calls this a *mystērion*—not just a mystery, as though it is a hidden secret, but a reality so intimate and personal that it defies explanation in rational terms.[7] "Christ in you, the hope of glory" (Colossians 1:27). It's about Christ being in us, Paul said, not just our believing in him. Through the Spirit of Christ, something of Christ himself is within us—not just a spiritual sensation but the very being of Christ is imparted to us through the Spirit. "Examine yourselves," Paul exhorts. "Do you not realize that Jesus Christ is in you?" (2 Corinthians 13:5).

Paul followed this with the corresponding truth that is equally a *mystērion* (though he did not use the word)—"Your life is hidden with Christ in God" (Colossians 3:3). When my mind attempts to grasp this truth it loses its grip, and I can only hold it in my hand like a living bird. It will perish if I clench my fist over it. If I am still and allow it to rest upon my palm, I feel its life quiver and the pulse of its rapid heartbeat. Not only has the Holy Spirit imparted to my inner soul some of the life of Jesus Christ, that same Spirit has taken a part of my soul and imparted into the life of God—I am hidden with Christ in God! I find it difficult to believe, but I know it to be true. Polanyi once said, "We know more than we can tell." There are truths that we know before we believe. He called this kind of knowledge "tacit knowledge."[8]

Emerging theology is about being in Christ, hidden with Christ in

---

[7]Karl Barth offers this explanation of the *mystērion:* "In the New Testament mysterion denotes an event in the world of time and space which is directly initiated and brought to pass by God alone, so that in distinction from all other events it is basically a mystery to human cognition in respect of its origin and possibility. If it discloses itself to man, this will be not from without, but only from within, through itself and therefore once again only through God's revelation. . . . Faith as a human action is nowhere called [in Scripture] a mystery, nor is Christian obedience, nor love, nor hope, nor the existence and function of the ecclesia, nor its proclamation of the Gospel, nor its tradition as such, nor baptism, nor the Lord's Supper" (Barth, *Church Dogmatics* 4/4, trans. Geoffrey W. Bromiley [Edinburgh: T & T Clark, 1969], pp. 108-9).
[8]Michael Polanyi, *The Tacit Dimension* (London: Routledge & Kegan Paul, 1967).

God. The Christ who is present to me and with me gives me presence to and with the very being of God. There is part of me that is already secure and safe with Jesus in heaven. I came to know that as a child; I am coming to believe it now.

Living the sacramental life of grace, not only dispensing sacramental grace. In the writings of Paul the word *grace* occurs eighty times. While he no doubt valued and taught the role of sacrament and symbol with regard to the community's life of faith, he did not bind grace to sacrament but sacrament to grace. Even in regard to baptism, he defers to others, though admitting that he did baptize some (1 Corinthians 1:14-16). Though the Latin translation of the New Testament made by Jerome used the word *sacramentum* to translate *mystērion* (the word that Paul used of marriage), Paul's other use of the same word does not denote a sacramental union, such as the church later developed. Members of the emerging church lived out grace in their daily life, and when they didn't, Paul rebuked them: "For by grace you have been saved through faith, and this is not your own doing; it is the gift of God—not the result of works, so that no one may boast" (Ephesians 2:8-9). To revert to life under the legalism of the law is to nullify grace, Paul reminds the Galatians (Galatians 2:21).

Grace is not a commodity that can be packaged and dispensed. It is the life of the Spirit that renews and transforms every facet of both the inner and outer life of those who belong to Christ. Paul's only reference to the Lord's Supper is in connection with the disorder at the common meal, in which the Corinthians were failing to practice the sacramental grace of sharing with one another. There is no suggestion in Paul's rebuke and instructions that the problem was in the act of dispensing the elements of bread and wine that represent the body and blood of Jesus. The sacramental act is participation in the meal itself, not in a ritual of administration.

We should understand that the grace of sacrament is Jesus himself, who unites the real presence of God with humanity in his own person. He is the primary sacrament from which all sacramental life flows and has its origin.[9] The essence of sacrament may be defined as a gracious invitation to participate in the life of God along with a gracious impartation of a spiritual benefit. When Jesus gave the invitation of grace, it included an impartation of grace. "Come to me, all you who are weary and are carrying heavy burdens, and I will give you rest. Take my yoke upon you, and learn from me; for I am gentle and humble in your heart, and you will find rest for your souls. For my yoke is easy, and my burden is light" (Matthew 11:28-30). Living a sacramental life of grace means living with openness to the needs of others and to persons who feel estranged from God. In our daily conversation we should speak with others so that our words "give grace to those who hear" (Ephesians 4:29). "Welcome those who are weak in faith. . . . [F]or God has welcomed them" (Romans 14:1-3). "Welcome one another, therefore, just as Christ has welcomed you" (Romans 15:7).

Our need does not cause the grace of God to be dispensed for us, but God's grace in our lives brings us to the altar. Grace lives on both sides of the altar, at both ends of the Table of the Lord. If we approach God, it is as those already graced with his love. When the prodigal son approached his father's home, he did not expect grace and asked only to be taken in as one of the servants. Jesus said, "But while he was still far off, his father saw him and was filled with compassion; he ran and put his arms around him and kissed him" (Luke 15:20). The sacrament was not in the celebration that followed but in the embrace on the road. I have been embraced with the arms of grace while still trying to find my way home.

Being a truthful church, not just the true church. Roman Catholic scholar Hans Küng drew a rebuke from the pope when he asked: "Is the church then credible, does she help men to be truthfully Christian, to be truth-

---

[9]Karl Barth speaks of Jesus as the one and primary sacrament from which all other sacraments find their reality. "A sacramental continuity stretches backwards into the existence of the people of Israel, whose Messiah he is, and forwards into the existence of the apostolate and the church founded upon the apostolate" (Karl Barth, *Church Dogmatics* 2/1, trans. Geoffrey W. Bromiley [Edinburgh: T & T Clark, 1964], p. 54).

fully human?" A truthful church, he argued, is a church that is provisional, that is, not an end in itself; unassuming, that is, to be constantly in need of grace rather than dispensing it; ministering, that is, taking the way of the cross rather than the way of triumphal procession; conscious of guilt, that is, exists in grace and not in righteousness; and finally, obedient, that is, remains free from all claims except the radical will of God as revealed in Jesus Christ. "Wherever, among individuals or groups, there is a truthful church," Küng added, "there occurs . . . a deepening and humanising of the world and of man; there dawns something of that complete justice, that eternal life, that cosmic peace, that true freedom and that final reconciliation of mankind with God, which one day God's consummated kingdom will bring."[10]

What caused the pope to censor Küng was the fact that he called into question the existence of a true church that was not also truthful in its daily life and practice. To be a truthful church is to make the truth of Christ an incarnational reality that is present in the world and to the world as the very presence of Christ. One of my former students, Todd Speidell, reinforced this point when he wrote:

> Christ presents himself in the depths of human need—the hungry, the thirsty, the naked, the sick, the imprisoned (Mt. 25:31ff.). The stranger among us, the homeless and psychologically debilitated, may be the place of Christ's presence among us. The Gospel of Matthew does not exhort us simply to be like Christ—ministering to the needy "as Jesus would" (which implies that he is not actively present but merely serves as a model for our social action)—but attests that Christ discloses himself through the stranger. We must be where Christ is, and act where he acts.[11]

---

[10]Hans Küng, *Truthfulness: The Future of the Church* (London: Sheed & Ward, 1968), pp. 126, 51, 215.

[11]Todd Speidell, "Incarnational Social Ethics," in *Incarnational Ministry* (Colorado Springs: Helmers & Howard, 1990), p. 146.

Emerging churches do not claim to be the one, true church, as though other churches are false or, even more to the point, as though it is true because it merely exists. The evidences for truth, as Paul argued, are not in one's own life but in the lives of those who are transformed by the life of Christ to serve the true God. Writing to the church at Thessalonica, he said that the message of the gospel came to them not only in words "but also in power and in the Holy Spirit. . . . [A]nd how you turned to God from idols, to serve a living and true God" (1 Thessalonians 1:5, 9). Truth is not something that the church possesses but what the Spirit produces. "When the Spirit of truth comes, he will guide you into all the truth; for he will not speak on his own, but will speak whatever he hears, and he will declare to you the things that are to come. He will glorify me, because he will take what is mine and declare it to you" (John 16:13-14).

The tragedy of truth is not the lie that contradicts it but its lack of incarnational witness. Jesus brought truth to humans through the incarnation of love and redemption. The truth is that God himself is given to us through the person of Jesus Christ, not just information about God. The apostle Paul presents a clear vision of this truth when he wrote, "When we cry, 'Abba! Father!' it is that very Spirit bearing witness with our spirit that we are children of God. . . . [T]hat very Spirit intercedes with sighs too deep for words" (Romans 8:15-16, 26). Paul reminds us that the language of the Spirit is the language of Jesus—it is the wordless language of the soul of God. The soul can bear things that seem unbearable to the mind. The soul can speak of things for which there are no words. When the church learns to be silent in the presence of the Word, it speaks the truth.

Being the church, not just going to church. If you were to ask the apostle Paul, Did you go to church today? he would stare at you dumbfounded! The people at Antioch did not just go to church, they were the church! Paul's analogy of the body of Christ was more than a metaphor of the church, it was meant to display the anatomy of belief. Believers *are* the body of Christ (1 Corinthians 12:27); they *are* a "holy temple in the Lord" (Ephesians 2:21); they *are* one body in Christ (Romans 12:5); their bodies *are* "members of Christ" (1 Corinthians 6:15). Jesus said, "Where two or three are gathered in my name, I am there among them" (Matthew 18:20).

The emerging church had its times of gathering. It was while they were worshiping the Lord and fasting that Saul and Barnabas were selected by the Holy Spirit to go on what would become the first mission journey (Acts 13:1-3). The church was not a place but an assembly of believers in a certain place. The human body, to follow Paul's analogy, is an assembly of parts that comprise the whole body. The parts of the human body are connected in such a way that "no assembly is required!" To press the analogy a bit further, we do say on occasion, "I had to pull myself together in order to get out of the house on time for my appointment." Or we might say, "I must have been out of my mind to think I could get away with that!" We all know what that means. We have all left our senses at times! Not that our brain is in the closet and one leg is in the bedroom while another in the family room, but that we have to let go of all the distractions and tasks that demand time and energy in order to focus on moving the body. In somewhat the same way, the anatomy of the church has many members that are all part of the body even though separated by time and space.

In the case of the body of Christ, some assembly is required! When Paul wrote to the Corinthian believers he said, "When you come together as a church . . ." (1 Corinthians 11:18). Did he mean that the church only came into existence when the members assembled? Hardly. The members themselves are the church (Ephesians 2:21; 1 Corinthians 6:19).

The emerging church is about being the church, like a family. It is an everyday reality with occasional gatherings and some celebrations. Being the body of Christ is a domestic as well as public practice of kingdom living. Being the church is as much a transformation of the secular sphere into sacred service as it is filling the sanctuary with ordinary saints. The Spirit of Christ has provided all the parts—some assembly is required.

BIBLIOGRAPHY

Anderson, Ray S. "An Emerging Church." In *Ministry on the Fireline: A Practical Theology for an Empowered Church*. Downers Grove, Ill.: InterVarsity Press, 1993.

———. *Minding God's Business*. Grand Rapids: Eerdmans, 1986.

———. *Ministry on the Fireline: A Practical Theology for an Empowered Church*. Downers Grove, Ill.: InterVarsity Press, 1993.

———. *The New Age of Soul: Spiritual Wisdom for a New Millennium*. Eugene, Ore.: Wipf & Stock, 2001.

———. "The Sociocultural Implications of a Christian Perspective of Humanity." In *The Shape of Practical Theology: Empowering Ministry with Theological Praxis*. Downers Grove, Ill.: InterVarsity Press, 2001.

———. *The Soul of Ministry: Forming Leaders for God's People*. Louisville: Westminster John Knox, 1997.

———. "Theology as Rationality." In *Christian Scholar's Review* 4, no. 2 (1974).

Anderson, Ray S., ed. *Theological Foundations for Ministry*. Grand Rapids: Eerdmans, 1999.

Barrett, C. K. *The Signs of an Apostle*. New York: Harper & Row, 1970.

Bartchy, Scott. "Power, Submission, and Sexual Identity Among the Early Christians." In *Essays on New Testament Christianity,* edited by C. Robert Wetzel. Cincinnati: Standard Publishing, 1978.

Barth, Karl. *Church Dogmatics* 1/1. Translated by Geoffrey W. Bromiley. 2nd ed. Edinburgh: T & T Clark, 1975.

———. *Church Dogmatics* 2/1, translated by Geoffrey W. Bromiley. Edinburgh: T & T Clark, 1964.

———. *Church Dogmatics* 4/1, translated by Geoffrey W. Bromiley. Edinburgh: T & T Clark, 1961.

———. *Church Dogmatics* 4/2, translated by Geoffrey W. Bromiley. Edinburgh: T & T Clark, 1958.

———. *Church Dogmatics* 4/3, translated by Geoffrey W. Bromiley. Edinburgh: T & T Clark, 1961.

———. *Church Dogmatics* 4/4, translated by Geoffrey W. Bromiley. Edinburgh: T & T Clark, 1969.

———. *Ethics,* edited by Dietrich Braun; translated by Geoffrey W. Bromiley. New York: Seabury Press, 1981.

Boer, Harry R. *Pentecost and Missions.* Grand Rapids: Eerdmans, 1961.

Bonhoeffer, Dietrich. *Christology.* New York: Harper & Row, 1966.

———. *Ethics.* New York: Macmillan, 1955.

———. *Letters and Papers From Prison.* New York: Macmillan, 1971.

———. *Meditating on the Word.* Cambridge, Mass.: Cowley, 1986.

———. *Sanctorum Communio: A Theological Study of the Sociology of the Church.* Minneapolis: Fortress, 1998.

Brooten, Bernadette. "Junia . . . Outstanding Among the Apostles." In *Women Priests,* edited by L. Swidler and A. Swidler. New York: Paulist Press, 1977.

Brunner, Emil. *The Christian Doctrine of the Church, Faith and the Consummation.* Dogmatics 3. London: Lutterworth Press, 1962.

———. *Man in Revolt.* Philadelphia: Westminster Press, 1979.

———. *The Misunderstanding of the Church.* London: Lutterworth Press, 1952.

Buxton, Graham. *Dancing in the Dark: The Privilege of Participating in the Ministry of Christ.* London: Paternoster, 2001.

Carr, Wesley. "Towards a Contemporary Theology of the Holy Spirit." In *Scottish Journal of Theology* 28, no. 7 (1975).

Carroll, Colleen. *The New Faithful: Why Young Adults are Embracing Christian Orthodoxy.* Chicago: Loyola Press, 2002.

Carson, D. A. *Becoming Conversant with the Emerging Church: Understanding a Movement and its Implications.* Grand Rapids: Zondervan, 2005.

Chandler, Russell. *Understanding the Age.* Dallas: Word, 1988.

Cox, Harvey. *The Secular City.* New York: Macmillan, 1966.

————. *Fire From Heaven: The Rise of Pentecostal Spirituality and the Re-shaping of Religion in the Twenty-First Century.* Reading, Mass.: Addison-Wesley, 1995.

De Mello, Anthony. *Song of the Bird.* New York: Doubleday, 1981.

Drane, John. *What Is the New Age Saying to the Church?* London: Marshal Pickering, 1991.

Ford, David F. "Faith in the Cities: Corinth and the Modern City." In *On Being the Church: Essays on the Christian Community,* edited by Colin E. Gunton and Daniel W. Hardy. Edinburgh: T & T Clark, 1989.

Foster, Richard. *Celebration of Discipline: The Path to Spiritual Growth.* San Francisco: Harper & Row, 1978.

Fox, Matthew. *Original Blessing: A Primer in Creation Spirituality Presented in Four Paths, Twenty-six Themes, and Two Questions.* Santa Fe, N.M.: Bear, 1983.

Franke, John R. *The Character of Theology: An Introduction to Its Nature, Task, and Purpose.* Grand Rapids: Baker, 2005.

————. "The Nature of Theology: Culture, Language, and Truth." In *Christianity and the Postmodern Turn: Six Views,* edited by Myron B. Penner. Grand Rapids: Brazos, 2005.

Franke, John R., and Stanley Grenz. *Beyond Foundationalism: Shaping Theology in a Postmodern Context.* Louisville: Westminster John Knox, 2001.

Gibbs, Eddie, and Ryan K. Bolger. *Emerging Churches: Creating Christian Community in Postmodern Cultures.* Grand Rapids: Baker, 2005.

Gibran, Kahlil. *Sand and Foam.* New York: Alfred Knopf, 1954.

Gillquist, Peter E. *Becoming Orthodox: A Journey to the Ancient Christian Faith.* Ben Lomond, Calif.: Conciliar Press, 1992.

Gillquist, Peter E., ed. *Coming Home: Why Protestant Clergy Are Becoming Orthodox.* Ben Lomand, Calif.: Conciliar Press, 1995.

Grant, Robert. "Trauma Spirituality," *The Orange County Register,* October 14, 1999.

Green, Michael. *I Believe in the Holy Spirit*. Rev. ed. Grand Rapids: Eerdmans, 2004.

Guder, Darrell L. *Be My Witnesses: The Church's Mission, Message, and Messengers*. Grand Rapids: Eerdmans, 1985.

———. *The Continuing Conversion of the Church*. Grand Rapids: Eerdmans, 2000.

Guder, Darrell L., ed. *Missional Church: A Vision for the Sending of the Church in North America*. Grand Rapids: Eerdmans, 1998.

Hanegraaff, Wouter J. *New Age Religion and Western Culture: Esotericism in the Mirror of Secular Thought*. New York: E. J. Brill, 1996.

Hauerwas, Stanley. *A Community of Character*. Notre Dame, Ind.: University of Notre Dame Press, 1981.

Heelas, Paul. *The New Age Movement: The Celebration of the Self and the Sacralization of Modernity*. Cambridge, Mass.: Blackwell, 1996.

Heidegger, Martin. *An Introduction to Metaphysics*. New Haven, Conn.: Yale University Press, 1959.

Heschel, Abraham. *The Prophets*. Vol. 2. New York: Harper & Row, 1962.

Irenaeus *Against Heresies* 1.3.17.1, Ante-Nicene Christian Library. Edinburgh: T & T Clark, 1868.

Jeanrond, Werner. "Community and Authority." In *On Being the Church: Essays on the Christian Community*, edited by Colin E. Gunton and Daniel W. Hardy. Edinburgh: T & T Clark, 1989.

Jones, Tony. *Postmodern Youth Ministry: Exploring Cultural Shifts, Creating Holistic Connections, Cultivating Authentic Community*. Grand Rapids: Zondervan, 2001.

Kim, Seyoon. *Paul and the New Perspective: Second Thoughts on the Origin of Paul's Gospel*. Grand Rapids: Eerdmans, 2002.

Kimball, Dan. *The Emerging Church: Vintage Christianity for a New Generation*. Grand Rapids: Zondervan, 2003.

Kraus, C. Norman. *Jesus Christ Our Lord: Christology from a Disciple's Perspective*. Scottdale, Penn.: Herald, 1987.

Küng, Hans. *The Church*. London: Sheed & Ward, 1967.

————. *Truthfulness: The Future of the Church.* London: Sheed & Ward, 1968.

Ladd, George. *A Theology of the New Testament,* edited by Donald Hagner. Rev. ed. Grand Rapids: Eerdmans, 1993.

Long, Jimmy. *Emerging Hope: A Strategy for Reaching Postmodern Generations.* Downers Grove, Ill.: InterVarsity Press, 2005.

Madeleva, M. "Ballade on Eschatology." In *The Four Last Things: Collected Poems.* New York: Macmillan, 1959.

Marsden, George. *Reforming Fundamentalism: Fuller Seminary and the New Evangelicalism.* Grand Rapids: Eerdmans, 1987.

McDonald, Gordon. *The Life God Blesses.* Nashville: Thomas Nelson, 1994.

McLaren, Brian. *A Generous Orthodoxy.* Grand Rapids: Zondervan, 2004.

————. *The Last Word and the Word After That: A Tale of Faith, Doubt, and a New Kind of Christianity.* San Francisco: Jossey-Bass, 2005.

————. *A New Kind of Christian: A Tale of Two Friends on a Spiritual Journey.* San Francisco: Jossey-Bass, 2001.

————. *Reinventing Your Church.* Grand Rapids: Zondervan, 1998.

McRoberts, Kerry D. *New Age or Old Lie?* Peabody, Mass.: Hendrickson, 1989.

Melton, J. Gordon, Jerome Clark and Aidan A. Kelly. *New Age Encyclopedia: A Guide to the Beliefs, Concepts, Terms, People, and Organizations That Make up the New Global Movement Toward Spiritual Development, Health and Healing, Higher Consciousness, and Related Subjects.* Detroit: Gale Research, 1990.

Middleton, J. Richard, and Brian J. Walsh. *Truth Is Stranger Than It Used to Be: Biblical Faith in a Postmodern Age.* Downers Grove, Ill.: InterVarsity Press, 1995.

Miller, Arthur. *After the Fall.* New York: Viking Press, 1964.

Miller, Keith. *The Secret Life of the Soul.* Nashville: Broadman & Holman, 1997.

Moltmann, Jürgen. *The Church in the Power of the Spirit.* New York: Harper & Row, 1977.

————. *God in Creation: A New Theology of Creation and the Spirit of God.* San Francisco: Harper & Row, 1985.

————. *Man: Christian Anthropology in the Conflicts of the Present,* translated by John Sturdy. Philadelphia: Fortress, 1974.

Murphy, Nancey. *Beyond Liberalism and Fundamentalism.* Valley Forge, Penn.: Trinity Press International, 1996.

Pannenberg, Wolfhart. *The Church.* Philadelphia: Westminster Press, 1983.

Pedersen, John. *Israel: Its Life and Culture,* vol. 1. London: Oxford University Press, 1973.

Pelikan, Jaroslav. *The Christian Tradition: A History of the Development of Doctrine.* Chicago: University of Chicago Press, 1971.

Penner, Myron B., ed. *Christianity and the Postmodern Turn: Six Views.* Grand Rapids: Brazos, 2005.

Percesepe, Gary John. "The Unbearable Lightness of Being Postmodern." *Christian Scholar's Review* 20, no. 2 (1990).

Peterson, Eugene. "Spirituality for all the Wrong Reasons." *Christianity Today,* March 2005.

Polanyi, Michael. *Personal Knowledge.* London: Routledge & Kegan Paul, 1958.

————. *The Tacit Dimension.* London: Routledge & Kegan Paul, 1967.

Rhodes, Ron. *The New Age Movement.* Grand Rapids: Zondervan, 1995.

Ritschl, Dietrich. *The Logic of Theology,* translated by John Bowden. Philadelphia: Fortress, 1987.

Smail, Thomas. *The Forgotten Father.* Grand Rapids: Eerdmans, 1980.

Spaulding, Paul L. "Proclaiming Christian Truth in a Postmodern Culture." D.Min. dissertation. Fuller Theological Seminary, 2005.

Speidell, Todd. "Incarnational Social Ethics." In *Incarnational Ministry: The Presence of Christ in Church, Society, and Family.* Colorado Springs: Helmers & Howard, 1990.

Thistelton, Anthony. *New Horizons in Hermeneutics.* Glasgow: Harper Collins, 1992.

Torrance, James B. "The Vicarious Humanity of Christ." In *The Incarnation—Ecumenical Studies in the Nicene-Constantinopolitan Creed A.D. 381*, edited by Thomas F. Torrance. Edinburgh: Handsel Press, 1981.

Torrance, Thomas F. "Service in Jesus Christ." In *Theological Foundations for Ministry*, edited by Ray S. Anderson. Grand Rapids: Eerdmans, 1999.

————. *Theology in Reconstruction*. Grand Rapids: Eerdmans, 1965.

Van Engen, Charles. *God's Missionary People: Rethinking the Purpose of the Local Church*. Grand Rapids: Baker, 1991.

Versényi, L. *Heidegger, Being and Truth*. New Haven, Conn.: Yale University Press, 1965.

Watzlawick, Paul, John H. Weakland and Richard Fisch. *Change: Principles of Problem Formation and Problem Resolution*. New York: W. W. Norton, 1974.

Weber, Otto. *Foundations of Dogmatics II*. Grand Rapids: Eerdmans, 1983.

Weber, Robert. *Ancient-Future Faith: Rethinking Evangelicalism for a Postmodern World*. Grand Rapids: Baker, 1999.

Willard, Dallas. *The Divine Conspiracy: Rediscovering Our Hidden Life in God*. San Francisco: HarperSanFrancisco, 1998.

Wright, N. T. *The New Testament and the People of God*. Minneapolis: Fortress, 1992.

Zizioulas, John. *Being as Communion*. Crestwood, N.Y.: St. Vladimir's Seminary Press, 1985.

Name and Subject Index

Scripture Index